Memories That Shaped an Industry

The MIT Press Series in the History of Computing
I. Bernard Cohen and William Aspray, series editors

The Computer Comes of Age, R. Moreau, 1984

Memories That Shaped an Industry, Emerson W. Pugh, 1984

MEMORIES
THAT SHAPED AN INDUSTRY

Decisions Leading to IBM System/360

Emerson W. Pugh

The MIT Press
Cambridge, Massachusetts
London, England

This book was computer composed by Caroline C. Coppola using YFL/PREP2 under VM/SP at the IBM Thomas J. Watson Research Center.

Printed and bound in the United States of America.

Library of Congress Cataloging in Publication Data

Pugh, Emerson W.
  Memories that shaped an industry.

  (MIT Press series in the history of computing)
  Bibliography: p.
  Includes index.

  1. IBM computers—History.   2. IBM 360 (Computer)—History. 3. Computer industry—United States—History.
I. Title. II. Series.
QA76.8.I1015P83 1984 001.64 83-18787
ISBN 0-262-16094-3

Contents

Series Foreword

Although it is generally recognized that the introduction of magnetic core memories revolutionized the computer, the actual steps by which this revolution occurred have not until now been recorded and analyzed. The new ferrite technology not only changed factors of reliability and ease of access but introduced a long-lasting feature of computers. In the current edition of the *Encyclopedia of Computer Science and Engineering* (Anthony Ralston, ed.; van Nostrand-Reinhold Company, 1983, p. 943), it is observed not only that ferrite cores provide "the oldest, still-current memory technology" but "magnetic core memories continue to exist" in spite of "the challenge posed by the later technologies," including plated wires, thin films, and semiconductors. This book is thus of more than ordinary value and interest in documenting a major new technology that has had a very long and active life.

The author, Emerson Pugh, is exceptionally well qualified to write this history. A research staff member at the IBM Thomas J. Watson Research Laboratory, Yorktown Heights, New York, he has not only an extensive background in the science and technology of computers but has also managed research and development projects leading to new computer memory technologies. His book, *Memories That Shaped an Industry*, is illuminated by the special insight that is possible only to someone who has participated in the kind of history-making events about which he writes.

One of the attractive features of *Memories That Shaped an Industry* is that it displays the interaction between scientific advances and technological developments in an industrial context. Here is an analysis of the complex interplay of the decisions and demands of management and the directions set by the state of the technology. Of great interest is the portrayal of the relations between industry, government, and academic engineering. Emerson Pugh has given us in cross section a picture of the complexities of the decision process that characterize the development and introduction of advanced technologies.

This book is the second to appear in a new series devoted to the history of computers and data processing. Future volumes will deal with various aspects of the development of systems, hardware, and software, and there will be both general works and specialized monographs. Some works being planned for the series will be of a biographical and even autobiographical nature, and others will concentrate either on a particular development, such as magnetic memory, or the technical history of an industrial company.

I. Bernard Cohen
William Aspray

Preface

Development of reliable, high-speed ferrite core memories that could be mass-produced at low cost was probably the most important innovation that made stored-program computers a practical, commercial reality. IBM's leadership in this development, beginning in the early 1950s, made possible the introduction in 1964 of the IBM System/360, which was so widely copied that it had the effect of a standard and contributed much to the rapid growth of the industry.

This book is about the technical innovations, the management decisions, and the people who contributed to the development of computer memories. The focus is on IBM, but important relevant activities of other organizations and individuals are described. In less than twenty-five years, the electronic stored-program computer was developed and marketed so successfully that it became an intrinsic part of American life.

I have chosen to tell this story not only because it is important in its own right but also because it provides a clear picture of the technological challenges IBM faced following World War II and the way it met those challenges. By focusing on the development of only one of the many computer technologies, I have been able to treat a full spectrum of IBM activities from the work of the scientists and engineers to the decisions of corporate executives.

Of the hundreds of engineers, scientists, and managers who made important contributions to computer memory development during this period, only a small number are named in this book. All of those identified are important in their own right, but they should also be thought of as representing the backgrounds and activities of many others whose contributions were essential to the development process.

The primary source materials for this book are internal IBM documents, such as project reports, technical reports, internal memorandums, and engineering notebooks. Some of these were provided by individuals and others I obtained from archival sources. Chapters 3 and 4 are based heavily on similar materials obtained from the MIT and MITRE Corporation archives. Patents and articles in the technical literature have been used to broaden the perspective and to provide readers with a means to pursue topics of special interest.

I have also made extensive use of personal interviews with more than seventy people who participated in the memory development effort in order to capture the flow of events and the attitudes of the participants. These interviews have proved to be invaluable in sorting out conflicting or misleading claims of contribution and inventorship and in providing leads to sources of information that might otherwise have been overlooked. Most of these interviews have been with former or present IBM employees, but a number have been with outside contributors, including R. B. Arndt (Remington Rand), J. P. Eckert (Remington Rand), J. W. Forrester (MIT), W. N. Papian (MIT), J. A. Rajchman (RCA), and A. Wang (Harvard). Background information has been obtained from a number of excellent books on the history of computing, especially *From ENIAC to UNIVAC* by Nancy Stern, *Project Whirlwind* by K. C. Redmond and T. M. Smith, and *The Computer from Pascal to von Neumann* by H. H. Goldstine.

I am deeply indebted to those who gave freely of their time, recollections, and personal records. My special thanks to Charles J. Bashe, Jean F. Brennan, Hirsh G. Cohen, I. Bernard Cohen, and Louis A. Russell for reading and commenting on early drafts of this book. I also want to express my gratitude to Ralph E. Gomory, IBM vice-president and director of research, for his support.

Emerson W. Pugh

Memories That Shaped an Industry

1
The Postwar Challenge

Thomas J. Watson, Sr., president of IBM from 1914 and president
of the International Chamber of Commerce from 1937, was an
ardent believer in world peace through world trade. It was a
belief he held, and attempted to validate, until the fall of 1939.
Then, as hostilities broke out in Europe and World War II spread,
he devoted his efforts to winning the war as fervently as he had to
maintaining the peace.[1]

Watson placed the entire company at the disposal of the War
Department, enlarged IBM's original plant in Endicott, New York,
and built a new plant in Poughkeepsie, New York, to produce 20
millimeter aircraft cannon, Browning automatic rifles, 0.30 calibre
carbines, aircraft supercharger impellers, and other munitions.[2]
He ordered IBM engineers and inventors to devote full time to the
war effort and to stop development of new commercial products.
Not wanting to profit from wartime production, he took the
unusual step of freezing his own salary at the 1939 level and
establishing a nominal 1 percent profit on munitions production.[3]

Important as the production of munitions was, IBM's main
contribution to the war effort was its own punched-card
equipment. Biographical information about millions of Americans
was stored by rectangular holes punched into IBM's eighty-column
cards. Punched-card equipment facilitated and recorded the
induction of men and women into the armed services and their
classification, training, and assignments. It was used at military
headquarters and on the battlefields to keep track of personnel
and supplies and to help guide and record the activities of a global
war. Calculations run on IBM machines helped break the
Japanese code before the battle of Midway, determined the
trajectory of artillery shells, and predicted the weather over the
English Channel.[3]

During the wartime years, from 1939 to 1945, IBM's factory space tripled, and its gross income increased from $40 million to more than $100 million.[4] Before the war IBM had been the major supplier of punched-card equipment. Now it had greatly increased production space and a tremendous backlog of orders for commercial punched-card equipment.

One might have expected IBM's only postwar challenges to be those of finding appropriate work for employees returning from the armed services, converting the new plant in Poughkeepsie, New York, from munitions production to the production of commercial machines, and reinitiating the development of new commercial products. Indeed these were major challenges and had to be met successfully.

The most crucial challenge was of a rather different kind, however; it was the challenge of new technology. During the war great strides had been made in electronics for military applications such as radar, sonar, communications, and specialized electronic calculators. After the war the military organizations continued to support the development of advanced electronics, including the development of electronic calculators with vacuum tube circuits capable of performing arithmetic hundreds of times faster than IBM's traditional electromechanical means. The competitive threat was recognized, and IBM began to implement electronic arithmetic functions in its punched-card line.

A more subtle threat was to the punched card itself. Ever since punched cards had been introduced by Herman Hollerith to tabulate the census of 1890, they had served as a convenient way of storing information.[5] Records were permanently and visibly stored by holes punched in the cards. Cards could be sorted by hand or by machine and fed into electromechanical tabulating equipment at speeds fast enough to keep up with the fastest mechanical counting mechanisms.

Now, however, electronic vacuum tube circuits could perform calculations much faster than data could be supplied by punched cards. Thus in a manner not fully comprehended at the time, vacuum tube circuits were beginning to make punched cards obsolete. The high speed of vacuum tube circuits had rendered punched cards inadequate as the direct interface to the arithmetic unit. What was required was an electronic means of storing and supplying data to electronic calculating circuits at a rate fast enough to match their own great speed. Such a memory should be inexpensive, reliable, and able to interface directly with high-speed electronic calculating circuits.

This requirement for high-speed memory was further increased by yet another innovation, this one related to the design of electronic calculators. Calculators designed according to this new concept were soon referred to as stored-program computers. It is a concept that underlies the design philosophy of most computers now in use.

A stored-program computer is one in which the high-speed memory is used to store both instructions and data. In this way the sequence of logical operations used in a long calculation can be made available as rapidly as the data. Furthermore the sequence of calculations can be altered automatically, based on intermediate results of the calculation. To hold instructions as well as data, the memory had to be larger and faster than those that would have been required for simple extensions of automatic calculators.

Although much of the excitement generated by new computer technology found expression in the phenomenal speed of calculation, the most critical technology was the high-speed memory. Without it, high-speed logic circuits would have been ineffective, spending most of their time waiting for more data or instructions. Getting a lead in the development of electronic computer memories therefore was one of the most crucial factors in IBM's success in the postwar era.

The Watson Legacy

IBM, prewar and postwar, reflected the ideas and beliefs of its leader, Thomas J. Watson, Sr. After a successful career that led to the position of acting sales manager of the National Cash Register Company, he was hired in 1914 as president of a small conglomerate, the Computing-Tabulating-Recording Company (CTR). Patched together out of three companies in 1911, CTR's primary products were scales that computed prices from weights, equipment that sorted and tabulated data stored in Hollerith punched cards, and clocks that recorded the time. In 1924 the company changed its name to International Business Machines. In that same year the office of chairman of the board was abolished, making Watson, at fifty, the chief executive officer and undisputed leader of IBM.[4]

Throughout his lifetime, Watson viewed IBM's business as that of supplying service—not just equipment—to customers, a successful formula. The sales of the company increased from $4.1 million in 1914 to $140 million by the end of the war. When Watson celebrated his fortieth anniversary with IBM in 1954, the company had achieved a gross income of $410 million and was reported to own more than 90 percent of all the tabulating machines in the United States.[6]

IBM's success with commercial punched-card equipment provided a customer base and sales force that was important to its subsequent success in marketing electronic computers. However, its initial thrust into large-scale calculating machines was largely the outgrowth of Watson's philanthropic support of scientific computation. This support began in 1928 when Watson agreed to assist studies of automatic test scoring and analysis proposed by the head of Columbia University's Bureau of Collegiate Educational Research.[7] In June 1929 the Statistical Bureau at Columbia University began operations with tabulating, sorting, and card-punch equipment contributed by IBM. The equipment was primarily used for analyzing test results, but its availability to other members of the faculty was at least as important. Punched-card machines had no arithmetic capability beyond simple addition, but a number of scientists learned how to take advantage of the speed of this one arithmetic operation to perform more complicated calculations.

One of these scientists, Wallace J. Eckert, a Columbia University astronomer later hired by Watson, recalls that after "doing computations the hard way, it was a great experience to see an accounting machine adding quantities in different counters at the rate of 150 a minute and printing the results, and sorting going on at a rate of about 20,000 cards an hour." By 1934 IBM had enlarged the capabilities of its punched-card equipment to include subtraction and multiplication as well as addition, and Eckert had devised a calculation control switch that IBM built for him to permit this equipment to be used to obtain numerical solutions to the differential equations of planetary motion.[8]

Numerical calculation techniques, developed by Eckert and others at Columbia using IBM punched-card equipment, were widely employed during World War II to solve military problems. After the war they helped provide the motivation for developing large electronic computers.[8] During the 1930s, however, growing interest in scientific computation had little economic impact on IBM. Few universities or industrial laboratories purchased electrical accounting machines for scientific computation. Nevertheless Watson persisted in his support. IBM's success in punched-card equipment had resulted in part from paying close attention to new applications and innovations of customers and then supplying the most promising of these in new products. Scientific computation and educational testing were two such requirements.

In 1937 IBM announced its first product resulting from the cooperative effort with Columbia University: the International Test Scoring Machine. In response to the concerns of salesmen that the machine would not be profitable, Watson reportedly responded, "Who wants to make money out of education?"[7]

That same year, Howard H. Aiken, an instructor and graduate student in physics at Harvard University, approached IBM with his ideas for building an automatic calculating machine capable of performing complex mathematical operations.[9] Watson was interested, and two years later a plan to design and build the system was initiated. Development and construction of the calculator took longer than anticipated and cost substantially more than the original estimate of $100,000.[10] The resulting IBM Automatic Sequence Controlled Calculator (ASCC) was completed and formally presented to Harvard on August 7, 1944.[9] It was developed and built at no charge to Harvard, but IBM did retain all patent rights for inventions resulting from its construction.[11]

The ASCC had two electromatic typewriters, two card-feed mechanisms, and a summary punch for its input-output. It had 3304 mechanical relays in its arithmetic section. Addition and subtraction were "accomplished with the aid of 72 adding counters, each consisting of 24 electromechanical counter wheels permitting computation to an accuracy of 23 significant figures."[12] The twenty-fourth counter wheel in each adding counter was reserved for indicating the algebraic sign of the number. Of major significance was its ability to perform many mathematical operations under one automatic sequence control. The main assemblage of the ASCC was 51 feet long, eight feet high, contained 530 miles of wire, and weighed about five tons.[12] Reportedly it is the largest electromechanical calculator ever built and the first machine actually constructed to exploit the ideas proposed one hundred years earlier by the British inventor, Charles Babbage.[13]

Watson was sufficiently proud of the ASCC that he had it housed in a stainless steel and glass case. Howard Aiken was so proud of *his* automatic calculating machine that he renamed it the Harvard Mark I, and a press release issued by Harvard prior to its dedication identified him as the sole inventor. Aiken had defined the architectural objectives and provided the motivation for the ASCC, but the actual implementation was the result of a cooperative effort. IBM engineers who had spent years on the project and were coinventors of the ASCC with Aiken were deeply distressed by lack of recognition for their contributions.[14]

Watson ordered numerous revisions of the ASCC brochure before it was issued in an effort to set the record straight. Then learning that Howard Aiken planned to build a more advanced machine without IBM's help, Watson responded by ordering his engineers to build a super calculator that would surpass the Harvard machine as well as any new versions Aiken might conceive.[10] The possibility that any other organization would develop a calculator superior to IBM's was unacceptable to Watson. He formed IBM's first Department of Pure Science, and in March 1945 hired Wallace Eckert as its director.[8] One of Eckert's new responsibilities was to help create specifications for the super calculator, later named the Selective Sequence Electronic Calculator (SSEC). Nine months later, in January 1946, specifications for the SSEC were approved, and construction was authorized by Watson, who ordered it to be completed in one year—an impossible task. But under pressure from Watson, the engineers did complete the machine in eighteen months.[10]

Critical to the performance of the SSEC was the use of high-speed vacuum tube circuits developed by IBM before the war and based on designs published in the technical literature during the late 1930s.[10] Two vacuum tube triodes were connected in a circuit in parallel so as to conduct electricity in the same direction but interconnected with each other so that only one of the two could be conducting at any one time. The voltage of the conducting triode was used to hold the other triode in the off state. This type of circuit came to be known as a flip-flop because external voltages could be used to cause it to flip-flop from one conducting state to the other.

The two stable states of the flip-flop circuit could be used to store information in much the same way that the holes (or lack of holes) were used in punched cards. Such circuits could also be used to create a binary counter by connecting a series of flip-flops so that two changes of the conducting state of the first flip-flop caused a change in the state of the second, two state changes in the second caused a change in the third, and so on. Because addition can be done by counting and carrying and multiplication by a sequence of additions, the flip-flop was able to serve as the basic building block for electronic computation.

The electronic vacuum tube circuits in the SSEC were able to perform fourteen-by-fourteen-digit decimal multiplication in 20 milliseconds, division in 33 milliseconds, and addition or subtraction of nineteen-digit numbers in only 0.3 milliseconds. According to IBM announcements the SSEC was "at least 250 times as fast" as the ASCC whose electromechanical arithmetic unit had required 6 seconds for multiplication and 16 seconds for division.[15]

The dramatic increase in speed at which arithmetic could be performed by vacuum tube circuits in the newer SSEC created a serious problem in storing intermediate results and supplying data and instructions fast enough for the arithmetic circuits. The designers of the SSEC described this problem as follows:

The critical problem in the design was to integrate satisfactorily a high-speed electronic computing unit with a sufficiently large number memory to keep the computing unit supplied with numbers and store the results as rapidly as they were produced. This calls for not only an effective computing and memory unit, but also a carefully worked out system for routing numbers to and from the computing unit, and a system of control and automatic instructions adequate to keep the machine in continuous operation for the rapid solution of a problem.[16]

Vacuum tube flip-flop circuits were used to provide high-speed memory for 160 decimal digits (equivalent to 640 binary digits, known as bits). Arranged in eight memory units of twenty decimal digits each, these units may be likened to the general arithmetic registers of a modern computer.[17] Mechanical relays provided slower access to 3000 decimal digits. These were organized in ten clusters of fifteen memory units each, and each relay memory unit was also able to hold twenty decimal digits. By operating many of the 150 mechanical relay memory units simultaneously, in an asynchronous manner, it was possible to supply and receive information from the eight higher-speed vacuum tube memory units at an adequate rate.

The 400,000 digits of data to which the SSEC had access "as rapidly as they are needed," according to the IBM brochure, were stored on paper tape consisting of standard, 80-column-wide IBM punched-card stock in continuous loops.[18] Three paper-tape punches and sixty-six paper-tape readers could be configured in a variety of ways to provide the needed flow of information in and out of the relay memory units.[19] Programming a problem to run correctly and efficiently on the SSEC with its complex storage hierarchy was not a trivial problem. Nevertheless, when properly programmed, it was able to handle problems that went well beyond the capability of any other automatic calculating machine then in existence.[10]

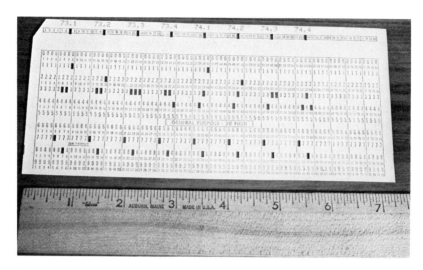

IBM punched card
An IBM eighty-column punched card typical of those in use during the
1950s.

SSEC memory components
The SSEC paper-tape reader, with its clutch mechanism exposed,
dominates the photograph. The paper tape actually consists of long
continuous loops of eighty-column-wide punched-card stock. Electronic
vacuum tubes used in flip-flop circuits for memory and logic are to the
lower right, and one of the electromechanical relays used for memory is
shown at the lower left. (Photograph courtesy of IBM Archives.)

Much of the credit for the architecture of the SSEC belongs to Robert R. Seeber, who was hired by Wallace Eckert in August 1945. Seeber had previously worked for Howard Aiken as a programmer on the Harvard Mark I (IBM ASCC) but decided to leave Harvard because of personality clashes with Aiken and disagreements over the proposed design of Aiken's next computer, the Mark II. Specifically Aiken rejected the idea of mixing data with instructions, saying Seeber's reasons for doing it "were pretty weak."[20]

Aiken's rejection of his ideas gave Seeber the "happy result" that he could use them at IBM in the development of the SSEC.[20] His proposal to have instructions stored in the same format as data and capable of being modified by the computer during a computation has caused the SSEC to be proclaimed the first stored-program computer to be implemented.[10] Formal dedication of the IBM SSEC took place on January 27, 1948. Headlined in the *New York Times* as a "mechanical brain" that "has incredible memory," a device that "can retain 400,000 digits, understand complex problems, and solve them," the SSEC occupied the periphery of a room approximately 60 feet long and 30 feet wide.[21]

The SSEC was so large that its dedication ceremonies were conducted inside the machine. In a gesture befitting Watson's pride in IBM and his sense of duty to society, the SSEC was made available for scientific calculations free of charge, and for problems of government and industry it was made available at a charge that covered only the cost of operation.[10]

Although few realized it at the time, the dedication ceremony marked a critical transition for IBM. The use of high-speed electronic vacuum tube circuits in the SSEC together with prewar electromechanical devices resulted in design complexities that highlighted the disparity in performance between these two technologies. In particular the small size of the high-speed memory that could be implemented economically and reliably using electronic vacuum tubes was a major constraint on the design of the machine and its subsequent use.

Seeber and his coworkers at IBM appear to have developed the SSEC architecture independently of outside efforts, thus giving them claim to independent conception as well as first implementation of a stored-program computer.[10] Questions concerning the priority of ideas in the history of technology are difficult to answer, however; the answers are seldom as simple as written history or patent documents imply. What is clear in this case is that the work of the IBM SSEC engineers, albeit a significant technical achievement, had less impact on the subsequent development of electronic stored-program computers than did work done by a group at the Moore School of Electrical Engineering of the University of Pennsylvania.

Developments at the Moore School

In February 1946, almost two years before the SSEC ceremony, the Electronic Numerical Integrator and Computer (ENIAC) was dedicated at the Moore School of Electrical Engineering of the University of Pennsylvania. Built under contract to the Army Ballistics Research Laboratory, it contained 40 percent more electronic vacuum tubes and performed arithmetic somewhat faster than the SSEC. In the computation of very large problems, however, the ENIAC was severely limited in working storage and by its dependence on manually plugged and switched sequence controls. In contrast the SSEC could function without operator intervention, under control of its modifiable stored program.

The senior member of the group at the Moore School was John William Mauchly, who had been interested in electronic means of calculation since the early 1930s. It was he who proposed and promoted the ENIAC project and provided the leadership. The second major contributor to the project was John Presper Eckert, Jr., apparently no relation to Wallace Eckert of IBM. Presper Eckert was a graduate student at the Moore School when he met Mauchly in 1941. Described by one of his colleagues as "the best electronic engineer in the Moore School," Eckert was brilliant and innovative and deserves much of the credit for the engineering success of the ENIAC project.[22]

Early in 1944, less than a year after the ENIAC project was started, Eckert and Mauchly had begun discussions concerning ways to provide more high-speed memory and superior operation of an electronic calculator.[23] In September of that year, John von Neumann, one of the world's most distinguished mathematicians, became involved in the project as a result of a chance meeting with Herman Goldstine, a mathematician and the Army Ballistics Research Laboratory liaison officer to the ENIAC project.

Von Neumann had come to the United States from Germany in 1930 as Adolph Hitler was rising to power. In 1933 he received a permanent appointment to the newly created Institute for Advanced Study at Princeton. During the war he consulted for numerous government agencies and helped develop mathematical models and numerical methods for solving problems on IBM punched-card equipment. His interest in higher-speed calculating equipment brought him in contact with the group at the Moore School in August 1944. Thus began an interaction among von Neumann, Mauchly, Eckert, Goldstine, and others associated with the ENIAC project that led to the design of a more advanced machine, the Electronic Discrete Variable Automatic Computer (EDVAC).[24]

The first document describing this machine, "First Draft of a Report on the EDVAC," was written in June 1945 as a preliminary internal report. Von Neumann was the sole author. Goldstine was sufficiently impressed with the draft document that he distributed it to approximately thirty people, some of whom had no prior association with the ENIAC or EDVAC. Subsequently, additional copies were distributed.[25,26] Distribution of von Neumann's report, with no credits to others, ended the productive and apparently harmonious working relationship that had existed.

A progress report on the EDVAC prepared by Eckert and Mauchly three months later appears to have received much less attention, partly because it was a classified government document with limited distribution. It contains a discussion of the new computer architecture with instructions and data contained in high-speed memory, and it has remarkably well-thought-out engineering solutions to many of the hardware requirements.[23] The two most important of these were a mercury acoustic delay line for high-speed internal memory and a magnetic tape storage device to be used instead of punched cards for input and output of data and instructions to and from the internal memory. Eckert and Mauchly noted, "Magnetic recording devices have been known for a long time, and recently commercial sound recorders using magnetic wire have been used for many purposes. The application of such methods to the recording of numerical data in digital form requires a few modifications and developments, but presents no formidable difficulties." In contrast they considered development of the required high-performance internal memory to be a substantial challenge.[27]

As early as 1942 Eckert had experimented with acoustic delay lines in which a transducer converted electric pulses into acoustic pulses (or waves) in a liquid. The acoustic pulses propagated from one end of the tank of liquid to the other at the speed of sound. Using mercury as the liquid and piezoelectric crystal transducers at either end, Eckert showed that half-microsecond pulses could be transmitted and detected reliably.[28]

A binary digit 1 was represented by a pulse 0.5 microseconds wide and a 0 by no pulse. With pulses spaced approximately 1 microsecond apart and traveling at the speed of sound, approximately 1000 binary digits (bits) could be stored in a tank 1.5 meters long. As the data stream was detected at the output end, it was either rewritten at the input end of the delay line or sent as electrical signals to the logic circuits of the computer. Only ten vacuum tubes were required to operate the memory delay line.[29]

Mauchly and Eckert were pleased that the magnetic wire (or tape) and the mercury delay line memory were both serial devices; that is, they transmitted or received data one bit at at time. This serial operation was consistent with their plan to reduce the number of vacuum tubes in the EDVAC by having it operate on data or instructions one bit at a time. The EDVAC was thus called a serial machine to contrast it with the parallel operation of ENIAC. The total saving in vacuum tube circuitry was such that their report of September 1945 predicted that 1925 tubes in EDVAC would permit three times faster addition and multiplication than the ENIAC, which had almost 18,000 tubes.[23] As finally completed, the EDVAC required 3600 tubes and was not quite as fast as anticipated; nevertheless, it was a significant improvement on the cost-performance of ENIAC and also offered the important advantages of stored-program operation.

In describing the importance of high-speed internal memory, von Neumann had used the term *memory* instead of *storage* because he likened the entire computer to the human nervous system. As time went on, the word *memory* was used primarily to describe the high-speed main memory, and the term *storage* was used for the lower-speed electromechanical magnetic disks and tapes; however, the terms *storage* and *memory* were often used interchangeably by workers in the field, and this book will frequently reflect this use.

Von Neumann's use of neurological analogies and neuron notation apparently enraged Presper Eckert, who viewed it as a technique whereby von Neumann could "go out and give talks on the work John [Mauchly] and I had done at the University of Pennsylvania without giving any credit to the University of Pennsylvania or to the people who had actually thought of the ideas."[30] Eckert and Mauchly were, of course, prevented from talking about their work because it was performed under a government security classification of confidential.

Although von Neumann did not claim the EDVAC design for himself, he did make use of the credentials gained from his draft report to establish his own computer project at the Institute for Advanced Study, the IAS computer. He sought funding from MIT, Harvard, the University of Chicago, and IBM.[24] Ultimately the IAS computer project was funded by $100,000 each from the army and navy ordnance departments and the institute itself.

Von Neumann also entered into a joint research and development contract with the newly established RCA research laboratories at Princeton, New Jersey, to provide the most critical hardware element: the main memory.[24] By the end of 1945 a plan evolved to use an electrostatic storage device called the selectron being developed at RCA. It consisted of a cathode-ray tube, similar to a television tube, with a highly specialized grid structure inside the tube just in front of the face.

An array of metallic eyelets served as the storage elements. Each could be held at one of two voltage levels. Read out of information was accomplished by directing the cathode ray beam of electrons through the hole in the selected eyelet. If the eyelet was at a positive voltage, the electrons passed through the hole and were detected by a readout plate. This was interpreted as a 1. If the eyelet was at a negative voltage, it blocked the passage of the beam of electrons and was interpreted as a 0. Writing the positive or negative voltage states of the eyelets was accomplished by a sequencing of electron beam bombardment while selecting individual eyelets by currents applied to appropriate wires in a grid of horizontal and vertical conductors adjacent to the eyelets.[31]

Unlike the mercury delay line, which read out the stored bits serially, the selectron memory provided random access to any bit in the tube. This provided access times of tens of microseconds to any bit in the memory and was at least ten times faster than could be achieved by the mercury delay line. All forty bits of a word in the IAS computer were to be obtained at once by storing each bit of a given word in a separate tube.[32]

UNIVAC, ERA, and Remington Rand

Meanwhile Eckert and Mauchly, incensed over what they perceived to be excessive credit taken by von Neumann, continued to develop the EDVAC.[24] Then in March 1946, less than two months after the ENIAC was dedicated, a change in patent policy at the Moore school precipitated the rapid departure of Eckert and Mauchly. As a continuing condition of employment, they were required to execute the university's newly created standard patent release and to "certify you will devote your efforts first to the interest of the University of Pennsylvania and will during the interval of your employment here subjugate your personal commercial interests to the interests of University."[33]

Having fought for ownership of the ENIAC patents and eager to have the EDVAC patents, Eckert and Mauchly refused to sign the required agreements and thus resigned from the university. Their

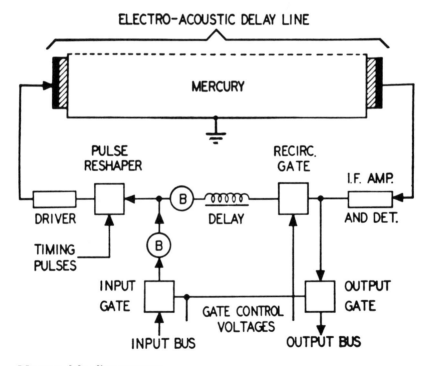

Mercury delay line memory
A mercury delay line memory tank used in UNIVAC is shown (above) with
one of the eighteen recirculation chassis mounted on the shell. A block
diagram of the memory is shown (below). (From J. P. Eckert, "A
Survey of Digital Computer Memory Systems," *Proceedings of the
Institute of Radio Engineers* 41, 1953, p. 1395, © 1953 IRE, now IEEE.)

resignations signaled the end of the preeminence of the University of Pennsylvania in the computer field.

Turning down an offer from Watson for their own computer laboratory at IBM, Eckert and Mauchly formed a partnership in June 1946 to undertake a research and study contract for the Census Department of the National Bureau of Standards. The contract, signed in September 1946 for a fixed fee of $75,000, called for them to provide specifications for two mercury delay tubes for storage and a magnetic tape drive system for their proposed EDVAC-type machine. In addition Eckert and Mauchly had been promised a subsequent design contract. Altogether the National Bureau of Standards agreed to provide $300,000 of the estimated $400,000 development cost of the new computer. Within a year the EDVAC-type machine was christened the Universal Automatic Computer (UNIVAC), and the partnership was soon converted to the Eckert-Mauchly Computer Company (EMCC).[24]

Additional funds were obtained by making a small UNIVAC-precursor computer (the BINAC) for the Northrop Company and by selling proposed UNIVACs to users such as the Prudential Insurance Company. Schedule slippages accompanied by development costs of more than twice the original estimate, however, finally forced EMCC to solve its financial problems by reaching an agreement on February 1, 1950, to be purchased by Remington Rand.[24]

The first UNIVAC was accepted by the Census Bureau on March 31, 1951, and within eighteen months two more UNIVACs were delivered to the government. These were relatively compact units, having only 5400 vacuum tubes versus the 18,000 in the ENIAC and occupying much less floor space.[24] Like the EDVAC the UNIVAC had a mercury delay line main memory and used magnetic tape units for many of the input-output functions for which punched cards had served in previous machines. Ultimately forty-six UNIVAC I's were built for government and commercial use.

Meanwhile John von Neumann's IAS computer had run into a number of engineering problems. Even limited operation was not achieved until the end of 1951, and public announcement was delayed until June 1952.[34] Difficulties with selectron tube memories caused a shift to a simpler electrostatic storage tube developed by F. C. Williams of the University of Manchester. However, the design of the IAS computer was so widely discussed that it became the model for several other computers, including IBM's first fully electronic, stored-program computer product, the IBM 701.

UNIVAC was the first electronic, stored-program computer to be produced and sold commercially. It so caught the public fancy that the word UNIVAC was used popularly to mean computer.

In signing its first contract for a UNIVAC with a commercial customer (the Prudential Insurance Company), EMCC had to agree to provide equipment to convert data stored on punched cards to data stored on magnetic tape and vice versa. Prudential, a major user of IBM punched-card equipment, was concerned about the lack of visibility of data on magnetic tape and about its uncertain long-term retention. Prudential therefore anticipated that all output from the UNIVAC would be converted back to punched cards from tape. Commenting on this cumbersome use of the magnetic tape-supported UNIVAC, Nancy Stern says, "It is ironic that Eckert and Mauchly had to agree to develop these converters in order to obtain the Prudential contract since their intention from the beginning was to provide a viable and vastly more efficient alternative to punch-card processing."[35]

To the market-conscious IBM management, customer desires were viewed not as ironic but as the primary basis for product specifications. Success in punched-card equipment had been achieved by careful adherence to customer requirements and preferences. Product engineers frequently got their assignments in the development organizations only after spending several years in the field installing equipment, servicing it, and listening to customer views, and salesmen were expected to advise the development organization of new applications and requirements.

The first three UNIVACs were delivered to government customers by the end of 1952, with more on order. They used punched-card equipment for long-term information storage, but they also used magnetic tape units for direct input to and output from the electronic computer. Magnetic tape storage units combined with the high-speed mercury delay line memory to make effective use of the vacuum-tube logic of the UNIVAC.

By the early 1950s stored-program computers had been shown to have application for very large scientific and commercial data-processing applications. The Eckert-Mauchly Computer Division, purchased by Remington Rand in 1950, appeared to be in a strong technical and financial position to exploit this market. Then in May 1952, James H. Rand, Jr., head of the Remington Rand Corporation, purchased another high-technology company, Engineering Research Associates (ERA). ERA, like EMCC, was the direct result of wartime research. It had been founded in January 1946 by Commander Howard T. Engstrom, who in peacetime had been a professor of mathematics at Yale, and by Lieutenant Commander William C. Norris, who in peacetime had been a sales engineer at Westinghouse. During World War II both had worked on advanced electronics technology in the secrecy-shrouded cryptologic establishment of the navy.[36]

The ERA company was founded with assurances of government research and development contracts because the Navy Department was desperate to find commercial firms willing to continue military electronics work. Six months after ERA was founded, it received a contract from the Office of Naval Research, without competitive bidding. A more substantial contract followed quickly from the Bureau of Ships, which provided the cover for secret contracts by the National Security Agency.[36] By 1952 ERA had 500 employees and was estimated to have produced 80 percent of the dollar value of electronic computers in the United States.[37] Its unique relationship with the National Security Agency had permitted it to become the dominant supplier of electronic computers for defense, but it lacked the capital or marketing skills required to move aggressively into the commercial market.

The purchase of ERA in 1952, following the earlier purchase of EMCC, provided Remington Rand with a significant portion of the experienced computer engineering manpower in the United

States, and Remington Rand appeared to be ready to provide the needed financial resources to move into the commercial market.[36] Through these two acquisitions, Remington Rand had become the unquestioned leader in electronic computers.

The technical strength of Remington Rand in the development of electronic computer memories was particularly impressive. ERA had built rotating magnetic drum memories using magnetic tape material developed in Germany during the war.[38] One of these served as main memory on ERA's first computer, the Atlas I, which was built with government funds and delivered to the government in December 1950. The commercial version, named the ERA 1101, was announced one year later.[36] UNIVAC was already being shipped with mercury delay line memories.

One could well wonder if IBM—with its business and technical leaders so firmly rooted in electromechanical technologies—could compete successfully with Remington Rand. Clearly new technical capabilities and new management insights were needed.

New Leaders at IBM

The end of the war brought back a number of employees who had gained new skills while serving in the armed forces. The most important of these to Watson was his older son, Thomas J. Watson, Jr. Known to his associates as Tom, he had worked as an IBM salesman for three years before being called to active duty. The younger son, Arthur K. (Dick), returned from the service to finish college before joining IBM.[39]

Tom Watson, Jr., was appointed vice president of IBM and member of the board of directors the first year after he returned from the army. In January 1952 he became president of IBM, but the shift of authority was still far from complete. Watson, Sr., retained the titles of chairman of the board and chief executive officer until one month before he succumbed to a heart attack on June 19, 1956.[39]

Long before Tom Watson, Jr., took over as president, he had become deeply involved in moving IBM into electronics technology. IBM's first electronic machine, the Type 603

An early magnetic drum

This magnetic drum memory was built by Engineering Research
Associates and delivered to the National Security Agency about 1948. It
was the first drum storage system delivered by ERA. The drum is shown
exposed, with a partial shroud for mounting the three heads for each
track: erase, write, and read. The oxide coating was obtained by gluing
magnetic tape to the surface of the drum. Tracks were on 1/16 inch
centers and data was stored at 80 bits per inch. (Photograph and
information courtesy of R.B. Arndt, Sperry Rand Corporation, St. Paul,
Minnesota.)

Electronic Multiplier, might never have been produced if it had not been for the personal sponsorship of the younger Watson who fought for funds to build the first production lot of fifty. The Type 603 thus became the world's first electronic calculator to be placed into production.[40]

It was a successful calculated risk. Before the first 603 was delivered in 1946, all fifty machines of the first production lot had been sold, and one hundred more had been ordered. However, the decision was made to limit production to one hundred units and replace the 603 with a more powerful machine.[40]

To help make and implement decisions, Tom Watson had begun to rely on a number of key people. There was James W. Birkenstock whom Watson, Sr., had dismissed as general sales manager of IBM in 1946 when Birkenstock was still only thirty-three years old. Watson, Jr., appointed him manager of the Future Demands Department in 1947 and later as his own executive assistant. In these positions, Birkenstock recalls that Tom Watson asked him to keep himself "continually involved in assessing the competitive threat from without."[41]

Another uniquely qualified person who influenced IBM's move into electronic computers was Cuthbert C. Hurd, who had joined IBM early in 1949. He had a Ph.D. in mathematics and had worked at the Oak Ridge National Laboratory where he helped introduce IBM machines for technical calculations. At IBM he was located at corporate headquarters, where he worked directly with Tom Watson and organized the Applied Science Department to serve as the technical arm of the sales organization.[42]

Important leadership and knowledge was also provided by Wallace W. McDowell, who replaced John McPherson as director of engineering in 1950. A 1930 graduate of MIT in administrative engineering, he served as assistant to the laboratory manager in Endicott from the time IBM's engineering was consolidated in that laboratory in 1933 until 1942, when he was promoted to laboratory manager.[43]

Tom Watson often told others that he did not consider himself to be particularly brilliant but that he prided himself on obtaining the best possible advice from those who had the expertise. In

January 1952 he hired John von Neumann as a consultant and spent a great deal of time with him.[44]   Watson and other executives used von Neumann to critique development programs and to referee some of the major technical decisions.[41] Watson also started an aggressive program to recruit college graduates in electronics, and, after the invention of the transistor in 1947, he ensured that specialists in solid-state physics and devices were recruited.[45] Following the long-established policy of building technical competence from within, he gave increased responsibility to IBM engineers who had returned from service with experience in electronics.

Ralph Palmer

The engineer who had the greatest impact on IBM's technical future was Ralph L. Palmer. He had joined IBM in the Endicott Laboratory in 1932 as an electrical engineering graduate of Union College. He was assigned to the electrical laboratory and became the manager five years later. There he had initiated work on the design of vacuum tube circuits that provided the basis for those used in the 603 Electronic Multiplier and the SSEC.[46]

In 1943 Palmer entered the navy and served as a technical executive officer in the Naval Computing Machine Laboratory on the grounds of the National Cash Register Company in Dayton, Ohio. In this assignment he was exposed to some of the most advanced electronic cryptanalysis devices, which contained thousands of vacuum tubes.[47]

Returning from the navy in late 1945, Palmer was eager to push IBM into advanced vacuum tube circuit technology. He was convinced that rapid advances in electronics would result in product capabilities far beyond those anticipated by customers. Therefore product developments would have to precede market demand. On this point, according to one of his colleagues, he was almost maniacal.[48]

Within weeks of returning from the navy, Palmer was asked to go to Poughkeepsie to build a group of engineers competent in electronics. He moved into an office at the head of the central stairway on the top floor of the main house on the 217-acre

Ralph Palmer
Ralph Palmer is shown (above, left) seated at the head table of a dinner
held in Endicott in 1946 to honor an IBM sales trainee class. In 1963
(below, right) Palmer is appointed an IBM Fellow by T. J. Watson, Jr.,
(left) as E. R. Piore (far left) looks on. (Photograph courtesy of the
IBM Archives.)

Kenyon estate in Poughkeepsie, purchased by IBM in 1944.[2] In makeshift facilities such as this, Palmer and the engineers he recruited started the projects that led to IBM's success in electronic computers.

Palmer's first product development project was to design an electronic calculator (later called the Type 604) with more function than the Type 603 Electronic Multiplier. The 604 had twice the storage capacity of the 603, and its plug-wire programming permitted it to perform several multiplications and divisions plus additions and subtractions at the same one hundred card per minute rate at which the 603 could perform only one multiplication.[40]

The circuit designs used in the 604 were similar to those in the 603, but they were implemented with miniature vacuum tubes that used less power and permitted a higher circuit density than had been achieved in the 603 or the SSEC.[49] The small interelectrode distances in miniature vacuum tubes made them very sensitive to contamination during manufacture, contributing to poor reliability. Ralph Palmer and his engineers quickly became involved in the design and specification of vacuum tubes, and a small production line was established. These activities caused GE and RCA to take seriously IBM's request for better vacuum tubes, permitting IBM to back away from manufacturing its own.[50]

Palmer insisted that the number of circuit types be kept small in order to reduce the number of different items that had to be manufactured, tested, and serviced. He also proposed that every vacuum tube and its closely associated resistors and capacitors be packaged separately in a pluggable unit that could be tested as a circuit before insertion into the machine. The resulting Type 604 pluggable unit was a significant contribution to digital electronic equipment design.[51] It increased circuit density, improved manufacturing efficiency, and reduced the time required to diagnose and correct circuit problems in the field. It became a common servicing technique to swap pluggable units between locations in order to isolate defective units. The improved manufacturability and serviceability of the pluggable unit became invaluable as more than 5600 of the 604 Electronic Calculating

Punches were shipped during a ten-year period following its announcement in July 1948.

The successful, rapid development of electronics capabilities, as evidenced in the 603 and 604 electronic calculators, played a major role in the selection of IBM to develop and manufacture computers for the SAGE Air Defense System, as described in later chapters.

Entering the Electronic Computer Market

In November 1946, ten months after Thomas Watson, Sr., had authorized construction of the SSEC, he was advised that the National Bureau of Standards had "embarked on a program of development of electronic digital calculating devices with funds from the Department of Commerce, War, and Navy." The advisory letter, written by John C. McPherson, director of engineering, and Wallace Eckert, described the Bureau of Standards program as "an outgrowth of the wartime demand for high-speed computing." McPherson and Eckert counseled that IBM not participate in the project because of possible adverse impact on the company's patent position. Instead they urged that IBM carry out enough basic development to provide the "vision to recognize important developments when they arise elsewhere" and to gain "sufficient know how to make quick and effective use of new developments."[52]

In assessing IBM's technical position, McPherson and Eckert expressed confidence that electronic vacuum tube arithmetic units being developed in IBM were adequate for the needs of future products, including very large calculators. However, they injected a serious caution concerning electronic memory, saying, "The problem of electronic storage of numbers during the calculation is of fundamental importance, and we have no adequate solution of the problem. This development should be pushed with all possible vigor."[52]

Less than two weeks later McPherson and his colleagues had identified fourteen areas of advanced electronics that needed to be considered.[53] All but three related to methods for high-speed storing and reading of information. None could be developed in time for use on the SSEC, whose design had been largely defined almost nine months earlier, nor were any of them ready for use on the Type 603 or Type 604 electronic calculators.

During 1948 Ralph Palmer learned about a new type of cathode-ray tube memory being studied at the University of Manchester in England by F. C. Williams.[54] Soon known as the Williams tube memory, the device used a conventional cathode-ray tube without any internal modification. IBM engineers began working on this device at about the same time as did the group under von Neumann at the Institute for Advanced Studies. Proceeding independently the two groups soon made the Williams tube memory their first choice for their respective applications.

By the end of 1949 Ralph Palmer and staff had achieved considerable success with Williams tube memories and had initiated work on magnetic drum storage similar to that being developed at ERA and on magnetic tape storage similar to that used on the UNIVAC. Palmer also had a project underway to design a computer that would use magnetic tape storage and a high-speed electronic memory. The requirements for this computer, which became known as the Tape Processing Machine (TPM), were documented in November 1949 and engineering designs were underway by the end of the year.[55] It was soon evident, however, that a less ambitious unit was needed to permit more rapid test of memory devices under development. The resulting smaller machine was known simply as the Test Assembly.

The Test Assembly was a complete computer. A 604 Electronic Calculator was used for the arithmetic element, the input-output was provided by a Type 519 that could read and punch cards, and the control unit was built with parts scavenged from a 604. The main memory of the Test Assembly consisted of twelve cathode-ray tubes operating in the manner proposed by F. C. Williams. It was capable of storing 250 words consisting of five-place decimal numbers with signs. Each decimal digit was stored in a separate tube, and a sixth tube stored the sign. Thus 125 words were stored in six tubes, and another 125 words in the other six tubes. In September 1950 the Test Assembly functioned well enough to run several test programs successfully, and by

March 1951 it had become a usable engineering tool.[56] Meanwhile, planning continued on the TPM.

Most of IBM's engineers and management were unimpressed. They believed large electronic computers were suitable only for very special scientific calculations for which few customers existed, and the use of magnetic tape to replace punched cards was contrary to the experience and expertise of most IBM engineers and salesmen. It was generally believed that no customer would pay a thousand dollars a month for any machine.[57] Jim Birkenstock recalls reviewing the results of an internal study in which the participants had voted 14 to 4 against there being any commercial application for calculating machines using magnetic tape.[58]

Various market forces, however, were beginning to cause Tom Watson to question prevailing views in the company. There was growing interest in using automatic calculators for scientific computations, and at the request of customers IBM had constructed a variety of special-purpose units. One of the most important of these was the IBM Card Programmed Calculator (CPC), which consisted of four individual units interconnected by cables: the 604 Electronic Calculating Unit, an accounting machine, a summary punch, and an auxiliary storage unit. Announced as a product in the summer of 1949, the CPC could call for numbers stored anywhere in the system, perform mathematical procedures defined by the control panel wiring, and transmit the result to a new storage location. The response to the CPC was unexpectedly good. Even at a monthly rental of $1500, over two hundred machines were installed between 1949 and 1952.[42]

With the outbreak of the Korean conflict in 1950, Watson, Sr., asked Birkenstock to organize a military products division for the purpose of providing the government with products for national defense. Birkenstock recalls that Watson, Jr., suggested this might be an opportunity to become involved with government agencies as a supplier of electronic computers. It was a crucial suggestion that might have been difficult for anyone other than Tom Watson. The older Watson had viewed wartime activities as patriotic endeavors rather than as a way to enhance IBM's products. But Tom Watson was able to convince his father that large-scale electronic computers might be crucial to the company's future.[41]

Birkenstock and Cuthbert Hurd toured numerous government agencies to learn of their requirements for electronic computation and concluded there was substantial similarity among the requirements of these agencies. Out of these visits evolved a recommendation to produce twenty identical scientific computers. These would be called Defense Calculators in order to satisfy Watson, Sr.'s, desire that the project contribute to the war effort. Politically such a name also had the advantage of avoiding any direct confrontation with the electromechanically oriented commercial product planning and development efforts.[58]

One member of Palmer's group who was particularly interested in the outcome of these considerations was Nathaniel Rochester, who had played a key role in designing the TPM and the Test Vehicle after joining IBM in 1948.[57] He vividly remembers a meeting chaired by Tom Watson in December 1950 at which a wild diversity of views had been expressed concerning the proposed Defense Calculator. According to Rochester, Tom Watson said, "Well now we've heard a proposal by the engineers represented by Nat Rochester and by the sales people represented by Cuthbert Hurd. They have a plan of action, and I'd like to know by a show of hands who's in favor of this and who thinks we should do something different or not do anything." This resulted in a show of hands each way, following which Watson said, "All right now all of you who voted against doing this and are in favor of doing something different will henceforth not be associated with this project until we get it going."[57]

It was one of the many critical decisions by Watson, Jr., that propelled the company into the field of electronic stored-program computers. From that day on there was a "green light to go ahead." Prior to this, Tom Watson had advocated hiring people qualified in electronics, but now he ordered an all out push to develop a strong electronic engineering arm in IBM.[59]

During the next two months Birkenstock and Hurd were able to get letters of intent from thirty government agencies and government contractors for estimated rentals of $8000 per month, enough to justify the project. But within a year it was recognized that the development and production costs had been badly underestimated. Customers were advised that a two times higher rental would be required. Many stayed with the project even at the higher rental, and new customers were added.[58]

The first Defense Calculator, renamed the IBM 701, was shipped to the IBM Technical Computing Bureau in New York City in December 1952, and the second IBM 701 was shipped to the National Laboratory at Los Alamos in January 1953.[42] Each installed computing system consisted of many boxes interconnected by electrical cables. Each box housed a separate functional unit, was fully tested prior to shipment, and was small enough to pass through standard doorways. The Type 701 Electronic Analytical Control Unit and the Type 706 electrostatic Williams tube memory were housed in separate boxes as were the punched-card reader, the punched-card recorder, the alphabetic printer, the magnetic tape readers and recorders, the magnetic drum reader and recorders, and the power supply and distribution.[42] Separately housed functional units were intended to facilitate shipment, installation, and service, as well as future system improvements. It was one of the many practical features that distinguished the new product from the one-of-a-kind SSEC.

After much debate, the name Electronic Data-Processing Machine was selected to describe the new electronic computer. The name was intended to suggest greater function than had been associated with previous calculators or computers. Birkenstock is credited with coining the name and the abbreviation EDPM in the hope of counteracting the increasing tendency of people to refer to all large computing systems as UNIVACs.[42]

The IBM 701 had been given high priority. It was developed in just two years under the direction of Nat Rochester and Jerrier Haddad, both of whom had gained experience in the design of production electronic calculators on the 604. The IBM 701 used Williams tube main memories, magnetic tape storage, and magnetic drum storage units based on designs first tested at IBM

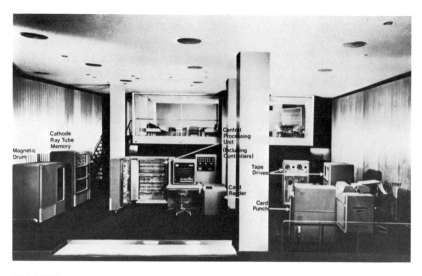

IBM 701 computer
A typical IBM 701 computer system configuration with a cathode ray
Williams tube memory unit to the left.

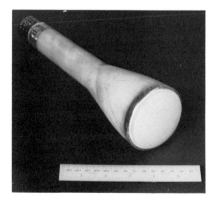

Williams tube memory
The Type 706 cathode ray Williams tube memory is shown with its 36
drawers of 2 tubes each.   The storage tube faces are visible through
circular openings in front of the drawers.   A single 3-inch-diameter
Williams tube is shown at the right.

on the TPM. The architecture of the 701 was similar to von Neumann's IAS computer.

The IBM 701 was formally dedicated on April 7, 1953. Its replacement of the SSEC as the showpiece of IBM's computer capability symbolically signaled IBM's transition to the new era of postwar electronic computer technology.

Engineers at ERA were intensely interested when in late 1951 IBM first announced its intention to build the Defense Calculator. They believed their Atlas II computer was better than the proposed IBM machine, but they had been prevented from making public statements by the classified nature of their government contract. By November 1952 they received permission from the government to announce an unclassified version of the Atlas II. They then revealed to top management at Remington Rand the existence of the machine. The unclassified version was called the ERA 1103, and the ERA engineers told their management it would be superior to the IBM 701. The surprised executives quickly approved a program to produce two machines and to buy parts to make two more. By February 1953 the ERA 1103 was officially announced and a modest marketing effort was initiated. By 1954 it was in production. Market success was almost immediate, and twenty ERA 1103s eventually were built.[36]

The predicted superiority of the ERA 1103s was not realized. In January 1954, for example, the Joint Chiefs of Staff requested that a comparison be made between the IBM 701 and the ERA 1103 for use by the proposed Joint Numerical Weather Prediction Unit. The results of a meteorological calculation run on both computers revealed that the "speeds of the two machines are comparable with a slight advantage in favor of the 701." The input-output equipment for the 701 was significantly faster, causing it to be selected unanimously for this application.[60]

In addition to stronger technical competition than expected, ERA was suddenly faced with a wholly new set of problems having to do with manufacturing a series of machines, setting rental and sales prices, installation, field service, and customer training.[36] IBM in turn was faced with almost instant competition for its first entry into the electronic stored-program computer business.

Meanwhile the TPM computer project was evolving into a machine that would be announced as the IBM 702. Using binary coded decimal and alphabetic symbols, it was intended more for commercial than scientific work. Like the 701 it had a Williams tube main memory and magnetic tape storage. The first of these was accepted by a customer in February 1955, and by the end of the year fourteen 702s had been produced.[60]

IBM had entered into the electronic stored-program computer market in head-to-head competition with the ERA 1103 and the UNIVAC I, both products of Remington Rand. IBM's computers used Williams tube main memories as did the ERA 1103, whereas the UNIVAC I used a mercury acoustic delay line memory. The reliability, cost, and performance of these memories soon became critical factors in the evolving competition.[61]

2
Searching For Memory

The search for memory technology in IBM was signaled by the November 1946 letter to Thomas J. Watson, Sr., from John McPherson and Wallace Eckert, urging that the development of high-speed memory "should be pushed with all possible vigor."[1] Two weeks later IBM engineers had identified eleven projects that might lead to improved memories, but none that could be developed in time for the SSEC.[2] Instead they were under consideration for future calculators to compete with those being developed by other organizations using government funds. At this stage IBM had decided not to seek government funding for development efforts for fear of jeopardizing its proprietary position in automatic computation.

The memory technology the engineers sought had to be fast enough to match the speed at which vacuum tube circuits did arithmetic operations. Such a memory was desirable for any electronic calculating machine, but the advent of stored-program computers made it imperative. John von Neumann had speculated that a memory with 4000 words of 40 bits each was more than adequate to handle the then-current calculations and that access times of 50 to 5 microseconds would reasonably match the electronic speed of vacuum tube logic. He also noted with a rather prophetic view of the future, "Ideally one would desire an indefinitely large memory capacity such that any. . . word would be immediately available."[3]

A First Choice

By 1948 IBM engineers agreed that the main memory technology would be some sort of special vacuum tube.[4] This judgment was based on the limitations of various alternatives.

Magnetic medium was attractive because it retained data even when the power was turned off, but the time required to access data mechanically was too long.[5]   Even the high-speed rotating drum introduced on ERA's 1101 computer in December 1950 required 17 milliseconds for one full revolution.   The mercury delay line memory developed for use on the EDVAC and UNIVAC computers by Eckert and Mauchly provided 1 millisecond access to data.   This was about ten times faster than the rotating magnetic drum but still much slower than the speed of electronic vacuum tubes.

Vacuum tube flip-flop circuits had been used in the ENIAC and the IBM 604 for very small memories called registers.   These vacuum tube memories provided the needed speed, but they were too expensive for large memories because the number of tubes increased almost in direct proportion to the number of bits of storage.

Jan Rajchman at RCA was attempting to reduce the cost of vacuum tube memories by storing hundreds of bits in one specialized cathode-ray tube, which he called the selectron.   His design required a rather complex structure inside the tube, making the practicality of his approach uncertain.   Nevertheless, because there were several other schemes for storing many bits in one tube, work on the general concept was promising.

At IBM Ralph Palmer assigned the job of developing the special memory tube to Philip E. Fox, who had a degree in electrical engineering from MIT and experience with vacuum tube circuits in the Army Security Agency prior to joining IBM in October 1946.   At IBM he had spent about a year and a half working on the SSEC and the 604 electronic calculator.[4] In his new assignment he purchased a large vacuum system, manufactured by RCA, and used it for the study of various tube designs.   He tried many ideas but none was right.   Then Ralph Palmer showed him a preprint of a paper to be presented by F. C. Williams and T. Kilburn of the University of Manchester, in November 1948, at a meeting of the Institute of Electrical Engineers in England.[6]   The paper described a scheme that Fox believed "really could store numbers."[4]

The storage method used a standard cathode-ray tube constructed much like a home television tube; but instead of creating pictures on the screen, the internal electron beam was used to store information on the tube surface. The beam was deflected to well-defined spots arranged in a rectangular array on the face of the tube. Each spot was used to store a 1 or a 0. A simple code was to have the beam on to write a 1 and off to write a 0. Visual readout could then be accomplished by interpreting a bright spot on the tube face as a 1 and a dark spot as a 0.

To accomplish the desired electronic readout of information, a characteristic of phosphor materials, unrelated to their luminescence, was employed: the capability of phosphor to emit more than one electron for each electron that strikes its surface with sufficient energy. The bombarding electrons are referred to as primary electrons, and those emitted from the material are called secondary electrons. Williams used this effect to create a very small region of positive charge at a spot on the cathode-ray tube face to which the electron beam was directed.

The creation of this positively charged spot was detected electronically by connecting an electronic amplifier to a conducting screen close to the exterior surface of the tube face. A positive signal was recorded by the amplifier when the electron beam knocked out secondary electrons from the surface of the tube. In contrast, if the beam was directed back to a spot from which the secondary electrons had already been removed, a negative signal was recorded by the amplifier. These positive and negative electrical signals were then associated with the 0s and 1s of digital information.

To change a stored 1 to a 0 required that the positive charge of the spot be neutralized. The problem was to replace the secondary electrons that had been emitted from the spot when the 1 was written. Williams had a clever solution. He observed that a positively charged spot could be discharged by directing the electron beam to a second spot nearby, typically just over one beam-diameter away. The secondary electrons released from the second spot were attracted to the first spot by its positive potential. Because these electrons did not have sufficient energy to cause secondary emission when they returned to the phosphor, they remained in the first spot and filled (discharged) it. The first spot of a pair of spots therefore could be left either charged positively (storing a 1) or discharged (storing a 0), depending on whether its companion spot was also struck by the beam.[6]

Williams and Kilburn proposed numerous variations of the pair of spots. In the version Fox selected, the beam was deflected from the first spot to the second spot, with the beam remaining on to store a 0 and turned off to store a 1. A similar beam deflection for readout produced a negative voltage followed by a positive voltage for a 1 and a positive followed by a negative voltage for a 0. The luminescence of the phosphor caused a 1 to appear as a dot and a 0 to appear as a dash. The code was therefore known as the dot-dash code.

The process of reading information stored in a given spot tended to destroy that information, however. Therefore a data regeneration, or rewrite process, was required after each readout. Furthermore electrons from surrounding regions would gradually leak into any spot that had been depleted of electrons. The leakage process took place in a few tenths of a second and even more rapidly when adjacent spots were read. These limitations of the phosphor storage material were overcome by designing the memory support circuits to regenerate information stored on the screen. This regeneration process was similar to that used with a mercury delay line in which the information stored in acoustic waves was continually detected at one end of the tube and written back into the other. However, the acoustic delay line required regeneration each time the data reached the opposite end of the tube, whereas the phosphor had to be refreshed only often enough, depending on its characteristics and the frequency of use.[6]

The Williams tube quickly became the primary choice of the IBM engineers for high-speed memory. Access times of the order of 10 microseconds were possible. This was nearly one hundred times faster than the access time of the mercury delay line memory used in the EDVAC and UNIVAC. By September 1950 a 250-word Williams tube unit built by Phil Fox had been successfully tested on the Test Assembly in Poughkeepsie.

Because it provided the same high-speed access to any storage spot that the RCA selectron offered but without such a complex internal structure, Fox expected it to be cheaper to manufacture and more reliable.

The group at Princeton under John von Neumann also learned about the Williams-tube and began working on it a few months before Fox started. The two groups appear to have worked quite independently of each other and to have separately chosen the Williams tube as the best electronic memory device at the time.[7]

The development and manufacture of Williams tube memories for use on the IBM 701 and 702 computers were aided by the hiring of Arthur L. Samuel from the University of Illinois in September 1948. Samuel had become interested in computers while helping to initiate the program to build a von Neumann-type computer (the ILLIAC) at the university. IBM hired him because he was a leading expert in vacuum tube design, with over fifteen years experience at Bell Laboratories prior to joining the University of Illinois.[8] Because Bell Laboratories and the University of Illinois had two of the finest programs in solid-state science and technology in the country, Samuel's ties with them were an important, and largely unexpected, benefit to IBM.

Shortly after IBM's decision to manufacture its own vacuum tubes became known, GE, RCA, and other suppliers became very responsive to IBM's special requirements, assuring IBM a satisfactory supply of conventional tubes designed and tested to meet rigid specifications. Thus the small manufacturing and development facility at IBM became available to work on improvements to the Williams tube.

In the spring of 1950, about two years after Bell Laboratories announced the invention of the transistor, Ralph Palmer was assigned responsibility for establishing a program in transistor and other solid-state technologies in the IBM Poughkeepsie Laboratories.[9] He placed this effort under Arthur Samuel, whose primary function was to locate and attract top technical experts to a company that lacked appropriate laboratory facilities and had virtually no previous experience in solid-state research and development. One of those he attracted was Munro King (Mike) Haynes.

Mike Haynes

Mike Haynes had a rare credential for that time: the Ph.D. in electrical engineering. Even more important his thesis work at the University of Illinois had dealt with the use of magnetic core elements for digital computer circuits. His thesis topic had been suggested by Ralph E. Meagher, of the University of Illinois, following a symposium in September 1949 at which An Wang had described his invention of a shift register storage device using doughnut-shaped cores of ferromagnetic material. Wang subsequently described his idea in a published article, saying, "Magnetic cores with a rectangular hysteresis loop are used in a storage system which requires no mechanical motion and is permanent. The binary digit 1 is stored as a positive residual flux and the binary digit 0 as a residual flux in the opposite direction."[10]

An Wang had used Deltamax, a new material fabricated by Arnold Engineering, a subsidiary of Allegheny-Ludlum. The critical characteristic of Deltamax was a sharp threshold for magnetization reversal when an external magnetic field was applied—for example, by electric current in a conducting wire wrapped around the sample.

Magnetic materials that possess this characteristic are referred to as rectangular or square loop materials because a plot of magnetization on the vertical axis and applied field on the horizontal axis has the shape of a rectangular or square loop. The word *hysteresis* is often inserted before the word *loop* to emphasize the fact that the magnetization reversal lags behind the applied current. The area in the hysteresis loop is important because it is proportional to the energy dissipated in the magnetization reversal process and is closely related to the stability of the storage state.

The Germans had used this type of material in magnetic amplifiers for fire-control systems in German naval vessels during World War II. It was an alloy containing 50 percent nickel and 50 percent iron that had been rolled very thin by a special Sendzimir mill devised in Germany. After the war U.S. naval scientific personnel brought samples of the material and one of the Sendzimir mills back to the United States and were instrumental in getting Arnold Engineering into the business.[11]

It was against this background that Ralph Meagher returned from the symposium at Harvard with news of the work of An Wang and proposed to Mike Haynes the topic for his thesis. Wang's results were so recent that Haynes believed he would be one of the first to work with these new devices. After passing his oral exams for the Ph.D. in October 1949, he ordered more of the material from Arnold Engineering and began studying the properties of doughnut-shaped samples consisting of ceramic bobbins wrapped with thin ribbons of Deltamax. Using experience gained from his assistantship on the ILLIAC project, he devised pulse equipment capable of testing cores for applicability in digital computer circuits. By December 1949 he demonstrated the same property of Deltamax that had been reported by An Wang of Harvard: electric current in a wire threaded through the hole of the doughnut-shaped sample could be used to magnetize the Deltamax material clockwise or counterclockwise about the hole.[12]

One of these states of magnetization could be associated with the binary digit 1 and the other with the binary digit 0. This information, stored in the core, could be sensed electrically by sending a current through the wire with the polarity for writing a 0. If the core was already in the 0 state, no magnetization reversal occurred; however, if the core was originally magnetized in the 1 state, the current caused a magnetization reversal to the 0 state. This in turn induced an electrical voltage in a sense wire threaded through the hole in the core. Voltage in the sense line indicated a stored 1, whereas no induced voltage indicated a 0. This was called destructive readout because the information was destroyed during the readout process.

Later in December Mike Haynes observed a new phenomenon: using small pulses of short duration he was able to detect the state of the core without destroying the information. The magnetization of the core was altered enough by the small pulses that its state could be determined, but apparently returned to its original state when the pulses were terminated.

The observation of nondestructive readout using small pulses led Haynes to the idea of switching the magnetization in individual cores by the coincidence of current pulses in two wires through the same core, neither current pulse being large enough by itself to switch the core. By Christmas 1949 he says he had shown that the clockwise or counterclockwise direction of magnetization in the doughnut-shaped cores could be reversed completely by a current that was less than twice as large as a current that did not reverse it at all.[12] With this property cores could be wired for individual selection in a two-dimensional array in which each core had one X and one Y wire through its hole. A current through one of the two wires would not switch the core, but a simultaneous current in the X and Y wires through a given core would switch it. Thus the magnetization state of any core in the array could be reversed by the coincidence of current through appropriate X and Y wires without altering the magnetization state of any of the other cores.

Learning through fellow graduate students about problems of Williams tube memories being developed for ILLIAC, Mike Haynes was eager to devise a substitute memory using coincident-current selection of magnetic cores. He recalls spending a lot of time during the Christmas holidays "in the lab, stewing and fretting. . . trying to invent something and figure out workable systems." But he was unable to devise a coincident-current memory that would be fast enough. The problem was that the current in each drive line had to be small enough that it alone would not switch a core. When two of these currents were applied coincidently, the sum was still too small to switch a core in less than a few milliseconds, too slow to be practical.

Mike Haynes therefore quit working on coincident-current magnetic core memory arrays, an invention that later played a major role in the development of electronic stored-program computers, and turned his attention to two ideas that never achieved commercial importance: nondestructive readout and magnetic logic.[13]

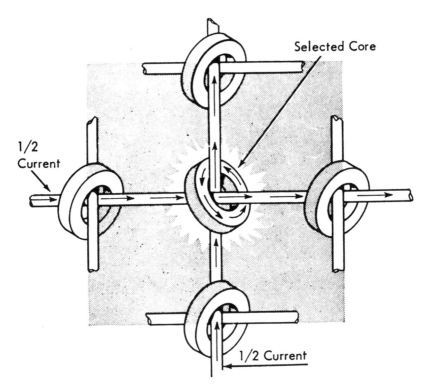

Selected Core

1/2
Current

1/2 Current

Coincident current selection
The half-select currents applied through the indicated vertical and horizontal lines are too small to switch the cores through which they pass. The one core in the center of the figure is switched, however, by the coincidence of the two currents. (Illustration from the *IBM News* of November 10, 1967.)

In April 1950 he described his memory ideas in a letter to Samuel at IBM: "I have found a way of sensing, or reading out, the information content (binary) of a core without the necessity of changing its state and subsequently regenerating. Using this, I have worked out a proposal for a static magnetic core storage system."[14] By June 1950 he had designed a complete arithmetic unit for a binary computer and had put together a "fairly substantial display of hardware," which he says, "comprised a number of shift registers interconnected together through an adder so that I could enter binary digits from a row of switches, store them in a register, then add another binary number to them and show that the sum came out correctly. There were no vacuum tubes except those that provided the pulse power for the whole unit. So I had a pretty convincing demonstration that magnetic cores had real potential for use in digital systems."[12]

When the dean of the College of Engineering raised the question of patenting these inventions, Haynes says, "I was completely floored because the idea of patenting anything was farthest from my thoughts." There was no patent department at the university. Work on the ILLIAC was free of government or industrial security and a very academic atmosphere prevailed. "I guess we thought we were working for the good of mankind," Ralph Meagher recalls.[15]

Mike Haynes and his adviser immediately set about to record the work and ideas related to shift registers, logic circuits, and the design of the arithmetic unit. But they did not record the memory invention because neither believed it was as important.[15] An Wang had already used magnetic cores to store information, whereas they believed they had achieved the first demonstration of magnetic core logic. Furthermore, Haynes believed the time required to write data in a coincident-current memory was "so long as to render it of little practicality."[13]

Logic and memory designs using magnetic core devices were the basis of Mike Haynes's Ph.D. thesis, "Magnetic Cores as Elements of Digital Computing Systems," completed in August 1950. The coincident-current memory operation of an array of magnetic cores proposed by Haynes was documented for the first time in a five-page section called "Static Magnetic Memory Proposal." The proposed memory, which he had not attempted to build, was expanded beyond his original ideas using a form of diode matrix selection to reduce the number of vacuum tube drivers needed to drive the word lines:

The basic idea is that of arranging the cores representing all the digits of each single word in a vertical stack, or word-column, with windings connected in series so that from two terminals (one on top, one on bottom) equal currents. . . may be supplied to all the cores of a word-column. These word-columns are then arranged in a square horizontal array such that, if the capacity is M^2 words, the M^2 word columns are in a square, M on a side. A corresponding array of current generator tubes, 2M of them at the top on one side, 2M of them at the bottom on the other side, is used in conjunction with an address switch and gates to deliver current pulses to the one and only word-column selected by the address switch. The top core in each column is regarded as representing the first digit of the corresponding word, and by passing a horizontal plane through the first digit core of any column we see that all possible first digit cores lie in this first digit plane. Similarly, all the cores which can represent the i-th digits of these M^2 words lie in a horizontal plane through the array at the i-th digit-level."[13]

.   Readout was to be accomplished either destructively by a large pulse on the selected word line or nondestructively by much smaller pulses. Writing was to be accomplished by a large word pulse to drive all cores to the 0 state followed by a half-select word pulse of opposite polarity coincident with half-select current pulses on bit lines where a 1 was to be written. Rectifiers were used in the digit-level interconnections to avoid interaction during readout, and rectifier pairs were used at the end of each word column to prevent multiple current paths through the array when only one word was to be selected.[13]

Haynes's thesis is the only written record of his work at the University of Illinois. Thus his claim, that he conceived a coincident-current-selection memory using magnetic cores before the end of 1949, can be verified only by the now-hazy recollections of his coworkers. He did, however, divulge many of his ideas during job interviews in the spring of 1950.[16]

His choice of IBM for a job was easy. He had worked briefly on a vacuum tube designed for the ILLIAC by Arthur L. Samuel at the University of Illinois, before Samuel left to join IBM. Samuel, along with Ralph Palmer and Nat Rochester, had attended the same September 1949 Harvard symposium on digital calculating machines at which An Wang described the use of magnetic cores for information storage in a shift register.[17] Samuel had also maintained his contacts at the University of Illinois and had followed Mike Haynes's work on magnetic core devices. Consequently, when Haynes's thesis was nearing completion, Samuel urged him to apply for a job at IBM.[18]

Mike Haynes received job offers from IBM, Bell Labs, and Hughes Aircraft. The Hughes offer was contingent on his obtaining security clearance for which they sent him the forms. The Bell offer was contingent on his passing a medical exam, for which they sent him the forms. The IBM offer had no conditions attached. The annual salary was $5,800.[19]

Haynes's response was just as unconditional. He arrived for work on October 2, 1950.

Magnetic Cores at IBM

Not long after joining IBM Haynes began seeing advertisements for ferromagnetic ferrite materials with hysteresis loops sufficiently rectangular to suggest their use in digital circuits. Ferrites, being poor conductors of electrical current, exhibited much faster magnetization reversal than metals in which induced eddy currents slowed the magnetization reversal process. The particular ferrites of interest had a complex cubic (spinel) crystalline structure and consisted of an iron oxide (Fe_3O_4) in which some of the iron was replaced by metals such as aluminum, magnesium, manganese, or zinc. Small additions of these metals critically affected the magnetic properties of the ferrites in ways that were not well understood.

Haynes ordered samples of every kind of ferrite in toroidal form made by General Ceramics. Typical cores were about an

Mike Haynes
M. K. Haynes (above) shortly after he arrived at IBM and (below)
celebrating his 32nd anniversary with IBM in 1982.

inch in diameter and cost several dollars each. All of them failed to exhibit magnetization loops rectangular enough for magnetic core logic or memory devices. Nevertheless, he enjoyed carrying around one of the smaller cores and telling his colleagues that it would, someday, replace the devices in the machine they were making.[12]

In December 1950 Haynes documented his project goals for the first half of 1951. They included improvements of magnetic core logic circuits as well as investigations of magnetic core matrix memories. Then in February 1951, he received an urgent request from Ralph Palmer to see him. Palmer was concerned about a project report from MIT describing some early work by J. W. Forrester on coincident-current magnetic core memories.[12]

Forrester clearly was not aware of Haynes's work; however, his report did acknowledge previous work on magnetic core storage, especially by An Wang at Harvard. Forrester asserted that all previous work had used cores as isolated digits or arranged in delay lines in which information was stepped from one core to another. His proposal, by contrast, made use of the steep switching threshold of the cores to permit individual core selection in an array of cores.[20]

He first noted how a two-dimensional array could be wired with two wires, an X and Y wire, passing through each core. Current in any selected X wire passed through all the cores in the selected row, and current in a selected Y wire passed through all the cores in the selected column; however, only one core, at the intersection of the selected row and the selected column, had both X and Y currents passing through it. He proposed that these currents be applied simultaneously and of such magnitude that the current in one line would be too small to switch a core (reverse the magnetization direction) whereas the coincidence of the two currents would switch a core.[20]

This was the same coincident-current selection scheme Haynes had conceived independently at the University of Illinois. Forrester, however, took the concept one step further: he proposed that several two-dimensional arrays be stacked, one on top of the other, to form a three-dimensional array. All cores in each planar array were wired by a single Z wire. Each X wire (or Y wire) was threaded serially through all the cores in the same row (or column) of each planar array. To select a single core in the three-dimensional array, Forrester proposed using the coincidence of a positive current through the selected X and Y lines and a negative current through all Z lines that were not to be selected. Negative current pulses in the Z lines were known as inhibit pulses. Individual core selection was thus achieved by the coincidence of three current pulses on three wires through the same core in the array. In contrast Haynes had used the coincidence of two current pulses at the selected core in conjunction with two-dimensional electronic selection of the word line to achieve a three-dimensional selection mechanism. Forrester's three-dimensional wiring scheme reduced the number and complexity of drive circuits required in large memory arrays, causing Haynes to give more thought to the problems of large memories.[20]

In the summer of 1951, Mike Haynes's project and other exploratory efforts were placed under the direction of Art Samuel in an organization devoted entirely to exploratory projects. It would have been called research except that Ralph Palmer, to whom Samuel reported, felt "the word research suggested work that was just wasting company money."[21] Haynes had also become a first-line manager. This was quite a challenge because, as he recalls, "I had absolutely no training or background that fitted me for that kind of activity. It was quite a shock to be put in the position of managing other people and not knowing how to go about it. There was no help from anybody in IBM for handling this kind of problem."[12]

One of his new employees was Richard G. Counihan, who had just received his bachelor's degree in electrical engineering at MIT.[22] Two months after joining IBM, Counihan had completed a report that contained an analysis of "all the major possible systems of magnetic storage known to date.[23] One of these systems was the Forrester scheme, which he called the direct switching MIT method, and another was Haynes's proposal, which he called direct switching using XY selection. Both schemes were suitable for driving three-dimensional (3D) arrays of magnetic cores, and both resulted in a reduced number of drive and sense circuits over simple two-dimensional (2D) schemes. Haynes's design made greater use of the external support circuits in selecting the desired core, thus putting less stringent requirements on the magnetic core characteristics.

Counihan noted that faster switching of the desired cores could be achieved by applying a positive half-select pulse to the selected Z planes in addition to the negative (inhibit) pulse on the nonselected Z planes. To read out stored information, only the XY word-selection drivers were used. In Forrester's scheme this pulse was the sum of two pulses, each small enough not to switch unselected cores on the planes through which they passed. In Haynes's scheme the readout pulse could be made as large as necessary for fast readout because only one selected word line was driven. Just as important, smaller electrical noise was expected in the IBM design because of the lack of half-select pulses during the read operation.[23]

The IBM method facilitated faster memory operation than the MIT method and could be implemented with somewhat poorer cores. Using switching data from magnetic cores then available, Counihan estimated memory cycle times as short as 50 microseconds could be achieved in a 4096×40 (163,840) bit array using the IBM approach. The MIT approach was expected to be more than ten times slower. In his report Counihan asserted, "The chief drawback to the 3D direct switching scheme of MIT is the time required to switch a core. . . . The XY selection direct switching system conceived by M. K. Haynes seems far superior to the MIT method in terms of functional simplicity, number of driving elements required, and speed of operation."[23]

For large, slow memories, the report proposed 4D and 5D wiring schemes. These extended the use of vacuum tube and diode selection schemes and further reduced the number of vacuum tube drivers required for large arrays. The IBM engineers thus believed they had superior schemes for driving low-performance and medium-performance memories. For ultra-high-speed storage, in the 5 microsecond cycle range, they

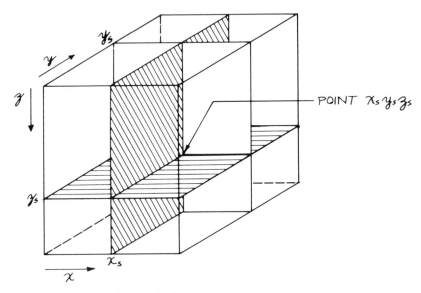

MIT memory selection method

The memory selection scheme attributed by Counihan to MIT was described by Forrester in the *Journal of Applied Physics* in 1951. All cores in each x plane are wired by a single x drive line, and all cores in each y plane are wired by a single y drive line. All cores in the selected planes x_s and y_s receive half-select pulses, but only those at the intersection of planes x_s and y_s receive the sum of these two pulses, i.e., a full-select pulse for readout. Writing is accomplished by pulses (of polarity opposite to that used for reading) on the same x_s and y_s planes to create all 1s, plus half-select pulses on selected z planes with polarity chosen to prevent cores from switching, thus storing 0s. The Forrester scheme requires the coincidence of up to three current pulses through each core to write information, causing it to be termed a 3D selection scheme. (Illustration from R. G. Counihan's internal IBM report of September 9, 1951.)

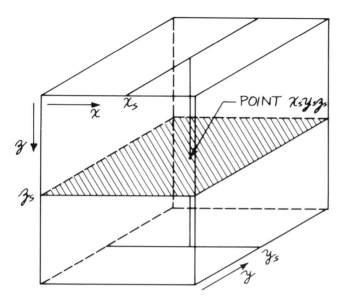

IBM memory selection method
The memory selection scheme attributed by Counihan to IBM was based
on the proposal in Haynes's thesis at the University of Illinois. An
electronic drive circuit on top of the array is activated to send current
through all word lines in plane x_s, and an electronic circuit at the bottom
of the array is activated to accept only current through word lines in
plane y_s. This causes current to flow only through one selected word line
at the intersection of planes x_s and y_s. For readout, all cores on this line
are driven to a 0 state, inducing a signal from cores originally in the 1
state and no signal from cores originally in the 0 state. (Haynes's thesis
proposed that readout be achieved nondestructively by using a very small
readout pulse on the selected word line.) Writing a word is accomplished
by an opposite polarity word-line pulse, large enough to drive all cores to
the 1 state, plus half-select pulses on selected z planes to prevent
selected cores from being switched to the 1 state, thus storing 0s. This
use of an inhibit pulse appears to have been suggested by Forrester's
work because Haynes's thesis proposed the use of half-select pulses of
like polarity on the word line and selected z planes. In either case
Haynes's method requires the coincidence of only two pulses through
each core to write information, causing it to be called a 2D rather than a
3D selection scheme in later writings. (Illustration from R. G.
Counihan's internal IBM report of September 9, 1951.)

proposed two more schemes, which they referred to as the transistor blocking oscillator and the pulse transformer systems.[23]

Feasibility Models

One of the problems in testing these designs was the lack of good magnetic cores. In the fall of 1951 Dick Counihan learned that General Ceramics had developed a magnesium-manganese ferrite material with superior properties for digital circuits. He quickly obtained samples and determined that they had reasonably good hysteresis loops. Using some of these new cores, with a 120 mil inside diameter (1000 mil=1 inch), 220 mil outside diameter, and a height of 60 mil, he built a small 2×2×2 ferrite core memory array. The 3D array was successfully operated using the IBM XY selection scheme in January 1952. Each of the eight cores was wired with three windings of twenty turns each. With drive currents of 0.1 to 0.15 ampere, memory cycles of a few microseconds were achieved.[24]

Counihan quickly followed this array with a larger 4×4×4 ferrite core array driven by the 5D drive system conceived by himself, Mike Haynes, and Gordon Whitney.[25] The cores in the array were wired and selected in the 3D manner proposed by Forrester, except that each of the X and Y drive lines was electronically selected by a 2D matrix of the type proposed by Haynes. Thus the memory array itself was wired and driven in a 3D selection scheme, but two additional dimensions of selection were provided by the organization of the vacuum tube drivers and diodes in the array wiring. The cores in the array had inside diameters of 175 mil, outside diameters of 260 mil, and a height of 60 mil. Because of the relatively low currents available from the drivers, the X and Y lines were threaded twenty times about each core and the Z lines ten times. With drive currents of 40 to 45 milliampere, a cycle of 160 microseconds was achieved. The memory was completed by mid-April and electrical tests were successfully concluded one month later on May 8, 1952.[24]

Haynes noted that the small 4×4×4 array driven in the 5D selection mode had demonstrated the feasibility of the scheme, but the real benefits of the concept could be achieved only in much

The first 4×4×4 core array

This 4×4×4 array of ferrite cores was successfully operated at IBM in May 1952. The core array was wired in the Forrester 3D selection manner, but two diode arrays provided external 2D selection of the X and Y drive lines, making it a 5D selection system by Haynes's terminology. Only two of the 4×4 core planes can be seen because the other two are hidden under the support plates.

larger arrays.[25] Specifically he hypothesized an array with 4096 words of 40 bits each in which the words were arranged in a 64×64 array. If driven in the 3D mode, 128 drivers would be required to drive the 64 X lines and the 64 Y lines; but by selecting the 64 X lines with an 8×8 diode matrix, only 16 drivers were required. Similarly 16 drivers could be used for the 64 Y lines. In this manner all the word lines could be driven by only 32 drivers as opposed to 128 drivers required in the 3D mode. Even greater savings would be realized in larger arrays.

Meanwhile Gordon E. Whitney, a 1950 graduate in electrical engineering and the first person to join Mike Haynes's group, was looking for possible users of the new magnetic core memory technology. His most enthusiastic contact was Edward J. Rabenda, who had begun his IBM career in 1924 in the Newark office servicing unit record equipment. With more than twenty-five years' experience as a successful IBM engineer and inventor, Rabenda had a lot of freedom to chose his own assignments. He proposed using a small magnetic core memory as part of a device for translating the code used on IBM punch cards to a denser, binary-coded decimal (BCD) code. This buffer memory had one storage location for each hole in the IBM punch card: 960 bits arranged in an 80×12 bit array.

In order to get enough good cores for this application, several orders of one thousand cores—150 mil inside diameter, 240 mil outside diameter, and 45 mil high—were placed with General Ceramics. A heavy-duty wire was threaded straight through each of the twelve rows of cores in the long (eighty core) direction. About 2 amperes were used to drive each of these lines. Each of the eighty columns was threaded by a fine number 32 (8 mil diameter) wire, which made fifty turns through the twelve cores in the column. With fifty turns through the cores, the 2.5 ampere turns required to drive the cores could be achieved with only 50 milliamperes in the line. This smaller current could easily be supplied by the card-reading brushes of the Type 405 accounting machine. The data in the core array were read from the eighty columns in parallel by driving the long straight wires, one at a

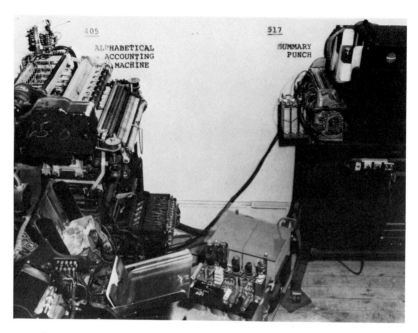

The first functional ferrite core memory
A ferrite core array is shown installed (above) in the IBM Type 405
alphabetical accounting machine. Its output was used to drive the Type
517 summary punch in April 1952. A closeup of a section of the 80×12
bit ferrite core array (below) shows the single drive lines through the
cores in the long direction and 50 turns in the short direction. The cores
are 150 mil inside diameter, 240 mil outside diameter, and 45 mil high.

time. The output signal was used to drive a Type 517 card
punch.[27]

Whitney assembled and tested the ferrite core array in April,
and on May 22, 1952, Rabenda conducted the first test of the
entire system. Forty-three of the eighty columns of ferrite cores
successfully accepted data from the card reader and then
transmitted them to the card punch. Rabenda continued working
on the buffer during the summer to improve its versatility—for
example, making it possible to punch many cards identically with
only one storage operation in the buffer. Because of poor
reliability and lack of uniformity of the available ferrite cores,
however, the buffer was not implemented in the Type 407
accounting machine product, a major disappointment.[27]

News of the core buffer quickly spread through the IBM
technical community. One of those to learn about the new device
was Werner Buchholz who had worked for almost two years as an
engineering planner (now called a systems architect) on the TPM.
He recognized the possibility of using ferrite core buffers to
synchronize the data rate of various mechanical units such as card
punches, card readers, printers, and punched tape. He discussed
his ideas with Haynes and Whitney, and by May 1952 they had
designed a ferrite core buffer for this function.[28] Their plan to
build a full-scale model for the TPM ran into trouble, however,
when General Ceramics was unable to maintain the required core
quality, causing Ralph Palmer to cancel the project.[12]

Meanwhile Rabenda continued to look for other applications
for magnetic core buffers in IBM equipment, and he filed a
number of patents for such applications. He demonstrated the use
of this 960 core buffer to IBM engineers and executives, as well as
to some outside visitors. He particularly recalls Tom Watson's
enthusiasm and his complaint that this new capability had not
been brought to his attention until seven months after the first
laboratory demonstration.[29]

In November 1952 the ferrite core buffer project that Haynes,
Whitney, and Buchholz had proposed the previous May was
reinitiated by Wayne D. Winger and Philip W. Jackson, who were
responsible for the development of the I/O (input/output) for the

IBM 702 computer. The 702 computer had evolved out of the TPM project and became IBM's first stored-program computer for commercial rather than scientific computation.

Jackson was responsible for the card reader, card punch, and printer for the 702. He had joined IBM as a customer engineer in 1949 and then transferred to the development group in Poughkeepsie to work on a rotating magnetic drum buffer, now proposed for use on the 702 computer system.[30] According to him, the big problem was "how to get data to stand still long enough to print it on a printer or to read it from a card when the buffer memory was a high-speed rotating drum with four read-write heads."[31]

The solution was to use a static buffer memory. Phil Fox and others suggested he use the Williams tube memory which had been successfully demonstrated on the TPM, but Jackson believed it would be too expensive for use as a small memory and he was not satisfied with its reliability. That September he had witnessed the operation of the buffer built by Whitney and Rabenda and had become convinced that magnetic core buffers should be considered seriously.[29] He asked Erich Bloch, a young engineer who had recently joined his group, to look into the problem.

Erich Bloch

Erich Bloch had joined IBM in January 1952 after getting his bachelor's degree in electrical engineering at the University of Buffalo, where he had taken one of the few courses in computer science offered anywhere in the country.[32] A careful, methodical person in planning and getting things done, he quickly acquired a reputation for hard work and long hours.[33] His thick German accent, the result of a boyhood in Germany and high school education in Zurich, Switzerland, seemed to enhance the precision with which he spoke.

Bloch's first assignment at IBM was to a programming group attempting to exploit stored-program computer concepts on the TPM. "After a while," he says, "I became interested in the hardware side of the business."[34] Learning of this interest and of

Bloch's knowledge of computer systems, Jackson asked him to look into the buffer memory for the IBM 702.

Bloch spent considerable time with Ed Rabenda, Gordon Whitney, and Mike Haynes learning about the ferrite core technology. He was told that Rabenda's ferrite core buffer was not reliable but that the problems were probably related to the large ferrite cores and the manner in which they were tested and characterized. Bloch was soon convinced that a reliable buffer could be made using improved smaller cores and improved core test procedures then available. He planned to rely on Haynes's group for ferrite core selection and characterization, as well as for help in circuit design. After initial discussions with Ed Rabenda, Bloch had little contact with him because he viewed the two projects as competitive. He wanted to be the first to make a magnetic core memory product in IBM.[32]

Both Wayne Winger and Phil Jackson were heavily involved in these discussions and in the decision to support the high-risk project. But because Jackson had responsibility for the card and printer systems that would use these buffers, he also remained involved in the buffer design work. One of the many uncertainties was that the buffer would be subjected to a noisy electrical environment in the card reader. Thus it might not function in the machine even if it functioned well in the laboratory.[32] Nevertheless, the possibility of achieving a buffer that would be cheaper, more reliable, and require less space seemed to warrant the risk.

Crucial to their planning was a smaller-sized core specified by Mike Haynes with an inside diameter of 60 mil, making the hole through the core smaller than the letter "o" printed on this page. With an outside diameter of 90 mil and a height of 30 mil, this core was difficult to handle and wire but required much smaller drive currents than cores previously available. The IBM engineers believed the smaller core size was an advantage because current in a single wire would be sufficient to switch the magnetization of the core from a 1 to 0. The use of wires straight through the core, without multiple turns, would make core wiring easier. General Ceramics agreed to fabricate the cores using dies ordered by

Haynes in March 1952, and paid for by IBM because General Ceramics refused to invest money in such impractical, small dies.[35] Later known as 60-90 mil cores (the dimensions of the inner and outer diameters), cores of this size were soon supplied by General Ceramics to engineers at MIT and ERA as well as IBM.[36]

The circuits selected by Erich Bloch to drive the ferrite cores in the small buffer memory employed magnetic switch cores driven by small thyratron vacuum tubes.[34] The magnetic switch cores were ceramic bobbins around which ferromagnetic metal strips were wrapped. They were very similar to the cores An Wang and Mike Haynes had first used for storing information except that the hysteresis loops were neither so wide nor rectangular as required for storage applications. Bloch used switch cores in his memory drive circuit in much the way a transformer is used. Primary windings driven by the thyratron supplied the current needed to switch the core, and voltage induced in the secondary windings was used to drive current through the ferrite cores in the memory array. The switch core thus provided the necessary impedance match between the thyratron vacuum tube circuit and the memory array line.

The engineering work proceeded in a highly empirical way. Little was known about magnetic core characteristics such as speed of magnetization reversal and sensitivity to changes in drive current or temperature. By February 1953 the 80×12 bit ferrite core card input buffer memory was operating reliably on a Type 407 printer attached to the TPM.[30] These buffer models were reworked by Erich Bloch during the final design effort for the IBM 702 during the summer of 1953.

The 2D buffers were released to manufacturing and marketed as part of the IBM 714 and 759 card reader and control unit, the 722 and 758 card punch and control unit, and the 717 and 757 printer and control unit. These machines, used with the IBM 702, 705, and 704 data-processing systems, are believed to be the first production use of ferrite core storage in computing systems.[37] Their first shipment to a customer was in February 1955 on an IBM 702 computer.

Erich Bloch
Erich Bloch reviewing semiconductor manufacturing facilities in 1970
when he was appointed vice president for operations of the IBM
Components Division. (Photograph courtesy of R. W. Collier, IBM East
Fishkill.)

This date is several months after ERA and International Telemeter Corporation had shipped larger ferrite core main memories on the ERA 1103 and the Rand Corporation Johnniac computers, respectively, and also after IBM had shipped the even larger main memories on the SAGE computer. However, these large main memories were not in quantity production in 1955, whereas Erich Bloch's 2D buffer memory was. In fact the 2D buffer was operational early in 1953 and engineered for production later that year.

During 1952 and 1953 Rabenda continued improving and demonstrating the ferrite core buffer attached to a card reader and card punch.[29] Working primarily alone in the traditional mode of an IBM inventor, he was not well situated to get ferrite core memories adopted by a product program. He controlled neither the basic technology (as did Haynes) nor the application (as did Bloch and Jackson).

It was not until late in 1953 that Ed Rabenda proposed a system that was accepted—not by IBM but by the National Security Agency. The system he developed for the agency contained a 120×12 bit array of ferrite cores that served to buffer data between magnetic tapes and punched-card equipment. In November 1955 it was announced as a commercial product (the IBM 774 Tape Data Selector) and was first installed in February 1957.[38]

Erich Bloch had beaten Ed Rabenda by two years in his race to have the first IBM product with a ferrite core memory. But Rabenda's pioneering work in ferrite cores was not forgotten in 1967, when he became an IBM Fellow, the highest engineering honor the company bestows. Announcing the appointment, Tom Watson said, "His over 60 inventions span the field from alphabetic accounting machines to tape controlled carriages, and he pioneered the use of magnetic core circuits in the company."[39]

3
A Memory From Whirlwind

In February 1951 Ralph Palmer asked Mike Haynes to assess an MIT report that contained the following thought-provoking statements:

The storage of digital information is more a problem of selection and switching than it is a problem of information retention. Many simple physical devices are available to store information, but most of them lack a suitable high-speed selecting system. . . . In an ideal storage system it should be possible to arrange elementary storage cells in a compact three-dimensional array. Storage elements inside the volume should be selected by suitably controlling three coordinates along the edges of a solid array.

First written by Jay W. Forrester in May 1950, these statements were modified for an article published in January 1951.[1] They describe a challenge Jay Forrester had issued to himself four years earlier when he attempted unsuccessfully to achieve his "ideal storage system."[2] Now he had a new device that showed promise of storing information in a three-dimensional array. It had a toroidal (doughnut) shape and was made of ferromagnetic material with a remarkably rectangular magnetic hysteresis loop characteristic.

Forrester's article immediately caught the attention of Ralph Palmer at IBM, and it influenced Mike Haynes's decision to expand his group's effort on magnetic core memories. But the true impact of Forrester's activities on the careers of Mike Haynes, Erich Bloch, and others at IBM was far greater than anticipated at the time. Indeed the impact extended far beyond individual careers. Forrester's dedication to developing his "ideal storage system" substantially altered the evolution of stored-program computers and, indeed, the entire computer industry.

Jay Forrester

Unlike Mike Haynes, who had limited funds for research at IBM and even less at the University of Illinois, Jay Forrester was accustomed to spending money in a big way. The product of wartime research, he was a natural technical leader.

Forrester received the Bachelor of Science degree in engineering at the University of Nebraska in 1939 and then went to MIT as a graduate student and research assistant in electrical engineering. He was one of the earliest members of the Servomechanisms Laboratory set up at MIT in response to technical requirements of the war effort. There he acquired extensive familiarity with servomechanisms and systems design and became an assistant director. He participated in the 1944 studies that assessed the feasibility of designing and building an aircraft analyzer into which constants for various types of aircraft could be set and was soon selected to lead the resulting Aircraft Stability and Control Analyzer project.

Jay Forrester was described by people in the project as brilliant as well as "cool and distant and personally remote in a way that kept him in control without ever diminishing our loyalty and pride in the project."[3] He insisted on finding and hiring the best people according to his own definition, people with originality and genius who were not bound by the traditional approach. "Oh, we were cocky," recalled one of his engineers. "But we had to lose some of the cockiness in the sweat to pull it off."[4]

In November 1944 the Servomechanisms Laboratory proposed to build a breadboard model in one year for $200,000. When subsequent discussions indicated this might not be nearly enough money or time, a feasibility study contract was signed with the Naval Office of Research and Invention. By August 1945 a formal proposal was made to carry the project to completion. The equipment was to be designed, built, tested, and delivered to the navy by March 1947 at a cost of $875,000.[5]

Two months after the formal proposal was made, Forrester attended the Conference on Advanced Computation Techniques at MIT in order to learn more about the design activity of the group at the Moore School of Electrical Engineering of the University of

Pennsylvania.[4] This group had just completed construction of the ENIAC, which made use of 18,000 radio tubes and 1500 electronic relays to perform digital electronic computations.

Forrester had already become interested in using digital electronic computation in the Aircraft Stability and Control Analyzer project as a result of conversations with Perry O. Crawford who, as a fellow graduate student at MIT in 1942, had proposed the use of digital computational techniques for automatic control of antiaircraft gunfire instead of the then-conventional analogue techniques.[5] Crawford cautioned Forrester that digital circuits were not yet well enough developed for his application, but when Forrester saw the digital circuit technologies developed for ENIAC, he was convinced they could be applied successfully to his project.

His decision to shift from analog to digital techniques was crucial to the future of his project, and it may also have been the first time a major control function was undertaken by digital techniques. By November 1945 Forrester was already looking for people with the special skills required for designing digital vacuum tube circuits, and by January 1946 he had made a new project proposal to the navy.

The project was to consist of two tasks: design of a suitable digital computer and adaptation of the computer to the analyzer problem. Both tasks were to be completed by December 1949 for a total of $2.4 million—almost three times the cost projected in the contract negotiated only five months earlier and ten times the estimate made fourteen months earlier. Moreover the proposed delivery date had slipped by two years.[4]

By March 1946 an agreement was reached with the navy in which the first task of designing a computer adequate for the aircraft analyzer problem was to be completed by June 1948 at a cost of $1.2 million. With its revised specifications, the project was renamed Whirlwind. It was one of a number of computer projects funded by the Special Devices Division of the Naval Office of Research and Invention.[4] It was not a small effort. During 1947 the Whirlwind project employed fifty people, half of them professional engineers or MIT graduate students.[6]

Jay W. Forrester
Forrester (above, left) in 1950 examines the MIT electrostatic storage tube his ferrite core memory replaced a few years later, and (below) pictured behind his desk in 1970. (Photographs courtesy of the MITRE Corporation Archives.)

Memory Considerations

The real-time response requirements of the aircraft simulator had placed a difficult requirement on information storage technology. The mercury delay line proposed for EDVAC and the rotating magnetic drum developed by ERA were too slow.

In February 1946 Jay Forrester attended a conference held at the Naval Research Laboratories to learn more about developments in electrostatic storage tubes. Six different applications for such tubes were cited at the conference, including use in electronic computers. Forrester carefully listed a number of desirable characteristics of storage tubes for computer application such as the ability to store 2500 to 10,000 yes-no signals per tube and to write such signals at the rate of 1 million to 10 million per second.[7]

Electrostatic storage tubes appeared to have the right characteristics for Forrester's aircraft simulator. In January 1947 Forrester attended a Harvard Computation Symposium where he outlined the objectives of the MIT Servomechanisms Laboratory effort on storage tube technology. After noting the speed with which the Whirlwind computer was to perform various calculations, he concluded that the associated high-speed memory would have to provide access to any of 640,000 bits in about 6 microseconds.[8]

Meanwhile Forrester was pondering other ways to provide the needed high-speed memory. In April 1947 he wrote a six page memo proposing his ideal storage system: data storage in three dimensions. He noted that digital storage had already advanced from the use of vacuum tube flip-flop circuits "to surface storage where a single circuit controls many points of information on an area." This method, embodied in the RCA Selectron and the MIT electrostatic storage tube, he asserted, "still falls far short of effective use of the volume occupied by the storage equipment. Efficient storage will be possible only if points can be closely spaced in a 3-dimensional (3-D) volume." Forrester then described how a low-pressure gas glow discharge tube could be employed as a double-valued impedance storage cell in a 3D array.[2]

Subsequent work showed, however, that variability among gas glow discharge tubes was too large to be satisfactory for use in the Whirlwind computer. Difficulty was encountered "due to random sparking, changes in cathode surface characteristics, and breakdown between leads inside the tubes."[9] Reluctantly, Forrester maintained the commitment of project Whirlwind to the use of electrostatic storage tubes being developed at MIT, but he also continued to look for alternatives.

New Objectives for Whirlwind

During the same period in which Jay Forrester was grappling with these critical technical problems, he found himself under increasing pressure to justify his $100,000 per month project. The Vinson bill, which created the Office of Naval Research and helped provide continuity for high-technology projects after the end of hostilities in 1945 also brought with it new ground rules and new people to evaluate projects.[10]

The massive expenditures of the Whirlwind project quickly brought it under scrutiny. An audit committee, headed by a professor of mathematics concluded, not surprisingly, that too little attention was being paid to mathematical issues. Concerning the five-times-higher level of expenditure for Whirlwind than for the IAS computer at Princeton, the committee concluded that the intended use of the two computers accounted for the difference. But John von Neumann, who headed the IAS project, stated less charitably that the differences in cost and approach resulted from the differences in people rather than from the intended use of the computers.[11]

The group Forrester assembled possessed strong engineering capability, but this was less evident to outsiders than was their cockiness and high level of expenditure. Unable to control ever increasing costs, their sponsors began to justify tight budgetary control of other projects by saying "We're not going to let it become another Whirlwind"[11] By the fall of 1948 the cost projected for Whirlwind exceeded $3 million.[10]

During 1949 pressure grew to terminate the Whirlwind project because no application appeared to justify such large expenditures.

Then in the fall of 1949 it was learned that the Soviet Union had detonated an atomic bomb, making government leaders increasingly concerned about the potential threat of Russian bombers. The Air Defense System Engineering Committee was created in January 1950 under the chairmanship of George E. Valley of MIT to study the problem and make recommendations. Shortly after the committee was established, Perry Crawford alerted Forrester to its formation, and within a week Valley was considering the possibility of using the Whirlwind computer for air defense. Not only was development of the computer well along, but project Whirlwind had the largest collection of digital computer engineers in the country.[12]

Based on the report by Valley's committee, the air force asked MIT to establish a laboratory dedicated exclusively to research and development leading to an adequate national air defense system, and by March 1950 Forrester was advised that his project would receive Air Force funding to develop the proposed system. The aircraft analyzer project was stopped, and the technical effort redirected to this new objective.[12]

The needs of the military and those of MIT's project Whirlwind had converged; money was once again assured for Whirlwind. The level of expenditure, to which Jay Forrester and his associates were accustomed, would continue.

A New Memory Proposal

Forrester was also deeply concerned about the slow progress in achieving reliable electrostatic storage tube memories essential to Whirlwind's success. Then in April 1949 he saw an advertisement for Deltamax, the ferromagnetic metal produced by the Arnold Engineering Company of Chicago, which had also interested An Wang and Mike Haynes. The magnetic characteristics of this material caused Forrester to reconsider the 3D memory array he had envisioned two years earlier. Instead of gas discharge cells, he now planned to use small rings of Deltamax for the storage devices. By June 1949 he began spending time alone in the laboratory working on these ideas.[13]

Forrester documented his ideas meticulously in his engineering notebook, as was his custom. His first entry, dated June 13, 1949, showed a nearly rectangular magnetic hysteresis loop and adjacent to it an XY array for addressing magnetic toroids. Entries made on June 13 and 14 include the following:

A method for using magnetic cores for data storage in three dimensions appears possible. The magnetic core material would be the non-linear type such as now being sold under the trade name Deltamax. . . .

In practice it may be possible to use a single conductor running straight through the core of the magnetic material instead of a coil around the core. Also it should be possible to make a three-dimensional array where one choice takes all cores in a given plane and the other two axes are selected to choose a single conductor running in perpendicular to all planes. Circular magnetic cores can be set in at an angle such that straight runs of wires could be used in both directions.[14]

By the end of June, Forrester had studied the characteristics of a number of magnetic cores. The cores were made with ceramic bobbins around which thin strips of Deltamax were wrapped. The cores were about 1.0 inch inside diameter, 1.25 inch outside diameter, and 0.125 inch high. His experimental results were not as good as he hoped. Among other problems he observed some peculiar characteristics of magnetization reversal in cores. Simple theory, he noted, suggested "the peak rate of change of flux would occur with the initiation of the current pulse. However, this does not seem to be true."[14]

Forrester began discussing his ideas and problems with Robert R. Everett, his associate laboratory director. He contacted outside laboratories trying to locate better magnetic materials, and in the fall of 1949 he selected William N. Papian, a graduate student in need of a thesis topic, to continue the search for magnetic core materials capable of functioning in his proposed 3D memory array.[15]

Bill Papian, an older student than most with a lot of practical experience when he began his thesis research, says, "Jay did feel that I could take on a good deal of responsibility, but he never for

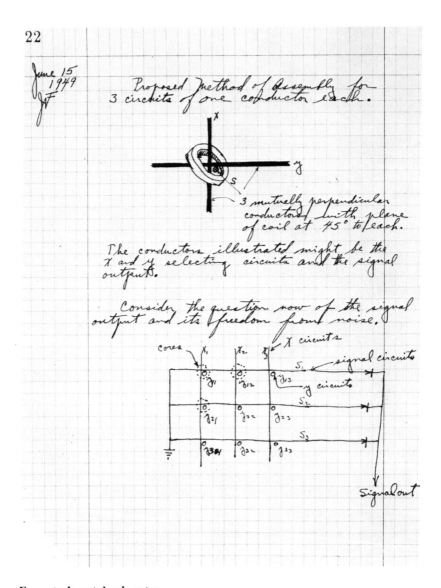

Forrester's notebook entry
Jay W. Forrester's entry in engineering notebook 47, page 22, dated
June 15, 1949, typifies the care with which he documented his ideas.
The top figure shows a toroidal magnetic core threaded and mechanically
supported by three wires passing perpendicularly through it.
(Photograph courtesy of the MIT Archives.)

an instant lost interest in the project. . . . I used Forrester's notebook 47 darn near as a Bible. . . . It was the boss's notebook for one thing, but also the notebook of the guy we all acknowledged was the most brilliant man around. Many of the ideas that came up later were already hinted at or fully discussed in that book."[16]

By January 1950 Papian had written his thesis proposal. It called for measurements of the properties of magnetic cores "made of Deltamax and similar alloys. Magnetic ferrites may be considered later." If magnetic cores with suitable characteristics were found and time permitted, he planned "to build a small (2×2) memory matrix with associated circuitry, and determine its operating characteristics." He estimated the total project would require about 400 hours of work. Forrester signed a statement that said, "The problem described here seems adequate for a Master's research"—in retrospect, a classical understatement.[17]

Papian completed a review of the literature on materials that might have the desired magnetic characteristics and contacted outside suppliers.[18] On April 13, 1950, he wrote in his engineering notebook, "First real gleam of possible future success came today." He had placed a large magnetic core on test for "permanence of storage in the face of repeated non-selected pulses" and found that the stored information was not destroyed even after "5 minutes of repeated nonselecting pulses at about one kilocycle."[19]

Papian also tested a number of cores made of magnetic ferrite materials, observing switching times as short as 2 microseconds. This was much faster than metallic cores, but the stability of stored information in ferrite cores was not good.[19] Major emphasis therefore continued to be placed on cores made by wrapping thin ferromagnetic metal strips around ceramic bobbins. The thinner the metal strips, the smaller were the induced electrical eddy currents and the faster the material could be made to switch from a 1 to a 0 state.

That spring Papian received the master's degree and became a full-time member of the Whirlwind project where he continued to work on magnetic core memories. In October 1950 he reported,

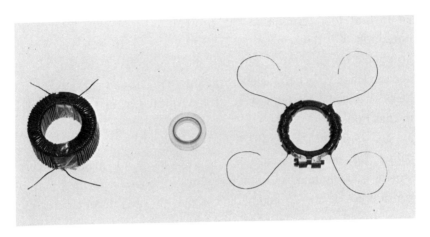

Early magnetic cores
These 1- to 2-inch-diameter magnetic cores were tested by W. N. Papian
as part of his thesis work in 1950. The wired core at right was made of
ferrite by the Ferroxcube Corporation, and Papian achieved the desired
switching characteristics by adjusting the screw of a nonmagnetic band
about the core to alter its internal stress. The wired core at left consists
of silicon-steel ribbons from Allegheny Ludlum encased in a transparent,
toroidal plastic case to prevent damage from the wires. At center is an
uncased metallic-ribbon core. (Photograph, taken in August 1950,
courtesy of the MITRE Corporation Archives.)

Metallic magnetic core array
A 16×16 plane of metallic cores tested at MIT near the end of 1951.
The cores are about 0.2 inch in diameter and consist of 0.25 mil thick
molybdenum-Permalloy ribbons wrapped on bobbins. (Photograph
courtesy of the MITRE Corporation Archives.)

"Preliminary operation of the $2 \times 2 \times 1$ array of cores has been accomplished. Perfectly successful storing and cycling of information throughout the array is indicated."[20] The model was referred to as a $2 \times 2 \times 1$ array, instead of simply as a 2×2 array (which it was) because each core was threaded by an inhibit line in addition to the X and Y drive lines, permitting the 3D array concept to be tested in the small 2×2 array.

Each of the four cores in the array was made of ten turns of 1 mil (0.001 inch) thick silicon-steel ribbon wrapped around a ceramic bobbin. The inside diameter of the ferromagnetic core was about 0.5 inch. Each core was driven by an X and a Y line wrapped twenty-five times about the core. This was twenty-five times the number of turns Forrester had proposed but was essential in this first crude magnetic core memory because of the large size of the cores and the small current available from the drive circuits. The combined sense-inhibit line also made twenty-five turns through each of the cores.[21]

By June 1951 Papian had completed his measurements on the primitive model. He had shown that drive currents could be increased or decreased by as much as 20 percent before a point was reached where information could no longer be retained. He had also determined that successive read-write operations on one core in the array disturbed the adjacent cores so that they exhibited a less certain 1 or 0 signal when interrogated. He concluded that the use of 3D arrays of magnetic cores for information storge was "fundamentally sound" but that arrays containing at least sixty-four cores were needed "to assess the ultimate practicability of arrays containing thousands of cores."[21]

Operation of the first array was unsatisfactory in at least one important respect. In the coincident-current mode, switching times were 30 microseconds or longer.[22] A memory constructed of cores this slow would fall far short of the performance requirements of Whirlwind.

Magnetic cores made of nonconducting ferrite materials had been shown to be at least ten times faster, but their output signals and resistence to disturb pulses were not as good. Consequently Forrester began to organize a small ferrite material development effort at MIT that Bill Papian reported would "involve Professor von Hippel's Laboratory, a small development firm in New Jersey (the Glenco Corp.), and ourselves."[20]

Finding a suitable material for Forrester's purpose would not be easy. Forrester was even beginning to discuss the possibility of using a ferroelectric material in place of ferromagnetic materials. He thought ferroelectric materials might be usable as memory elements because they could store an internal electric field much as ferromagnetic materials stored an internal magnetic field.

Meanwhile improvements continued to be made in electrostatic storage tubes for Whirlwind. By the end of March 1951 Forrester was able to advise the Office of Naval Research that Whirlwind had become "a reliable operating system," experiencing 90 percent useful operation during a scheduled thirty-five-hour week. Several times the computer had achieved as many as seven consecutive hours of error-free operation.[23]

Early in the year, the Whirlwind computer was coupled with the prototype Microwave Early-Warning (MEW) pulsed radar to track single aircraft and to perform a computer-controlled, collision-course interception. On April 20, 1951, three such interceptions were successfully completed.[23] With continuing improvements in electrostatic storage tubes and other components, there was reason to believe the system could be made as reliable as needed.

The successful preliminary operation of Whirlwind with electrostatic storage tubes diminished the need for a new memory technology. Nevertheless Forrester and Papian continued their efforts. By the end of 1951 they had demonstrated the operation of a 16×16 (256) bit array of metallic cores.[24] By May 1952 a 16×16 bit array of ferrite cores had been operated as a memory with adequate signal and much higher performance.[25]

Joining Forces

Also in May 1952 Norman H. Taylor, a key design engineer for Whirlwind, advised Forrester that he had talked with John McPherson of IBM about the production problems of the air

Ceramic Memory I
Wired ferrite cores in the 16×16 core array, Ceramic Memory I, which
was successfully tested at MIT in May 1952. The cores have an outside
diameter of about 0.14 inches, and the heavy X and Y wires are 20
gauge or about 0.038 inches in diameter. The thinner Z inhibit and
sense lines thread all the cores in the plane. (Photograph courtesy of the
MITRE Corporation Archives.)

defense computer.[26] The result was that in July 1952 Jay W.
Forrester, Robert R. Everett, Norman H. Taylor, and C. Robert
Wieser of the MIT Lincoln Laboratory visited IBM's
manufacturing and development facilities in Poughkeepsie, New
York, to evaluate IBM's capability for developing and
manufacturing the sophisticated air defense computer proposed by
MIT.[27] Their visit included Ed Rabenda's laboratory, Mike
Haynes's laboratory, and the main Poughkeepsie plant where they
observed neatly dressed men and women assembling IBM
machines on freshly polished wood parquet floors. Much
impressed, Norman Taylor was heard to exclaim, "Oh, Karl Marx,
where are your dark satanic mills?"[28]

That fall Bill Papian and Kenneth H. Olsen also visited IBM
development facilities to learn more about IBM's work on ferrite
core memories. They came especially to see the IBM 405
accounting machine equipped with the 960 bit ferrite core buffer
built by Gordon Whitney and Ed Rabenda. Shortly after the visit
IBM received a subcontract from the MIT Lincoln Laboratory to
provide engineering services and to conduct research and
development studies "to assist MIT in determining the Air
Defense System's requirements of a digital computer and related
terminal equipment, including study of present developments."[27]
Forrester was to be in charge of the MIT effort.

IBM's work on magnetic core technology appears to have been
only a secondary reason for MIT's decision to select the company
to work on the Air Defense System. Nevertheless, it is interesting
to compare the status of this technology at IBM and MIT in the
fall of 1952.

Bill Papian at MIT had operated his first 16×16 bit ferrite
core memory array in May 1952, the same month Ed Rabenda and
Gordon Whitney of IBM had successfully tested their nearly four
times larger 80×12 bit ferrite core memory array as a functional
part of the IBM Type 405 accounting machine. The IBM test was
probably the first test anywhere of a ferrite core memory
performing a useful function. It was also in May 1952 that Ken
Olsen at MIT had described the use of a magnetic matrix switch to

drive a core memory array and Counihan, Haynes, and Whitney at IBM had used a type of diode matrix switch for the same purpose.

Here, however, the similarities of the two programs end. The IBM effort under Mike Haynes consisted of a number of small experiments to test a variety of concepts for magnetic core memory and logic. In contrast the MIT effort under Jay Forrester focused almost entirely on the single purpose of developing a large main memory for Whirlwind. Limited work on core logic did not begin at MIT until the summer of 1952.[29] Even more important, Jay Forrester could call on help from highly skilled professionals throughout the MIT organization; and the Digital Computer Laboratory, which he headed, had approximately four hundred employees, about twenty of whom were already involved in various aspects of magnetic core memory technology.[16, 30] This included Forrester himself; Bill Papian, an engineer with a master's degree from MIT and considerable practical experience; David R. Brown, who headed the magnetic core materials development effort; and Kenneth H. Olsen, who had submitted his master's thesis that spring.

Ken Olsen in particular typified the unique resources available to Forrester. One of the brightest graduate students at MIT, his thesis work was performed under the direction of Robert R. Everett, the associate director of the Digital Computer Laboratory. It dealt with the use of magnetic matrix switches to drive a coincident-current magnetic core memory. By using saturable-core transformer elements, the switch provided a relatively fixed drive pulse to the memory lines even when the vacuum tube driver outputs varied. More important it permitted the electrical voltage and current capabilities of the vacuum tube drivers to be matched to the requirements of the memory lines, and it reduced the number of vacuum tube drivers.[31]

Long-term problems relating to drive and sense circuits, wiring schemes for noise cancellation, and core materials were assigned to other graduate students. Full-time employees were assigned to solve more immediate problems and to provide continuity to the effort. It was a technical manpower resource far beyond that available to Mike Haynes. Even if such a resource had been available, Haynes was too inexperienced to manage it. Furthermore nobody at IBM was working on the magnetic materials themselves. Ralph Palmer and Art Samuel had begun to recruit such specialists, but the first of these did not arrive until August of 1952.[32]

First Ferrite Core Main Memory

In the September 15, 1952, *Quarterly Progress Report* of MIT's Digital Computer Laboratory, Bill Papian reported that three 16×16 magnetic core arrays were in operation. The first array had been made with magnetic cores of thin strips of molybdenum-Permalloy metal wrapped around ceramic bobbins. With improved support circuits it was now operating with a 16 microsecond read-write cycle. The second 16×16 array used ferrite cores purchased from General Ceramics. The drive lines passed straight through the cores as proposed by Forrester. This array had first operated in May 1952 with a 13 microsecond cycle but was now operating with a 5 microsecond cycle. The inhibit line, recently installed, caused the improved performance and also permitted full test of the 3D wiring concept. The inhibit line was driven directly from the plate of a vacuum tube, as were the other lines. Experiments were also being done to drive the lines through a saturable magnetic transformer core similar to the type Olsen discussed in his thesis. A third 16×16 array also used ferrite cores. Its X and Y lines were driven by transformer cores but was only partially operational.[33]

During the third quarter of 1952 a decision had been made to build a full-sized memory large enough to replace the electrostatic storage tubes in the Whirlwind I computer. A 32×32×17 bit array was to provide 1024 registers of 17 bits each. Each 17 bit register was divided into a 16 bit word plus a parity bit. A parity bit, used to check errors in the electrostatic memory and now in the magnetic core memory, performed its function as follows:

Just before each 16 bit word was written into main memory, the logic of the memory counted the number of 1s in the word. If the number of 1s was odd, the parity bit was set as a 1; if the number of 1s was even, the parity bit was set as a 0. This way, the number of 1s stored in any 17 bit register was always even. If a register in the main memory was subsequently interrogated and found to have an odd number of 1s, an error was recorded. This was called a parity check.[34]

Debugging a memory with 1024 registers of 17 bits each was a major problem. The number of different patterns of 1s and 0s that could be stored in the 17,408 individual magnetic cores was enormous. Merely to check all worst-case conditions was a major undertaking. Therefore, it was agreed that an electronic computer should be built to do this job—in itself a major development effort indicative of the increasing complexity of the project.

Norm Taylor had spent much of the previous quarter of 1952 working with Ken Olsen to design the needed Memory Test Computer (MTC).[33] Construction of the MTC, using standard circuits of the type in Whirlwind, was expected to take six more months. Jay Forrester assigned Olsen to build the MTC and Papian to build the magnetic core memory.

Sixty assorted molybdenum-Permalloy cores, fabricated by Magnetics Incorporated of Butler, Pennsylvania, were tested that summer. The outside diameters of these cores ranged from 1/8 to 1/4 inch, the width from 1/16 to 1/8 inch, and the ribbon thickness from 0.12 to 0.25 millimeters. The ratio of 1 to 0 signals was greater than thirty and switching times were less than 6 microseconds. According to the September 1952 *Quarterly Progress Report*, "Some of the cores were the most satisfactory so far received. . . . Metal-ribbon cores, because they have reached a higher state of development at the present time, will be used for the MTC.[33]

Nevertheless because of the superior performance ultimately expected from ferrite cores, Dave Brown, who headed the magnetic core materials development effort, began to establish a pilot-production plant for them. A subcontract had also been awarded to the General Ceramics and Seatite Corporation of Keasby, New Jersey, to continue the empirical development of ferrites for use in digital computers.[33]

By May 1953 the MTC and the $32 \times 32 \times 17$ bit memory were both completed. The memory was the first magnetic core memory

Core plane for Whirlwind
A 32×32 ferrite core plane of the type used in the MIT Whirlwind I computer. The cores have a 90 mil outside diameter and are threaded by a 32-gauge (10 mil diameter) magnet wire with Formex insulation. The frame's outside dimensions are about 9.5 inches. (Photograph courtesy of the MITRE Corporation Archives.)

ever built with sufficient capacity to serve as the main memory of a computer. Runs as long as four to five hours were reported without a single parity check.[34] In July the memory was removed from the MTC, and on August 8 it was placed in operation in the Whirlwind computer side by side with an electrostatic storage tube memory of the same capacity. The core memory was reported to be "operating very reliably" by the following week.[35] The group responsible for electronic storage tube memories also noted that "storage-tube reliability has become excellent," but their effort was in vain. The shift to ferrite core memories was by now inevitable.

Contrary to initial predictions, the magnetic core memory was made of ferrite instead of metal-ribbon cores. The ferrite cores supplied by General Ceramics were the 60-90 mil size originally specified by Mike Haynes. Ferrite cores of this size had first been used by Erich Bloch in a small 80×12 bit 2D, memory which was operating reliably on the IBM TPM in February 1953.

In September 1953 a second bank of ferrite core memory with a $32 \times 32 \times 17$ array was inserted into the Whirlwind computer. In addition to improved reliability, as observed by the smaller number of parity checks, the magnetic core memory provided faster access to stored information.[36] This accomplishment occurred just four years after Mike Haynes, at the University of Illinois, and Bill Papian, at MIT, had independently begun their thesis projects on magnetic cores.

The Disputed Invention

Forrester's careful documentation of his proposed 3D memory array using magnetic toroids began in June 1949, several months before Haynes had begun working with magnetic cores at the University of Illinois. The priority of Forrester's work seemed to be clear.

Haynes and Forrester were not, however, the only ones considering the use of magnetic cores for information storage. Jan A. Rajchman at RCA was independently developing similar concepts at about the same time. Once he read about the square-loop magnetic sheets developed by the Germans, he says,

"It was completely obvious that you could make a memory with this material. I had worked on resistor matrixes for read-only memory, so I was quite familiar with the problems of half-select."[37,38]

By September 1950 Rajchman had given sufficient thought to the subject that he filed a patent describing what he called simply a "Magnetic Device."[39] A proposed embodiment of his idea consisted of an 8×8 array of small magnetic cores made of rectangular loop material such as Deltamax. These magnetic cores were not shaped like the toroids used by Wang, Forrester, Papian, and Haynes. Instead they were short cylindrical posts sandwiched between two flat blocks of magnetically soft material that provided a return path for the magnetic lines of flux emanating from the cylindrical cores. These magnetic lines of flux flowed upward through a cylinder to store a 1 and downward to store a 0. The cylindrical cores were arranged in an XY array between the flat blocks. Coincident-current selection of any desired cylindrical core was achieved by means of separate X drive lines that passed around each row of cores and Y drive lines that passed around each column of cores.

Rajchman's invention was structurally very different from the 2D arrays proposed independently by Forrester and Haynes, but he used the same fundamental concept to store information in a coincident-current selection mode. His patent application was filed on September 30, 1950. Forrester did not file for a patent until May 11, 1951.[40]

Less than three weeks after filing his patent claims, Rajchman was appointed to the Paper Review Committee of the Institute of Radio Engineers (IRE).[41] In this capacity he became aware of the paper submitted by Bill Papian for presentation at an IRE conference the following March. After that Rajchman and Papian communicated with each other quite freely, consistent with the "spirit of cooperation that remained from the war."[37] There was soon enough information exchange among a growing number of workers that the origin of ideas was increasingly hard to determine. Even the independence of Rajchman's invention is

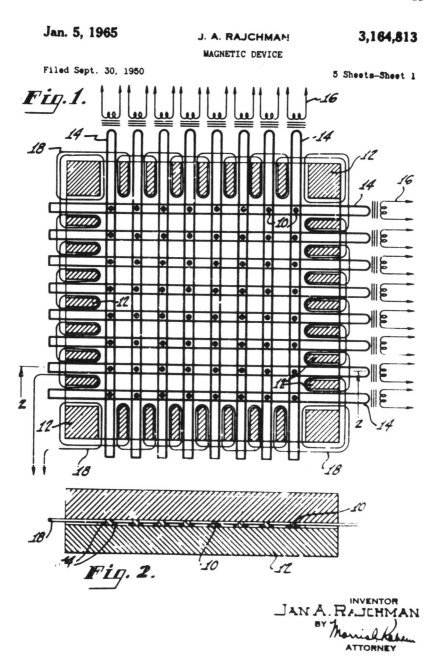

Jan. 5, 1965   J. A. RAJCHMAN   3,164,813

MAGNETIC DEVICE

Filed Sept. 30, 1950   5 Sheets—Sheet 1

Fig. 1.

Fig. 2.

INVENTOR

JAN A. RAJCHMAN

BY

ATTORNEY

The Rajchman patent

A specific embodiment used by J. A. Rajchman to illustrate his magnetic memory invention. The small 8×8 array of cylindrical magnetic storage cells (10) are selected by the coincidence of current in orthogonal drive lines (14). Note that the patent did not issue until 1965, almost fifteen years after it was filed.

questioned by Papian and Forrester who still believe that he was fully aware of their work before he started his own.[16,43]

Rajchman's proposed memory structure appeared to be easier to build than Forrester's because wires did not have to be threaded through individual toroidal-shaped cores. However, it suffered from problems of signal attenuation in conductor lines sandwiched between the blocks of magnetically soft material, and the assembly process affected the performance of the individual cylindrical memory cores. Because of these problems, Rajchman gradually moved toward the use of toroidal cores as proposed by Wang, Forrester, Papian, and Haynes.

Rajchman first tried etching cores out of a sheet of permalloy glued to a plastic substrate because he felt "it would be much too tiresome to wire individual cores. But, the results were miserable." Then he obtained some thin German-type magnetic ribbon wrapped on ceramic bobbins from Armco in Philadelphia. By February 1952 the small RCA effort had assembled a 16×16 bit memory.[44] Jan Rajchman says, "It worked like a charm right away. The thing that surprised me was how little effort there was in assembling 256 discrete cores in a memory."[37]

To reduce the cost of the cores, Rajchman asked the RCA department that made ferrite for television tubes to try to make square-loop cores. They succeeded in this effort but were not interested in making cores commercially unless they could sell more than a million per year. When asked if he thought they would sell that many Rajchman says, "I took in my breath and said, 'Yes,' although I thought a million was completely out of the question."[37]

Early in 1952 Rajchman had built and operated a 16×16 memory array in a 2D coincident-current mode. It was made with relatively slow switching metallic cores using three wraps of $1/8$ mil molybdenum-Permalloy ribbon on ceramic bobbins. Then in October 1953 he reported on the design and operation of a 100×100 bit array made with manganese-magnesium ferrite cores fabricated at RCA. The toroidal-shaped cores were 34-54 mil (inside-outside diameter) and 16 mil high. These cores were substantially smaller than the 60-90 mil General Ceramics cores used in the $32 \times 32 \times 17$ bit array for Whirlwind. Rajchman used a 9 mil, number 32, double-formex insulated wire passing straight through the cores for the row and column wires. These also supported the cores.[45]

Rajchman did not use Forrester's 3D wiring concept to reduce the number of drivers. Instead he devised a scheme in which the 100 X lines were driven by the output signal from a smaller 10×10 matrix of magnetic switch cores. The smaller matrix of magnetic switch cores was driven by ten vacuum tube drivers on one side and ten on the other. Thus only twenty drivers were required to address the 100 X lines of the storage array. The 100 Y lines were similarly selected. Only forty drivers were needed to access the 10,000 ferrite cores in the array—five times fewer than would have been required without the use of the magnetic core matrix selection scheme. (His matrix selection approach was similar, but not identical, to the one Olsen had proposed a year and one half earlier in his master's thesis at MIT.[31]) The read-write cycle of Rajchman's memory was reported to be 25 microseconds.[45]

Rajchman's memory array was tested at about the same time that the MIT $32 \times 32 \times 17$ bit memory was placed on the MTC. Rajchman had to make do with less sophisticated test equipment; nevertheless he felt he had shown the feasibility of large ferrite core memory arrays using his drive scheme.

On September 25, 1956, an interference was declared between the Forrester and Rajchman patents. The brief for Rajchman stated, "Forrester concededly was the first to conceive, and Rajchman's position is that Forrester failed to sustain his burden of proof concerning reduction to practice."[47] In particular, the brief asserted that the 2×2 metallic array constructed by Bill Papian in the summer of 1950 did not constitute a reduction to practice. To this the Board of Patent Interferences concurred, noting that even Forrester did not claim these tests had proved magnetic core memories were satisfactory for the Whirlwind application.[46] Rajchman's brief further claimed that Forrester's invention had been abandoned "until Papian discovered at an IRE meeting in March 1951 that Rajchman was working along the same lines and that this knowledge spurred Papian into renewed activity."[48]

The board noted that Forrester had the burden of proof because he was the junior party to the interference; that is, he had the later filing date. In the opinion of the court, Forrester had failed to demonstrate adequate diligence throughout the period including January, February, and at least the first sixteen days of March 1951. On October 18, 1960, the Board of Patent Interference awarded to Rajchman what many believed were the ten broadest claims of the Forrester patent.[49] These claims dealt with coincident-current or coincident-voltage selection of bistable storage elements having rectangular hysteresis loops. The remaining claims of the Forrester patent covered the inhibit drive, 3D selection of cores, coordinate wires threaded straight through the cores (instead of having multiple turns), and certain aspects of output signal sensing.

Research Corporation, which handled all patent licensing and negotiations for MIT and was assignee of the Forrester patent, immediately initiated a civil action to regain the ten claims. RCA countered with a civil action to obtain the claims awarded to Forrester. In addition Research Corporation filed civil suits against RCA and IBM for patent infringement on the presumption that it would win in the courts.

These proceedings were of interest to everyone in the rapidly growing computer industry. Research Corporation was offering to license the Forrester patent at a price of two cents per core, which would add substantially to the cost of making magnetic core memories. The events were also a stark reminder that issued patents are subject to legal challenge and that failure to document or pursue an idea diligently can result in loss of patent rights—even to a person who, admittedly, was not the first to conceive the invention.

Prior to 1957 IBM had entered into patent cross-licensing agreements with RCA covering only special technologies such as electron tubes. The interference between the Rajchman and Forrester patents made a broader agreement with RCA desirable. In July 1957 IBM negotiated a cross-license with RCA which enabled each party "to practice patent methods and processes of the other party in the manufacture and use of Data Processing Machines and Systems."[50] This, of course, included the Rajchman patent. Birkenstock and others involved in the IBM negotiation with RCA were pleased when the ten broadest claims of the Forrester patent were awarded to Rajchman in 1960. If this decision was upheld in the civil actions, IBM would be free to use these patent claims.

More Inventors

The financial importance attached to the outcome of the Forrester versus Rajchman patent litigation tends to obscure the fact that no one person invented magnetic core memories. Like so many other technologies, magnetic core memories resulted from the contributions of numerous individuals. As early as 1935 K. J. Sixtus (of General Electric Research) had described coincident-current excitation of magnetization reversal in wires exhibiting rectangular hysteresis loops.[51] Although he did not suggest a practical application, one could conclude that the use of coincident-current selection of magnetic cores in a storage array was obvious to anyone familiar with his work.

During the 1940s a number of apparently independent proposals were made to use ferromagnetic loops or toroids to store information. The minutes of a two-day meeting at the IBM Watson Laboratory in June 1948 record such a proposal by the IBM scientist Llewellan H. Thomas and his engineering colleague Robert Walker. The meeting was attended by John McPherson, Wallace Eckert, Ralph Palmer, Rex Seeber, and several other IBM technical leaders. Convened about five months after IBM's SSEC had been dedicated, the meeting was held to discuss specifications and technologies for IBM's next large-scale calculator.[52]

Thomas and Walker had been experimenting with information storage in 1.5 inch diameter ferromagnetic metal rings. Each ring was wired with two input lines, but apparently coincident-current selection was not considered. Thomas and Walker continued work on ferromagnetic ring storage until they learned about the work of An Wang at Harvard. Then because Wang's work was more advanced and was believed to predate the IBM effort, Thomas terminated the project.[53] One can now ponder the wisdom of that decision because the experiments of Thomas and Walker were documented in the same month in which An Wang says he conceived his magnetic storage invention.

An Wang, who founded Wang Laboratories in 1951, had just completed his Ph.D. studies in May 1948 when he joined the staff of the Harvard Computation Laboratory, headed by Howard Aiken.[54] Wang recalls Aiken urging him to think about ways to use magnetic media for information storage without the use of mechanical motion. He says, "I was intrigued by his suggestion. . . . [but] the problem of how to get the magnetized information out—without motion and without destroying its magnetic property—baffled me, and maybe others before me."[55]

It was early in June 1948, about a month after Aiken suggested the problem, that the solution occurred to An Wang. He saw he need not worry about destroying the information stored in the core during readout as long as he properly detected the information and was able to write it back into the core if he desired. "The idea," An Wang recalls, "is that by destroying the information—I know it." With this insight, he quickly developed his shift register memory using magnetic cores.[54]

In 1947, two years before Wang filed for his patent, Frederick W. Viehe had filed a patent application on an electronic relay circuit that described the storage of information in a single toroidal magnetic core wired by a primary input wire, an auxiliary winding, and an output.[56] Unlike the well-educated Wang, Frederick Viehe had no formal training in electronics except as an electrician's mate in the navy. "Very much an individualist [and] difficult to live with," according to his son, he had a small electronics laboratory in his house where he conducted his studies.[55]

During the patent dispute that ensued between Wang and Viehe, IBM in 1956 purchased Wang's patent for $400,000. IBM also hired Viehe as a consultant and purchased his patent as well.[57] Under Birkenstock's leadership, IBM's commercial development department thus had positioned IBM to be able to use both of these patents, no matter who won the interference. In 1959 the patent interference case was settled with Wang winning fifteen of the sixteen disputed claims.[55]

In 1945 several years before either Wang or Viehe filed their patent claims, J. Presper Eckert and Chuan Chu of the Moore School of Electrical Engineering at the University of Pennsylvania had proposed the storage of information in a 2D array of toroidal ferromagnetic cores. Each core in the array was wound by a wire (in series with an oxide rectifier) which was connected between an X and a Y drive line. Separate drive circuits for each X line and each Y line thus made it possible to pass current through any one selected core in the array. This technique for using external circuitry to select individual cores in an XY array was similar to the scheme Mike Haynes proposed five years later for driving individual columns of cores in a 3D array.

These ideas were documented in the report of June 30, 1946, on EDVAC, the computer developed by Eckert and others at the Moore School.[58] Although the EDVAC report was classified, it was distributed widely enough to cast doubt on the independence of proposals made by others at a later time. J. Presper Eckert says he told a number of people about this work, including Jay Forrester and Richard L. Snyder; and Jan Rajchman remembers Snyder communicating this idea to others in 1947, about two years before Forrester first documented his ideas for 3D arrays of magnetic cores.[59] In 1948 a graduate student of Snyder at the University of Pennsylvania developed a 2D magnetic core memory array in which the cores were selected by a multicoordinate selection system similar to that described in the EDVAC report.[60,61]

In addition to the many activities that predate the work of Forrester and Rajchman, many more innovations subsequently were required in order to make magnetic core memories a practical reality. These innovations relate to ferrite core materials and processes, noise reduction schemes, electronic support circuits, component and array packaging, array wiring, and manufacturing and test techniques.

A Retrospective View

Jay Forrester's role as a promoter and a technology champion far overshadows his role as an inventor. By promoting and building Whirlwind, he created the pressing need for a large, fast, reliable, random-access memory. Moreover he had the resources to develop the first large memory using magnetic cores, and he made the decision do just that.

Forrester also had a clear vision of the ultimate form of ferrite core memories: a simple 3D array of magnetic doughnuts with three drive wires strung straight through each doughnut. His observation that nonmetallic ferrite cores might be more suitable than metallic cores was particularly significant. Unlike Mike Haynes, Forrester spent little time considering alternative selection schemes for memory or studying magnetic core devices for logic. He had a single purpose, knew what he wanted, and believed he could obtain the type of magnetic core he needed. He did not plan to compromise his simple design.

Forrester started a search for appropriate materials that led to E. Albers-Schönberg, who had observed square hysteresis loop ferrite materials as early as 1949. Albers-Schönberg had recently come from Germany to join General Ceramics in New Jersey. In 1950 he was approached by the MIT group and urged to begin work on square-loop ferrite cores for use in memories. This was the beginning of ferrite core work throughout the world.

An interesting example of how rapidly these technical developments were disseminated is related by Heinz E. Billing of the Max Planck Institute in Germany:

At the end of July 1952, Prof. Weizsäcker, at that time visiting his brother-in-law Albers-Schönberg in the USA, sent me some ferrite cores, developed by Albers-Schönberg. In the accompanying letter he pointed out that these cores had a rather square shaped hysteresis loop and might be of great interest as memory components. Their magnetization could be switched in a few microseconds. For someone working on the problems of computer memories, this information was sufficient to make him immediately think of a memory element selected by two coincident currents. . . I myself had, only 4 months later, a small two-dimensional test matrix running with 16 rows of 10 bits each with a 5 microsecond access time.[62]

From his account, one might infer that Billing was the first to fabricate a ferrite core memory array. Indeed he was one of the first; however, his array of 160 bits was actually completed more than six months after Ed Rabenda and Gordon Whitney demonstrated a 960 bit ferrite core array on the IBM 405 card reader, Mike Haynes and Dick Counihan had operated a $4 \times 4 \times 4$ array of ferrite cores, and Jay Forrester and Bill Papian had operated a 16×16 ferrite core array with an inhibit line to show 3D memory capability. It was almost one year after Haynes and Counihan had demonstrated what may have been the first 3D array of ferrite cores in a small $2 \times 2 \times 2$ array.

The question of priority on later innovations became even more confused as Forrester's articles on magnetic core memories attracted new people to the field. This problem was aggravated by the secrecy surrounding most efforts. IBM did not encourage engineers to publish their results, nor was the predominantly government contract work at ERA publicized.

Exploratory work on ferrite core memory devices was started at ERA immediately after Forrester's paper appeared in the *Physical Review* in January 1951. By July 1952 the navy had contracted with ERA to develop a ferrite core memory to replace the electrostatic memory on the ERA 1103 computer. Roland B. Arndt, who served as project engineer for this effort, had worked on selectron memory applications at RCA before joining ERA. On July 7, 1952, his first day of work at ERA, Arndt was told that his assignment was to put ferrite core memories on the 1103.[63]

Thus a competitive ferrite core memory effort was initiated by the navy at ERA almost as soon as Forrester and Papian successfully operated their first 16×16 bit array of ferrite cores under contract to the Air Force and at about the same time IBM was selected to work with MIT to develop a computer for the air defense system. The technical direction of the ERA memory development effort, like that at IBM, was based largely on the work at MIT. ERA had access to the MIT reports and held open discussions with the technical people there.[63]

The air defense system itself was classified, but the Whirlwind computer and the magnetic core memory developments were not. The publicity given the nonclassified work at MIT was extensive. In September 1953, for example, MIT sponsored A Symposium on Magnetic Cores—Their Application, Fabrication, Testing, and Handling. The list of invitees included representatives of seven companies that produced ferrite cores, five companies that produced metal-ribbon-wrapped cores, and eight companies that were using magnetic cores in computer development. Representatives from universities and government were also invited.[64]

Without the Whirlwind effort, large ferrite core memories certainly would have been developed, although somewhat later. IBM, with its early start, surely would have produced one of the first large commercial ferrite core main memories. But this more gradual development did not occur; instead publicity given the technology by MIT, competitive pressures, and the availability of government funds brought a number of companies into the ferrite core memory business, and the presumed requirements of national defense caused IBM and MIT to work together in a crash effort to develop large ferrite core memories for the air defense system.

4
Project SAGE

"One of the best payoffs that belonging to a professional society could produce," John McPherson recalls. "I should have gotten a finder's fee."[1] His "inconsequential committee meeting" in June 1952 to organize the second Joint Computer Conference had resulted in a discussion of consequence. Norm Taylor of MIT had advised him that the MIT Digital Computer Laboratory was looking for a commercial concern to manufacture the proposed air defense system. Was IBM interested?

McPherson returned to IBM headquarters at 590 Madison Avenue to advise Jim Birkenstock and others of his discussion. The executives quickly determined that IBM was interested. It appeared to be the opportunity Tom Watson was looking for—an opportunity to rebuild the military products division and to strengthen IBM's capability in electronic technologies.[2]

Selecting IBM

During July 1952 Jay Forrester and his associates reviewed a list of fifteen to twenty companies as potential manufacturers of the digital computing equipment needed for the next phase of the Whirlwind project. Preliminary meetings were arranged with representatives of the five companies that appeared to be most promising.[3] The Bell Telephone Laboratories and RCA chose to withdraw from further consideration because of prior commitments. The remaining three companies were visited at several locations by Jay Forrester, Robert Everett, Norm Taylor, and Robert Wieser. According to Forrester, these four representatives of MIT were unanimous in their ranking of the companies and in the view that a wide margin existed between them. Their order of choice was (1) IBM, (2) Remington Rand,

and (3) Raytheon. IBM was formally notified of its selection that October.

In reporting on negotiations with IBM Norm Taylor had said, "The IBM administration, right up to Thomas J. Watson, is very interested in this job."[4] Apparently Remington Rand was also interested. According to Birkenstock they "attempted to use the political clout of General MacArthur," whom they had recently hired, "to unhook the MIT-IBM agreement."[2] In response Forrester documented his reasons for selecting IBM:

At all points of contact we observed certain fundamental differences between the two companies. . . . In the IBM organization we observed a much higher degree of purposefulness, integration, and esprit de corps than we found in the Remington Rand organization. Also, of considerable interest to us, was the evidence of much closer ties between research, factory, and field maintenance in IBM. Many of the comparative shortcomings in the Remington Rand organization can be traced directly to the very recent acquisition of their two strongest electronic groups and the fact that the two had not yet worked with each other or with a Remington Rand factory. The ERA organization, which we considered the best of the Remington Rand company, had been so recently acquired that it was almost impossible to tell what its future in the rest of the company would become.[3]

Forrester then cited other factors that led to the selection of IBM. These included greater experience in transferring electronic equipment from development to the factory, over 3 million vacuum tubes already operating in IBM equipment at customer locations, superior technical ability among key technical staff members, superior field service force, and closer proximity to MIT.[3]

Staffing the Project

Some IBM employees had been assigned to the project as early as September 1952 in anticipation of the contract.[5] One of these was John M. Coombs, who became the IBM project manager. He had joined IBM in January 1952 from ERA a few months before the purchase of ERA by Remington Rand was consummated.[6]

Office space was rented on the third floor of a necktie factory on High Street in Poughkeepsie, New York, where work on the TPM previously had been concentrated. The IBM part of the project got its first name, Project High, from this location. The overall project continued to be referred to by the MIT designation of Whirlwind II, but as IBM became more deeply involved, it was clear that a name less closely identified with MIT was needed. The name SAGE (Semi-Automatic Ground Environment) was adopted and remained the designation to the end of the project. The large SAGE computers received the service designation AN/FSQ-7 (Army-Navy Fixed Special Equipment); and the first prototype AN/FSQ-7 computers were designated XD-1 and XD-2.[7]

By the end of November, fourteen staff-level employees had been assigned to the project. One of their major activities was to define the responsibilities of IBM and to help formulate the contract with MIT. This was completed by the first of the year and IBM began staffing in earnest. By July 1953 there were 203 technical and 26 administrative people on the project. By November the planned level of about 300 had been reached, which consisted of 17 supervisory and administrative, 162 professional-level technical, 65 technical support, and 52 clerical persons.[8,9]

An early recruit to the program was Nathen P. Edwards, whose first assignment at IBM had been with Phil Fox, developing the Williams tube storage for the TPM and the IBM 701. He joined Project High in December 1952 and was soon placed in charge of memory systems.[10] Edwards immediately hired two engineers from Mike Haynes's group: Robert L. West and Gordon E. Whitney.[11] Then in September 1953 Richard Counihan was also recruited from Mike Haynes's area. Haynes himself remained in commercial development activity to work on magnetic core logic and small buffer memories and to recruit and educate more people in magnetic core technology.

Another important recruit to Project High was Wilford M. Wittenberg. He replaced Edwards as manager of memory development for SAGE one year later when Edwards became one of three members of the newly formed Engineering Design Office reporting to John Coombs.[12] Wittenberg had previously worked for Edwards on Williams tube memories for the TPM and 701 and before that he had been an IBM customer engineer.[13]

Edwards moved to Boston for a few months beginning in January 1953 to work with Papian and to learn all he could about the MIT ferrite core memory project. He also observed the operations room for a sector of the North American Air Defense System, where air force personnel were taking data supplied by radar screens and manually tracking the various airplanes in their sector on a large Plexiglas screen. The information collected at this location was also being used to test the experimental Cape Cod System, which served as a prototype of the proposed air defense system.[10]

The proposed system was to have large digital computers at many sites around the country in constant communication with each other to share data automatically, to calculate the paths of all aircraft over the country, and to determine if hostile aircraft were present. The manual plotting Edwards observed was to be done automatically in real-time by the new system.

The system was to be implemented with electronic vacuum tube logic and ferrite core memory. The computers proposed for the air defense systems would each require ten to thirty times as many vacuum tubes as the 1400 then used in each IBM 604, and all had to function reliably at the same time.[6] Although such a high degree of reliability in vacuum tubes had never been achieved, the demonstrated reliability of vacuum tube circuits at that time far exceeded the reliability of transistors, which had been invented only five years earlier.

Edwards thought the proposed use of ferrite core memory was speculative. Testing of the first prototype ferrite core main memory was not to begin for several months. "We all shared Forrester's optimism and arrogance to some extent," he recalled. "Yet I wondered at the self-confidence that man must have to convince military leaders to entrust the nation's air defense to such a grandiose collection of basically untried and untested technologies."[14]

Cooperative Design Effort

Designing the main memory for the SAGE AN/FSQ-7 computer was a cooperative effort by MIT and IBM engineers. Effective organization and strong leadership were required. Referring to this problem, Jay Forrester wrote to all AN/FSQ-7 engineers in July 1953:

> The AN/FSQ-7 equipment is an essential part of an important defense program, and overall has been planned on a very tight time schedule allowing no wasted effort and time. . . .
>
> The difficulty in accomplishing the program on time is increased inevitably by the fact that two organizations are doing most of the work together. The relationship between them is new, many of the people in the groups are new to the problem and to the ways of attacking it. . . . In addition, the interdependence of the various parts of the work is very complex, and this condition is made more difficult to cope with because of the sharing of the work between IBM and MIT, and within MIT among the various divisions of the Lincoln Laboratory.[15]

During the first nine months of Project High, IBM personnel spent 950 man days at MIT learning about the Whirlwind system and about the proposed air defense system. At the same time MIT personnel spent 340 man days at IBM. IBM received over 500 technical documents from MIT, and submitted over 60 in return.[8] The MIT engineers were particularly interested in the IBM 604 calculator and the IBM 701 computer.[16] The pluggable vacuum tube units designed for these machines provided a basis for those designed for SAGE and were important for achieving reliable, manufacturable, and repairable systems.

Detailed technical interaction continued throughout 1953 and 1954. During this period project members spent 2000 man days at each other's locations; IBM received 1000 technical documents from MIT and sent 400 of its own.[8]

During early 1953 Edwards devoted much of his time to memory drivers. High-powered vacuum tubes were expensive and unreliable. The use of magnetic transformer coupling between the vacuum tube drivers and the memory lines was proposed as a way to reduce the current needed from the vacuum tubes.[17]

Wittenberg studied various drive circuits for memory arrays, while
Edwards and others contacted GE and RCA to determine what
type of vacuum tubes would most likely meet their requirements.[18]
Studies at IBM by Bob West indicated forced-air cooling of all
vacuum tube drivers would be necessary.

Numerous technical choices had to be made such as size of
ferrite cores, array wire diameter, electronic component types, test
procedures, drive and sense circuitry, and memory structure and
packaging. There were many uncertainties. Major design changes
were considered, including alternatives to Forrester's proposed
memory drive and selection scheme.[19]

In May 1953, for example, Ken Olsen wrote to Norm Taylor
saying, "It has been pointed out by several people that many of
the problems in the coincident-current magnetic memory would be
simplified if each word in the memory were read out
independently by driving that word with a single winding." This
was a significant change from Forrester's proposal and was much
closer to the 3D XY selection scheme Haynes had proposed in
1951. The advantage of such an approach, Olsen noted, was that
the sensing winding "only picks up a signal from the core in the
selected word because none of the other words are pulsed—not
even with half select current."[20] To reduce the number of vacuum
tube drivers required for direct drive of each word line, Olsen
proposed the use of a matrix of switch cores. Each switch core
would drive one word line and would itself be selected by what he
called the anticoincidence of currents applied to the X and Y wires
of the matrix.

But consideration of such major changes from Forrester's
memory array wiring proposal were terminated following
successful tests of the 32×32×17 bit memory array on the
Memory Test Computer (MTC) in May and June 1953. The SAGE
development schedule did not allow consideration of major
alternatives once an acceptable approach had been found. Many
problems remained to be solved, but the general direction of the
memory development effort was now defined.

Papian and the MIT engineers were to study the feasibility of
fundamental design decisions. In particular they were to build

feasibility models of 64×64 core planes and large 3D arrays in order to measure operating characteristics and problems pertaining to array drivers and sensing. Edwards and the IBM engineers primarily were expected to address issues of manufacturability, reliability, and maintainability. Drive and sense circuits had to be designed that performed the specified functions and could be maintained in the field. Vacuum tubes, germanium diodes, capacitors, and other components had to be specified and suppliers found. Means for testing all components used in the memory had to be constructed, including devices for counting, handling, and testing the hundreds of thousands of individual ferrite cores. Finally a manufacturing organization had to be established and trained.

In order to exchange information and to make decisions rapidly, a series of monthly meetings was established. The first of these, held on January 20, 1953, midway between MIT and IBM in Hartford, Connecticut, was attended by fourteen MIT and thirteen IBM representatives.[21] This series of meetings soon became known as Project Grind as the attendees "ground out" technical decisions and schedules. Excerpts from the minutes of the second day of the Project Grind meeting in June 1953 give some sense of the technical issues and discussions:[22]

It was generally agreed that no more than two hours a day will be available for the process of marginal checking. . . . if a part starts to deteriorate or is different from other circuits, it should be replaced.

Whole circuits must be marginal checked. It is not necessary to locate an error more precisely than to the pluggable unit containing it.

It is fairly well established that the magnetic memory will contain 4,096 registers, 33 bits each (including one parity bit) in a 64×64×33 core array. . . .

It was generally decided that a few spare planes should be wired into the memory array for emergency use.

It was definitely decided that everything should have sufficient capacity so that a complete second memory can be added later without redesigning of logic, air conditioning, power supply, room space, etc.

A crystal translator (matrix switch) will control cathode drivers which drive the driving transformers. IBM will study the 6146 and 7AK7 tubes as transformer drivers and MIT will study the 5998 tube.

The sensing amplifier will use a balanced input and amplifier, full wave rectification taking place immediately preceding strobing gate.

A memory cycle was proposed which required 7 3/4 microseconds for a complete read-write time from one strobe to the next. It was agreed. . . . to make the memory cycle faster if it is possible to eliminate: the post write disturb pulse which requires 1/4 to 3/4 microsecond. . . and the staggering of read pulses which requires an additional 1/2 microsecond. . . .

Postwrite disturb and staggered read were two techniques that had been proposed as a way of reducing the delta noise in the array at read time. Delta noise was a problem unique to Forrester's 3D wiring approach. In Forrester's scheme one core in each of the thrity-three core planes received a full-select current pulse at read time by the coincidence of half-select pulses in the appropriate X and Y lines. Necessarily all the other cores on the driven X and Y lines received half-select current pulses. Although the magnetization in these half-selected cores did not flip from one storage state to another, there was a small change in magnetization as the current pulse was turned on and off. Each half-selected core therefore induced a small delta noise into the sense line. In the memories for SAGE, each sense amplifier was subjected to delta noise from sixty-three half-selected cores on the X line and sixty-three on the Y line. The total delta noise therefore might be larger than the signal from the one fully selected core and thus make it impossible to distinguish between a stored 1 or a 0.

The first solution to this problem, proposed by Jay Forrester in an early notebook entry in June 1949, was to wire the sense line through each of the cores in a given plane in a diagonal pattern so that the delta noise was positively oriented for half the cores and negatively for the other half. It was an effective solution if the cores had nearly identical delta noise characteristics. This in turn depended on the squareness of the hysteresis loops.[23]

It was later observed, however, that cores emitted more than the normal delta noise immediately after being switched to a 1 state. The delta noise of cores just switched to the 1 state did not balance that of other cores even when the basic core characteristics were the same. Certain patterns of information storage therefore resulted in poor cancellation of delta noise and in an incorrect memory readout, even when all the cores had identical characteristics.

The proposed solution was to subject every core to a half-select disturb pulse immediately after storing a 1. In this way all cores in the 1 state were half-selected at least once before a read pulse was applied. The corrective half-select pulse, called a postwrite disturb pulse, was applied by driving those inhibit lines that had not been driven at write time.

Staggered read was independently proposed by Haynes and Forrester for further reducing delta noise.[24,25] The concept was quite simple. The read current in one of the drive lines was initiated and held on until the resulting noise subsided. Then while current was still flowing in the first line, current was initiated in the orthogonal line to switch the core. Delta noise at switching time was thus reduced by about a factor of two. The disadvantage of staggered read and of postwrite disturb was a longer read-write cycle for the memory. More information about ferrite core characteristics and memory support circuitry was needed before a decision could be made concerning the necessity of using these techniques.

A decision that staggered read was not needed was made in September 1953 following measurements on a 64×64 bit array at MIT.[26] The decision to use postwrite disturb in SAGE memories was made near the end of 1953 when debugging efforts revealed that a postwrite disturb pulse was essential even to the operation of the smaller core arrays on Whirlwind.[27] Prior to extensive debugging of the two memory banks on the Whirlwind computer, the testing of the arrays had not been adequate to evaluate this infrequent error mode.

Project members at IBM and MIT believed in the urgency of national defense, experienced the uncertainties of a new technology, and shared a common sense of commitment.[14] But there were conflicts. "We had a good working relationship with the MIT people, especially Bill Papian," Wittenberg recalls, "but sometimes we got the feeling they believed all we had to do was package Whirlwind circuits and then manufacture them. . . . They were good technical people, but they didn't understand the practical problems of manufacturing and maintaining such systems. Every time Bill Papian came, he got upset about the changes being made to his designs. We got annoyed because we couldn't make them understand the problems."[28]

A memo written to Jay Forrester by one of his associates in June 1953 provides a somewhat different perspective: "Despite well established principles known to our people at the very start of our joint work with IBM, many months were required to haggle over relatively minor details before IBM agreed to adopt the proposals of the MIT people as the basis for proceeding."[29]

Progress at MIT

The IBM development organization was in a state of turmoil during the end of 1952 and the first half of 1953. Engineers were being pulled off other projects and placed on the rapidly expanding Project High. Key engineers were recruited from Haynes's group, and Haynes himself was increasingly busy consulting with Project High, recruiting more engineers, and supporting Erich Bloch in the development of small ferrite core buffer memories for the IBM 702 computer. Meanwhile momentum in the memory development group at MIT was picking up rapidly. Planning for a larger memory for Whirlwind II was started even before the first $32 \times 32 \times 17$ bit ferrite core array had been successfully tested with the MTC.[30]

Edwards was assigned fulltime in Bill Papian's group during early 1953 and participated in many of the planning and engineering decisions.[14] They wanted to use ferrite cores with as small a diameter as possible in order to reduce both the size of the memory and the power to drive it. The wire selected was as thin as the technician at MIT could string by hand without breaking. They then calculated how large the inside diameters of toroidal-shaped cores of various heights would have to be to permit the X and Y wires to pass perpendicularly through them. It was also necessary to allow room for the sense and inhibit wires. The outside core diameter was then determined based on electrical and magnetic considerations. The resultant cores had 50-80 mil diameters and were 25 mil high, enough smaller than the 60-90 mil cores used in the first $32 \times 32 \times 17$ array to permit a 10 to 15 percent reduction in drive current.[30] This smaller core size was first used in the second memory array installed in Whirlwind I in September 1953.

By the end of July 1953 the first 64×64 plane of ferrite cores was nearly assembled. Papian was working to complete a full $64 \times 64 \times 17$ bit array for insertion into the MTC by November. He wanted to test as many features of the proposed XD-1 memory for the AN/FSQ-7 computer as possible in this array.[31]

The use of saturable pulse transformers to couple the vacuum tube drive circuit to the memory drive lines was an important feature for several reasons. The transformer provided impedance matching by transforming the high-voltage capability of the vacuum tube into the high current required to drive the magnetic cores. Previously the two internal plates of the 5998 tubes had to be used in parallel to supply sufficient drive current. Now transformer coupling permitted a two-to-one reduction in current required from the tube, making it possible to couple the 5998 plates to the transformer so that one plate provided a positive drive current and the other provided negative current. A factor of two reduction in the number of drive tubes resulted.

The reduction in the number of tubes originally was thought of as a way to save cost and space in the memory. It enabled the vacuum tube drive circuitry for the $64 \times 64 \times 17$ bit array to be mounted in the same space previously used to drive the original, four-times smaller array. Even more important, however, magnetic cores were found to be so reliable that a reduction in vacuum tubes led to a nearly proportionate improvement in memory reliability.

By September good progress had been made in showing feasibility of pulse transformer drive and in achieving the associated factor-of-two reduction in drive tubes.[32] It had also been demonstrated that an entire 64×64 plane of cores could be wired by one continuous sense line and sensed by only one sense amplifier circuit. Previously there had been concern that 64×64 bit planes were so large that they would have to be segmented in two or four parts, each part with its own sense winding and sense circuit.

Although technical progress was being made, the schedule was slipping. Mounting the large memory in the MTC was planned for November 1953, but the unit was not operational in the MTC until February 1954.[27,33] Even the straightforward job of assemblying a memory this large took much longer than anticipated.

Five professional technical people plus support personnel in the MIT organization spent two months testing each of the 200,000 cores supplied by the General Ceramics Corporation. Almost 100,000 good cores were needed to wire seventeen planes (plus four spares) of 64×64 (4096) cores each. Cores were rejected whose output signal varied from the nominal value by more than 15 millivolts when a nominal drive current of 0.82 amperes was sent through the core. All cores in a plane were retested after the X and Y wires were strung. On average six cores per plane were replaced. Perhaps half of these had been improperly tested the first time and half had been damaged during wiring.[27] The sense and inhibit lines were then wired through all the cores and the planes retested. Replacement of bad cores was much more difficult at this stage and fortunately much less frequent.

The performance of the 64×64×17 bit memory array in the MTC was judged to be satisfactory. It served as the prototype for the larger 64×64×36 bit array now planned for the first SAGE

AN/FSQ-7 computer prototype called the XD-1. Memories designed for the XD-1 and XD-2 prototype computers in turn were to serve as prototypes for the production memories for SAGE.

Ferrite Core Procurement

The study of ferrite material for use in a coincident-current selection memory began in 1950 when Jay Forrester learned that the General Ceramics Corporation in Keasbey, New Jersey, could produce ferrite materials with rectangular magnetic hysteresis loops. At his request a development program was set up by General Ceramics under E. Albers-Schönberg who had made the first rectangular loop material. Beginning early in 1952 the General Ceramics work was supported by a subcontract from the MIT Lincoln Laboratory.[34]

In March 1952 Haynes ordered a die for pressing cores that General Ceramics believed was too small to be practical. This die was used to produce the first 60-90 mil cores for IBM.[35] In the summer of 1952 the Lincoln Laboratory contracted for improved core materials for this small core size, apparently unaware of the fact that the dies were originally ordered by IBM.[36] Dave Brown's group also entered into a materials development effort that fall and consulted with General Ceramics on core processing and testing procedures.

By the end of 1952 a satisfactory material was developed. Known as Ferramic S-1 material, it was a magnesium-manganese ferrite material covered by E. Albers-Schönberg's patent, which was assigned to General Ceramics.[37] The first use of 60-90 mil cores made with Ferramic S-1 material was by Erich Bloch in the buffer memory for the IBM 702 computer. This buffer was successfully tested on the TPM in February 1953. Bill Papian also used these cores in the first ferrite core array tested on the MTC in May 1953 and then transferred to Whirlwind I in August. This same S-1 material, with continuing refinements, was used to make the smaller 50-80 mil cores used in subsequent MIT prototype memories.

RCA, which manufactured magnetic ferrite yokes for the deflection circuitry of television tubes, entered the ferrite core fabrication business through the urging of Jan Rajchman.[38] By mid-1953 RCA had made small quantities of 34-54 mil cores—smaller than any cores made by General Ceramics to that time—for Rajchman's 100×100 bit memory.

Thus in the summer of 1953 the two most promising suppliers of ferrite cores were General Ceramics and RCA. Plans for the first SAGE prototype computers, the XD-1 and XD-2, were falling rapidly in place. Ferrite cores had to be ordered quickly if they were to be fabricated, tested, and wired into arrays to meet the XD-1 prototype build schedule proposed by Forrester in May 1953:[39]

Specifications for cores	July 1, 1953
Specifications for memory circuits	August 1, 1953
Specifications for mechanical design	October 1, 1953
All cores and other parts procured	January 1, 1954
Construction complete	May 1, 1954
Testing of memory as independent unit	July 1, 1954
Test memory in system	August 1, 1954
Ship to Lexington, Massachusetts	August 15, 1954

In July 1953 IBM requested RCA and General Ceramics to give quotes on 250,000 cores each, a total of 500,000 cores. Specifications for these cores were based on experience with the MTC and were defined by agreement between the MIT and IBM engineers.[40] Experience with the MTC indicated that only 28 percent of the cores received from General Ceramics were good, even after a preliminary screening by General Ceramics in which 60 percent of their batches were completely rejected.[41] If 28 percent of the 250,000 cores received from each of the two vendors were good, there would be just enough good cores to populate one XD-1 array.

RCA, however, was not willing to quote on the requested basis. Instead they offered to supply only 50,000 untested cores but with a guaranteed yield of at least 25 percent.[42] This guarantee was risky because RCA had much less experience than General Ceramics in meeting specifications for ferrite core memories. Furthermore electrical specifications for good cores were still imprecise, and electronic test equipment was limited in its ability to test many of the parameters believed to be important.

That September Bob West of IBM personally calibrated the test equipment at the two vendors using specially calibrated test equipment and a standard core.[43] But not only was it difficult to maintain the calibration of the testers, it was soon found that the specifications for the cores were inadequate. They had been written to eliminate bad cores from good cores produced by General Ceramics, but RCA cores were made by a different process and performed somewhat differently from those made by General Ceramics. Most RCA core batches failed the specifications altogether, but even those that did not fail were found to be unacceptable in the memory array.[44,45] The ferrite core specifications had to be rewritten, and MIT began wiring and testing arrays using RCA cores in an effort to relate their characteristics to the properties required in an XD-1 memory array.

The schedule for the XD-1 prototype computer called for all cores for the first $64 \times 64 \times 36$ array to be tested by January 15, 1954. Although General Ceramics was the only supplier that could meet this schedule, other vendors, such as RCA, Ferroxcube, and IBM (which had begun to establish a core pilot line production facility in the summer of 1953), were encouraged to remain in the competition to supply cores for the production AN/FSQ-7 units.[46]

Core Testing and Wiring

Jay Forrester required that each electrical component be tested for satisfactory operation even when it and its interacting components were operating at the marginal range of their specifications. This process was called marginal testing. Marginal testing of ferrite cores originally required three separate tests on each core with different drive and disturb pulse settings. This sequence of tests was soon replaced at IBM by a single test that Mike Haynes devised: all drive currents were set 10 percent low, all disturb pulses were set 10 percent high, and the output signal required of each core was set 10 percent above the nominal design value. This one test simulated all worst-case conditions simultaneously and greatly simplified the test procedures. Subsequently it was adopted throughout the industry.[11]

Testing so many cores was a problem. The semiautomatic tester employed at MIT permitted an operator to test each core in about five seconds.[41] Testing 500,000 cores would require twenty-nine days of twenty-four work hours each, uninterrupted by coffee breaks or equipment failure.

To remedy this problem, MIT had developed electronics that automatically rejected bad cores without operator intervention. The semiautomatic testers, in contrast, displayed the output signal of the core on an oscilloscope and the operator accepted or rejected cores based on this display. Automatic testing was faster and less fatiguing but had the disadvantage that important, unexpected information was sometimes lost which might have been observed by the operator.

Development of automatic mechanical core handlers for use with automatic and semiautomatic test electronics was undertaken by IBM, which also had responsibility for building all the core test equipment needed by Project SAGE. Design of the core test probe, a single wire to be inserted through the hole in the core, was assigned to the electronics group by Edwards. The probe had to be able to carry the large drive current required to switch the core and yet be able to detect the very small output voltage induced by the flux reversal process.[47] The tool engineering group designed the automatic core handler, consisting of a chrome-plated disk with holes in the periphery into which cores fell as the disk rotated. The test probe was then automatically inserted, by a solenoid from above, through the core for electrical test.[47] By April 1953 the first model was built and the engineers reported, "We are proceeding to eliminate the bugs."[48]

In September 1953 Dave Brown reported that they had used the automatic core handler successfully with the MIT automatic core selection electronics. He urged IBM to hasten construction of the ten automatic handlers, which were needed by General Ceramics for preliminary screening of ferrite core batches and by IBM and MIT for final core tests.[49]

By early November 1953 MIT had one semiautomatic and one fully automatic tester in operation, and IBM had three semiautomatic testers running two shifts per day, each producing an average of 1000 good cores per day.[50]   Core breakage and mechanical failure of these handlers were common, but enough good tested cores were on hand by February to populate the first memory array.   Tests of partially wired arrays led to new test specifications for future cores that rejected about 10 percent of the cores previously accepted.

Core testing continued with monotonous persistency.   By mid-July 1954, 486,000 good cores were available and nearly half of these had already been wired into fifty core planes of 64×64 cores each.[51]

The wiring of the core planes was a particularly laborious task requiring great patience and skill.   A long hypodermic needle was probed by hand into a glass dish containing the cores until sixty-four cores were loaded onto the needle.   Then a copper wire was inserted through the hypodermic needle and the needle withdrawn to cause the sixty-four cores to be strung on the copper wire.   The wire was attached to the terminals of the memory array.   A total of sixty-four wires, with sixty-four cores each, were so attached.   These were the X wires.   The sixty-four orthogonal Y wires then had to be threaded through each of the cores at ninety degrees to the X wire.   As each core was approached, it was hand manipulated to ensure a proper orientation in the array.

When all wires were threaded in this manner, a core mat of 4096 cores having an X wire and a Y wire through each core was ready for insertion of the third and fourth wires (inhibit and sense).   Before this was done, the array was tested to be sure that all cores were good.   A bad core was removed by cutting the X and Y wire through it.   Then new X and Y wires were restrung through the cores in the row and column containing the removed core, and a new core was inserted during the restringing operation. The inhibit and sense lines were then strung through each core in the plane.

Assembly time for the X and Y wires alone was about twenty-five hours for skilled operators.   Stringing the third and

Semiautomatic core test apparatus
Operators of this early core test apparatus used at IBM studied the
electrical characteristics shown on the oscilloscope before deciding to
accept or reject a core.

Wiring core planes
Women in the IBM Poughkeepsie plant wire 64×64 core planes for use
in the XD-1 computer of SAGE. It took more than forty hours to string the
X, Y, inhibit, and sense wires through a core plane by hand, using
tweezers to manipulate the cores.

Wired ferrite cores
The corner of a 64×64 core plane used in the XD-1 computer shows how
the four wires threaded through each core reached electrical terminals on
the core frame. The U.S. ten cent coin provides a sense of size for the
cores, which are 50 mil inside and 80 mil outside diameter.

fourth lines required another fifteen hours.[52] Occasionally the women assembling the core frames broke down and cried when a final inspection revealed a fault in the wiring that required the wires be removed and restrung. The emotion of seeing so much labor lost was too much for the conscientious people needed for this exacting work.[53]

XD-1 and XD-2 Memories

In the fall of 1953 Ken Olsen and a number of other MIT staff members were assigned to IBM in Poughkeepsie to help in final testing and debugging of the XD-1 prototypes.[54] In spite of close cooperation and increased effort, some slippage of the schedule was detected as early as January 1954.[55] In May it was noted that the first XD-1 core frame had been assembled four weeks behind schedule, but the level of activity at IBM was described by MIT representatives as "very encouraging."[56] By June the estimated slippage for shipment of XD-1 was six weeks, and by September the original ship date of August 1954 had slipped to January 1955.[57,58] The January shipment date was actually met—in retrospect, a remarkable feat considering the complexity of the project and the use of previously untried ferrite core memory technology.

The design specifications for the memory elements for XD-1 and XD-2 had been documented by Wil Wittenberg of IBM and Bill Papian of MIT and approved by Jay Forrester in April 1954.[59] Each of the two prototype computers was to have two banks of ferrite core memory. Each memory bank had thirty-six planes of 64×64 (4,096) ferrite cores each, for a total of 147,456 good cores per array. Three of the planes were spares and would not be connected electrically except to replace a faulty plane. This way it was expected that the ferrite core array would never have to be replaced.[60]

The thirty-three operable planes provided words of thirty-two bits plus a parity bit. Before entering a word into memory, it was first placed in a vacuum tube flip-flop buffer where the number of 1s in the word were counted. The parity bit was then set either to a 1 or a 0 as required to give an odd number of 1s in the thirty-three bit register. Each time a word was read out, it was checked to see if the number of 1s was still odd. If not, a parity check (error) was registered.[61]

The ferrite cores had 50-80 mil diameters and were 25 mil high. They had four wires through them: the X, Y, inhibit, and sense line. The drive lines were number 33 gauge (7.1 mil), and the sense line was number 36 gauge (5.0 mil).

Drive currents of 0.41 amperes and about 2 microseconds in duration were supplied by large push-pull cathode follower vacuum tubes through a transformer. The output signals from the cores were 0.15 volts. The read and write functions were carried out under the control of a vacuum tube clock, read-write gate, sense amplifier, digit driver, sample gate, sample flip-flop, and associated cathode followers and pulse amplifiers. The selection plane equipment comprised 673 vacuum tubes and 1071 diodes, and the control circuits and digit plane circuits comprised 103 tubes and 292 diodes. Each memory therefore had 776 vacuum tubes, and the two memories used in each AN/FSQ-7 computer had just under 25 percent of the total tubes used in the computer.[61,33]

To facilitate service, all SAGE memory drive circuits were in pluggable units that could be replaced quickly when a malfunction occurred. These pluggable units were huge by today's standards: about 1.5 feet long, 1 foot high, and 2.5 inches wide. Each unit had eight to ten vacuum tubes plus ten to fifteen circuit cards. Large vacuum tubes (rather than the newer miniature tubes) were selected for the memory support circuits as well as for logic because the large glass surface area facilitated cooling and because it was easier to achieve the required internal grid tolerances.[62]

Forced-air cooling with a laminar flow of air about each tube plus a temperature monitoring system made it possible to maintain a temperature of 24°C to within plus or minus 1°C.[59] The use of staggered read had been found to be unnecessary.[63] A postwrite disturb pulse, first found to be necessary in the Whirlwind memory late in 1953, was used to reduce the delta noise in the array from partially selected cores.[27] The agreed-to cycle time of 7.5 microseconds was expected to be achieved, but by July there was

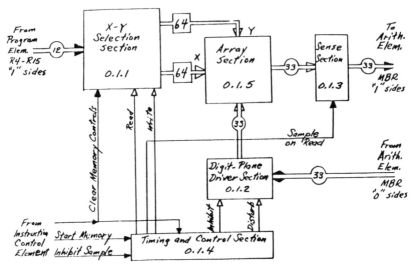

SAGE memory block diagram

This block diagram from an internal IBM report of July 12, 1954, shows the memory element for SAGE to consist of two identical memory banks, each organized into five functional sections: X-Y selection, array, sense, digit-plane driver, and timing and control.

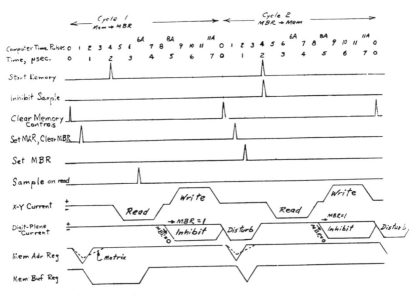

SAGE memory timing chart

This timing chart from an IBM report of July 12, 1954, shows among other things the timing of the inhibit and post-write disturb pulses. A memory cycle in excess of 7 microseconds is indicated, but a cycle of only 6 microseconds was achieved less than three months after this report was issued.

increasing pressure from the designers of the AN/FSQ-7 computer to shorten the memory cycle.[64]

By mid-October 1954 the the first memory bank was completed and operating with a faster-than-projected cycle of 6 microseconds. This was in fact the speed MIT had originally requested but one to which the more conservative IBM engineers had been unwilling to commit themselves. Satisfactory margins were achieved even with somewhat narrower read, write, and inhibit pulses.[64] Minor improvements in the second and third memory banks caused IBM to use these in the first SAGE prototype computer (XD-1) shipped to Lincoln Laboratories in January 1955.[65] The XD-1 prototype computer replaced Whirlwind in the Cape Cod System in 1955. The first and fourth banks of memory were placed in the XD-2 computer, which IBM retained to support software and system development.[6]

In spite of these significant accomplishments, the company's management was concerned in late 1954 by competitive accomplishments. That November International Telemeter had installed a 4096-word ferrite core memory on the Rand Corporation Johnniac computer, and ERA (absorbed by Remington Rand in 1952 and merged with Sperry in 1954) had shipped a ferrite core main memory on its 1103 computer.[66,67] Both of these events occurred two months before IBM shipped the XD-1 computer to the MIT Lincoln Laboratory with two ferrite core memory arrays. The ERA ferrite core memory was designed and built for NSA but was regarded as a forerunner to commercial use of ferrite core memories on the ERA 1103. It thus posed the major competitive threat.

IBM management took some comfort from the fact that the ERA ferrite core memory was neither as fast nor as large as the SAGE memories. It had an 8 microsecond cycle versus 6 microseconds for the SAGE memory, and the ERA memory was four times smaller, containing thirty-six planes of 32×32 cores each. The cores were the same 50-80 mil size used in SAGE and were also purchased from General Ceramics. The ERA memory occupied two boxes, each 8 feet long by 2 feet wide and 6 feet high.[67]

ERA 1103 core plane

This type of ferrite core plane was used in the Remington Rand Univac 1103 series of computers. The first two were built by Engineering Research Associates (ERA) for the National Security Agency under code name Atlas II and the first commercial machines were called ERA 1103s. The 32×32 bit core plane uses 50-80 mil cores supplied by General Ceramics. A continuous inhibit line passes through each core twice, once in the X direction and once in the Y direction. The diagonal sense line passes through each core only once. (Photograph and information courtesy of R. B. Arndt, Sperry Corporation, St. Paul, Minnesota.)

The ERA memory had been designed, built, and installed by Roland B. Arndt, a man who did not know what a ferrite core memory was when he started the project in July 1952. There were never more than ten to fifteen people on the project, including the woman who did most of the core stringing. The memory delivered to NSA had not been specially designed for mass production and could not provide the basis for large-scale manufacturing.[67] But IBM corporate managers had only limited knowledge of the size of this effort and were concerned by the potential competitive threat presented by Sperry Rand's technological achievement.

Core Fabrication in IBM
During the spring of 1952 Ralph Palmer had rejected product proposals for using ferrite core memories because of the poor quality and lack of uniformity of available cores. By June he decided to establish a ferrite core development activity at IBM to facilitate the development and manufacture of commercial memory products. Materials, furnaces, ball mills, and presses were ordered and the recruitment of key technical personnel was begun.[68]

Lloyd P. Hunter, who had been hired in 1951 to head IBM's physical science and components work under Arthur Samuel, was in charge of the project, with two new recruits, M. Clayton Andrews and Andrew H. Eschenfelder, under him. The first task was to purchase ferrite cores from General Ceramics and make equivalent cores. They mixed ferrite materials and pressed and fired cores ranging in size from 0.5 to 1.25 inch in diameter. By February 1953 they had fabricated cores with square magnetic hysteresis loops that "looked good on Mike Haynes's pulse tester."[69]

More rapid progress was made following James M. Brownlow's arrival in March 1953 with a lot of practical knowledge about the fabrication of ceramics. When Andrews was unable to press cores with the desired rectangular cross section, Brownlow got a box of detergent from the janitor's closet and added some to the ferrite powder. The detergent helped disperse the ferrite in the ball mill and served as a lubricant during pressing. The next batch of cores came out with the desired shape.[70] Brownlow quickly converted these makeshift procedures to more conventional methods such as the use of polyvinylalcohol to serve as a binder and lubricant for the ferrite.

The IBM development of ferrite core processing technology was in an embryonic state when Project High was initiated, but management was eager to expand it. A proposal for IBM to undertake development work to become a second source of ferrite cores for SAGE was drawn up, and by May 1953 Jay Forrester had approved the plan.[71,72]

That June Project High established a subcontract with the IBM Research Department. Basic studies were to be undertaken in Lloyd Hunter's Physical Research Department and a pilot line was to be established in John B. Little's Component Research Department. Little had joined IBM from Bell Laboratories in 1950 to establish vacuum tube manufacturing and had been responsible for mechanical assembly techniques developed in IBM for the Williams tube memory units. In mid-1953 he had about 25 people working for him on a variety of component development projects. Now his top priority was to find someone capable of establishing a facility to make the new ferrite core devices. He recalls a telephone call from the laboratory manager to inform him of a job applicant, John W. Gibson, who "might be of interest for the ferrite core program."[73]

John Gibson
Gibson had a round boyish face and easy manner that masked only partially his intellect and deep inner drive. He had completed a four-semester year at John Hopkins before enlisting in the navy as an electronics technician at age seventeen. After two years in the navy, he took a standard electrical engineering course when he returned to Johns Hopkins and received his master's degree in 1951. He then worked at the Naval Research Laboratory for a year before returning to Johns Hopkins where he obtained the Ph.D. about a year later.[74] When he joined IBM in June 1953, his immediate assignment was "to develop the materials, techniques,

and equipment for production and testing of ferrite cores for Project High."[73]

Gibson made several visits to MIT to learn as much as possible about ferrite core processing procedures. Information about the MIT work was available to anyone, whereas the General Ceramics effort on ferrite cores was proprietary. It was important to IBM to develop a process independently of General Ceramics in order to be able to use it for commercial as well as military products. Assuring that this restraint was not violated was a continual administrative responsibility because the memory designers for Project High had frequent contact with General Ceramics.[73]

In order to achieve the necessary uniformity of all cores in a memory array, the MIT engineers had chosen to fire enough cores at one time to populate an entire array. They had a massive furnace, perhaps ten feet square, which required several days to cycle. The heat treatment required more than a day and consisted of heating the pressed cores to about $1300°C$, holding them at that temperature, and then slowly cooling them. The cores were then given a short-cycle heating and cooling treatment to reduce the oxygen content.[75]

After reviewing these procedures, Brownlow and Gibson agreed that they would try to implement a single, fast-fire sintering process to replace this relatively long one. They planned to make cores in small batches and to control the processing steps well enough that cores made in different batches would have the same properties.[75] They placed cores in a small platinum boat that they could insert into a two-inch diameter furnace, heat to the desired temperature of about $1300°C$, and then draw out of the center of the furnace at a controlled rate.[76] After much experimentation, they found a good cycle that produced cores superior to those received from General Ceramics.

Prior to firing, the ferrite powder was pressed into the desired toroidal shape. MIT used a single station press, which was adequate for their development work but would never meet the requirements of making millions of cores of uniform quality.[45] William J. Walker, a mechanical engineer and first employee of

John W. Gibson
Gibson shown in a components laboratory of the Data Systems Division in November 1960, nine months before he was named manager of the newly formed IBM Components Division. (Photograph courtesy of the IBM Archives.)

John Gibson, undertook the development of high-speed core pressing equipment. He and Gibson noted that ferrite cores were similar in shape and size to the porous sintered bearings used in various electromechanical instruments. They got quotes from General Motors in Detroit on the cost of making such bearings and used this as a measure for their own cost projections. From General Motors they also learned that sintered bearings were pressed on rotary presses. This information led them to the Colton Company and to a company in Philadelphia that made presses used in the pharmaceutical industry to produce aspirin tablets.[74]

The first attempts to press cores with a rotary press were only moderately successful. The ferrite material was so abrasive that it quickly wore out the metal dies. After several attempts, Walker bought standard Colton rotary presses and modified them using tungsten carbide dies. The modified Colton press had eight sets of pressing tooling with upper and lower punches that moved around the periphery of the circular press table. The ferrite power was inserted in the dies in the periphery of the press table and then compacted by the punches to form a toroidal core. The modifications were completed in 1954. The eight-station press was capable of pressing the newly defined 50-80 mil cores for SAGE at a rate of thirty cores per minute.

Cores produced on John Gibson's pilot line were evaluated by Project High as having "exceptionally good characteristics with good uniformity between firings."[77] These findings were verified by the MIT group, which still had technical responsibility for the SAGE development effort. Their quarterly progress report of September 15, 1954, describes the MIT evaluation of cores from three potential vendors:[58]

Ferroxcube Cores —
A lot of 1000 cores supplied by Ferroxcube has been evaluated. . . . These cores would require considerable alteration in properties in order to meet the present memory-core specification but would be usable in slower-access memories.

RCA Cores —
Several lots of RCA cores have been evaluated to determine the

Colton rotary press
This is the first single-punch, modified Colton rotary press used by IBM
for the manufacture of ferrite cores. It was part of the manufacturing
line established in the IBM Poughkeepsie plant in the fall of 1954 to
produce cores for Project High and for the memories used on the IBM
704 and 705 computers.

reproducibility characteristics from lot to lot. . . . On the basis of the lots tested, it would appear that RCA core production is not stabilized and that insufficient control of processing variables is the underlying cause.

IBM Cores —
A core pilot plant at IBM has produced three lots of 740 cores each. Upon test by IBM, the yield of acceptable cores for the three lots averaged about 95 percent. Samples from each lot have been tested in Group 63, and the results are in agreement with IBM's. On the basis of these preliminary lots, IBM appears a very probable second source of supply of ferrite memory cores.

The success of this effort had long-term importance to IBM in the development of computer memories for commercial computers, but its immediate importance was in solving a problem that had become increasingly important to the SAGE project: General Ceramics was the only commercial source of satisfactory ferrite cores. Dave Brown noted with pride that General Ceramics' success was due in part to "working in close cooperation with Lincoln Laboratory."[27]   More recently he had begun to work closely with RCA in Camden, New Jersey, to help them become a second source of supply. Tests of individual cores had been made, and 4096 cores out of 10,000 had been selected to wire a 64×64 memory plane. The results were disappointing. The cores required a higher drive current and had poorer operating margins than those received from General Ceramics. Nevertheless Brown reported in March 1954, with more optimism than future events warranted, "The progress of RCA in ferrite synthesis is encouraging, and ultimate success seems certain."[33] By the end of July success of the RCA effort appeared less certain, causing Brown to report, "General Ceramics is still the only source of memory cores in production quantities."[78]

Three months earlier Forrester had written to IBM, "A few components are so critical in nature that we strongly feel that they should receive attention to a high enough level to assure that early action is taken to provide adequate insurance for a continuous source of supply." Then placing ferrite cores at the top of his critical list, Forrester continued, "The core activity at IBM should definitely be aimed at providing facilities which can provide adequate quantities to supply the duplex machines' requirements in case the General Ceramics effort should run into difficulty."[79]

In response to Forrester's request and to Palmer's desire to produce all critical components for IBM's products, John Gibson not only established a core fabrication facility, but he also contracted to design and build two prototype automatic testers with improved electronics and ferrite core handlers for SAGE. Eugene F. Brosseau, hired by IBM in July 1954 with a degree in electrical engineering, was responsible for completing these testers. In the summer of 1955 two completed testers were shipped to temporary facilities in Kingston where construction had just begun on a 320,000 square foot plant for the manufacture of the SAGE computers.[80] Two more automatic testers were built for testing cores made in the Poughkeepsie plant. These improved testers had a vibratory bowl to feed the cores to the tester station instead of the rotating corn-planter mechanism of the earlier handlers.[81]

In one year John Gibson had established a pilot line capable of producing over 5000 cores of superior quality per day, and in the next year he had supplied the first automatic testers for production use. These were major accomplishments, the first of many that propelled Gibson to the position of manager of IBM's newly formed Components Division in August 1961.

Realizing the Dream
IBM received the first production contract for SAGE computer systems in February 1954. To produce these systems, IBM built a new factory, which was opened in Kingston, New York, early in 1955; and on January 1, 1956, all IBM Project High personnel, including those in Poughkeepsie, "came under the procedural guidance of the Kingston Military Products Division."[82] By now 670 IBM professional, technical, and administrative persons were involved in SAGE development plus an additional 817 involved in manufacturing.

The first production AN/FSQ-7 system was shipped to McGuire Air Force Base in June 1956 and was immediately put to work on

XD-1 memory prototype
The first prototype memory for SAGE is shown at the left, partially
assembled. The glassed-in space will hold 36 ferrite core planes,
mounted horizontally. Sense amplifiers are in a separate box to the
right. The other units contain memory test equipment.

SAGE memory
"The heart of the AN/FSQ-7 air defense computer is the magnetic core
memory," said the announcement literature. The memory array is to the
left, the memory frame in the center, and the power module to the right.

air defense systems check-out and program development. This air
defense site was declared operational on July 1, 1958.[82] The final
sector in the SAGE system within North America was completed
five years later.[83]   Twenty-eight systems ultimately were
manufactured for SAGE.

Each system had two computers, and each computer had
25,000 vacuum tubes and two main memories. Each memory
weighed 5272 pounds and had 147,456 ferrite cores. The memory
capacity was later increased eight-fold.[84]   Each AN/FSQ-7 duplex
system used 3 million watts of power and occupied 40,000 square
feet of floor space. The system was sufficiently reliable that less
than two hours per year of air defense time was lost.[83]

Commenting on IBM's effort on Project SAGE, Forrester said,
"I think the remarkable thing is the broad support that the
company gave to the program: the willingness of the company to
take what would be seen as risks to make it successful, building a
factory, for example, before there was a contract for the
product. . . to go ahead even in the absence of certainty of
financial remuneration was indicative of the kind of top level
support that helped a great deal to bring the whole thing off
successfully."[85]

Project SAGE represented a major gamble for the IBM
Corporation.   A high percentage of the company's technical
resources were committed to a single project in the still-uncertain
electronic data-processing field.   The gamble was successful.
During the 1950s SAGE provided IBM with half a billion dollars of
revenue. More important it was a training ground for many young
engineers who gained experience with the first large, real-time,
on-line computer system, as well as with a number of new
hardware technologies including magnetic core memory.

By early 1955 most of the IBM engineers were working on
less exciting jobs of increasing production and reducing costs.
Others had been moved to small commercial or military
development projects. A few, under the leadership of Nate
Edwards, began to define exploratory projects to provide future
enhancements to SAGE. However, little money was available for

improvements to SAGE until late in 1956 when the Air Force made a substantial amount of money available for this purpose.

SAGE enhancement projects were started sooner at MIT. Construction of an experimental ferrite core plane with 128×128 bits was begun in June 1954 while IBM personnel were still wiring and testing the four-times-smaller core planes for XD-1 and XD-2. By September the 128×128 bit plane was completed, and by the end of the year Bill Papian reported, "Design and development of a random-access $256 \times 256 \times 33$ core memory with a 6 microsecond cycle time is becoming the major goal of this section."[58,65] This was sixteen times the size of the memories used in the XD-1 and XD-2 prototypes and in SAGE itself. These memories provided a partial basis for the larger SAGE memories, which ultimately were developed and placed into manufacture by IBM in 1957.[84]

The advanced computer development work at the MIT Lincoln Laboratory continued to be followed closely by engineering groups throughout the country, but at MIT the excitement was beginning to wane. Building larger arrays and replacing vacuum tube circuits with transistor circuits seemed to be minor accomplishments compared to building the first large magnetic core memory. The engineers were increasingly caught up in a difficult race with the many ferrite core development activities that their own technical work and publicity had helped to create.

In 1956, the year in which the first SAGE production computers were shipped to McGuire Air Force Base, Jay Forrester left the MIT Lincoln Laboratory to become a professor of management at the MIT Sloan School. Forrester says he "had come to the conclusion that great technological successes depended more on the managerial environment then they did on the underlying science. If you had the right environment, you would get the science, but you could easily have the science in an environment that did not make it effective." At the Sloan School he began promoting System Dynamics, his own approach to the modeling of societal systems using feedback loops similar to those used by engineers in the design of servomechanisms.[85]

Ken Olsen used the knowledge he gained from SAGE to found the Digital Equipment Corporation in 1957. In 1958 a portion of the Lincoln Laboratory was incorporated as the MITRE Corporation, and many MIT engineers joined the new organization. Robert Everett was named vice president of technical operations in 1959 and president in 1969. Bill Papian and others remained at the Lincoln Laboratory to take charge of efforts in advanced computer technologies, but in 1964 Papian also left, first to Washington University in St. Louis, Missouri, and later to the real estate business in Washington D.C.[86]

5
Commercial Ferrite Core Memories

The year 1953 marked IBM's rapidly growing commitment to electronic stored-program computer technologies. Manpower on Project High was increased from fourteen in January to three hundred by the end of the year, and in April the company dedicated its first commercial stored-program computer, the IBM 701. Work on the experimental Tape Processing Machine (TPM) was continued toward the development of the company's second commercial stored-program computer, the IBM 702. Unlike the 701, which was developed for scientific calculations and defense applications, the 702 was intended for commercial data processing, a field then being served by punched-card equipment.

Rapid and effective response to customer requirements had been the hallmark of IBM's success in commercial punched-card equipment, and it characterized the company's mode of entry into commercial electronic data processing. Product decisions and engineering efforts frequently were direct responses to customer requests. IBM's first ferrite core memory products were no exception to this mode of operation.

A Small 3D Array Memory Product
"IBM cannot hold its Commonwealth Edison account," Wayne Winger was told, "unless this problem is solved—and it is your job to solve it."[1] The problem was a performance limitation of the IBM 702 in applications involving heavy use of magnetic tape storage. Winger and his colleagues concluded that a small buffer memory, designed to receive data from magnetic tape at tape speed and transmit it to main memory at memory speed, could solve the problem. This would permit almost complete overlapping of tape reading, data-processing, and tape writing functions.[2]

Bloch was given the assignment to develop the required buffer memory toward the end of 1953 after he had completed work on the 2D ferrite core buffer memories for the card reader and punch and the printer control units of the IBM 702 computer. The large size of the proposed magnetic tape buffer made Forrester's 3D wiring scheme more attractive than the 2D scheme Bloch had used on the earlier buffers. The buffer size finally selected was 800 characters of seven bits each.[3] This was achieved in an array of seven planes of 40×20 cores each. If wired in Forrester's 3D manner, sixty drivers would be required for the X and Y lines plus seven more for the inhibit lines.

Bloch believed that this was still too many vacuum tube circuits for such a small memory. He noted that the 5D address scheme employed by Haynes and Counihan in their 4×4×4 array in May 1952 would require many fewer drive circuits. This had been accomplished by using vacuum tube drivers and a type of diode matrix to select the X and Y lines.

A similar approach, using a matrix of magnetic switch cores instead of semiconductor diodes, had been investigated in 1952 by Ken Olsen at MIT as a means of selecting the X and Y drive lines of the 16×16 ferrite core memory array constructed by Bill Papian.[4] Olsen's technique not only reduced the number of drive circuits, but the switch cores facilitated impedance matching between the vacuum tube drivers and the memory lines. Similar techniques had been also reported by Jan Rajchman of RCA at the IRE meeting in March 1952 and then in 1953 as the means of driving his 10,000 bit memory array.[5]

The success reported for these experimental efforts encouraged Bloch to use the same techniques in his buffer memory product. Using switch cores wired in 4×5 matrixes, he was able to drive twenty memory lines with only nine vacuum tube drivers. Thus, only twenty-seven drivers were required to drive the 20 X and 40 Y lines of the memory in contrast to sixty drivers that would have been required using the simple 3D drive scheme employed in the SAGE memories. Bloch chose to refer to his memory as a 3D memory with matrix selection rather than calling it a 5D selection memory. His terminology was thus consistent with that of Olsen and Rajchman as opposed to that of Haynes and Counihan.

Bloch also made use of the selection scheme in the switch core matrix, which was first described by Ken Olsen.[4] In this approach the four bias lines in the matrix were driven with current pulses of such polarity that the cores were driven more into their saturation state. The five orthogonal set lines were driven so as to switch the cores. A particular core in the matrix was selected by the *absence* of a pulse on one of the four bias lines combined with the presence of a *positive* pulse on one of the five set lines.[6] Known as the anticoincident-current selection scheme, it resulted in faster switching and permitted the use of looser tolerances in the switch cores and drive circuits.

The ferrite core size, wire size, and wiring configuration in the memory array were chosen to be the same as those used in SAGE. This reduced costs substantially. No new core type had to be developed, and many of the same procedures and fixtures for core testing and wiring could be used. A number of modifications were also made to the vacuum tube drive and sense circuits to reduce the cost of the memory.[3]

To reduce costs further, grade B cores from General Ceramics were used. These were rejects from core batches intended for SAGE.[3] The large variability in characteristics of these cheaper cores resulted in undesirable electrical noise in the memory, which was overcome by the use of two IBM innovations. The first was staggered read, proposed independently by Mike Haynes and Jay Forrester and patented by Haynes.[7] In this scheme a time delay between initiation of the two read pulses permitted the noise induced by the first pulse to decay before the second pulse switched the core. The second innovation was disturbance cancellation, in which an additional core of the same material as the memory cores was driven by the X and Y lines and coupled to the sense amplifier so as to counterbalance the disturb noise of the nonselected memory cores.[8]

Development of circuit and array technologies for the 3D ferrite core array tape buffer was initiated in Haynes's group in February 1954 in support of Erich Bloch.[3] The $20 \times 40 \times 7$ bit memory was assembled and debugged during May and shipped to Commonwealth Edison in June 1955 as the IBM 776 tape buffer.[2] This basic buffer design was modified during the ensuing years, resulting in the 775, 776, 777, and 760 buffers. Large numbers of these buffers were produced to satisfy a variety of system needs. The popular 760 buffer, for example, provided one thousand 7-bit characters using a $25 \times 40 \times 7$ bit ferrite core array.[9]

The IBM 776 tape buffer was the first 3D ferrite core memory IBM produced for a commercial customer. It was shipped about seven months after ERA shipped its six times larger ferrite core memory to the National Security Agency and about six months after the 24 times larger SAGE memories were shipped to Lincoln Laboratory by IBM. With a memory cycle of 23 microseconds, the 776 tape buffer was approximately two times slower than the ERA memory and four times slower than the SAGE memory. Nevertheless it was an important accomplishment because it was in volume production and incorporated engineering features that reduced its costs below those of other memories.

Indecisions on Main Memories

By the end of 1953 IBM commercial products had been defined with 2D ferrite core arrays of approximately 1000 bits and 3D ferrite core arrays of 5000 to 7000 bits. There were vigorous discussions, however, concerning the viability of ferrite cores for computer main memories having of the order of 100,000 bits.

These discussions revealed the rather different missions of IBM and MIT. The MIT mission was to develop and promote new technologies. Bill Papian and many of his colleagues therefore viewed IBM as an unimaginative bureaucracy that was moving too slowly in using ferrite core memories in commercial machines.[10] IBM in contrast, considered its primary mission to be one of satisfying customer needs and desires. Its leaders were concerned that MIT's promotion of ferrite core memories was causing some customers to desire such memories before they had been fully developed as a manufacturable, reliable product.

Within IBM, discussions concerning the use of ferrite core main memories had already begun early in 1953 when Haynes and others proposed that they be used for the main memory of the IBM 702 computer.[11] They argued that Bloch's 2D buffer on the TPM in February 1953 proved that cores could be operated reliably, and successful operation of the first $32 \times 32 \times 17$ bit ferrite core array on the MTC at MIT three months later was an even clearer indication of the technical feasibility of large ferrite core memories.

Many people believed ferrite cores were fundamentally more reliable than electrostatic storage tubes, but in early 1953 there was little data to support this. By June 1953 the MIT ferrite core memory on the MTC was reported to have achieved several error-free runs of four to five hours.[12] This was better than results typically reported for electrostatic storage tubes of more than one error per hour, but the test conditions were not directly comparable.

By the end of 1953 two banks of ferrite core memory had been in operation in the Whirlwind computer for three months. While these memories were being debugged on Whirlwind, a postwrite disturb pulse was added that greatly improved operating margins. Thirty-seven days of error-free operation were reported, in which a parity-check system had ensured detection of any errors.[13] It was not until August 1954, however, that the first quantitative analysis was made of the relative reliability of electrostatic storage versus ferrite core memories. Eight months of operation of magnetic core memory had produced thirty-five parity checks, whereas the previous eight months of operation with electrostatic storage had produced 900—one error per week for ferrite core memory versus five errors per day for electrostatic storage.[14]

These data were not available during 1953 when memory technology decisions for IBM's commercial products were being made. But even if they had been available, they might not have altered the decisions. The greater reliability of ferrite cores on Whirlwind could be attributed in part to eight more months of debugging and fine tuning of the computer. If electrostatic storage had been retained on Whirlwind and refined during this period, it too would have achieved better reliability. Furthermore

Phil Fox and other IBM engineers were convinced that the IBM Williams tube storage was superior to the electrostatic storage tubes used by MIT. Finally the Whirlwind air defense application placed a premium on reliability with little regard to cost, whereas IBM's commercial customers were very cost conscious.

Ferrite cores were expensive. Cores purchased from General Ceramics cost thirty-one cents each. By the time they were individually tested, wired in a core array and tested again, and then connected to vacuum tube circuitry needed to operate the memory, the cost of the memory exceeded one dollar per bit. Added to this high cost was concern that outside organizations and individuals held critical patents. One of these, An Wang at Harvard, already had initiated negotiations for large royalty payments.[15]

At this time IBM was manufacturing superior electrostatic storage tubes based on the RCA 3-inch tube. IBM's manufacturing cost was about forty dollars per tube, almost twice as much as RCA charged, but the yield was 80 percent for IBM tubes versus less than 10 percent for RCA tubes when tested for use as electrostatic memories.[16] The cost per bit of a fully assembled and tested Williams tube memory was estimated at about one dollar per bit on the IBM 701, and this cost was projected to come down as manufacturing volume increased.[17]

The argument in favor of Williams tube memory for the IBM 702 was clinched when Phil Fox proposed using an improved version of the storage tube that could store ten times as many bits per tube. Called the barrier-grid tube, it had a conducting wire mesh over the storage surface that increased the storage retention and resolution. Although this tube was more complicated than the ones used on the IBM 701, the tenfold increase in storage capacity was expected to result in a major cost savings. A decision was made to ship the first IBM 702s with storage tubes similar to those on the 701. Future 702s would use the higher-density barrier-grid tube. Fox was pleased that his barrier-grid proposal had "pulled the rug out from under cores for the 702.[11,18]

This decision was soon reassessed for three reasons. First, the IBM 702 sales efforts were meeting stiff competition from the Remington Rand UNIVAC. Engineering design teams put in place to meet this challenge developed new computer designs, which became the IBM 704 and 705 computers. The designers immediately reopened the question of memory technology, influenced in part by International Telemeter's offer to build ferrite core memories as replacements for Williams tube memories on the IBM 701 computers.[19]

Second, Tom Watson urged Palmer to reconsider greater use of cores. Following a visit to MIT in April 1954, Watson wrote: "I recognize that the use of cores in IBM as a commercial end product has been limited by patent problems, problems of uniformity of quality, etc. Nevertheless, if the problem of stringing the cores can be licked, it seems to me, as a layman, that the cost of storage using these cores would be far less than using anything else. . . . I think a tremendous amount of thought should be put into the decision as to how many cores will be used in the 702 in the first models and how quickly we can get them into use on a very broad basis in this machine."[20]

The third reason for reassessment resulted from Watson's decision to carve out of IBM a new organization with resources to design, manufacture, and sell electronic data-processing machines. He made this change in recognition of the potential importance of electronic computers and in direct response to the growing success of Remington Rand's UNIVAC. As Watson recalls, "The loss of our business in the Census Bureau [to the UNIVAC] struck home. We began to act. We took one of our best operating executives, a man with a reputation for getting things done, and put him in charge of everything which had to do with the introduction of an IBM large-scale computer—all the way from design and development through to marketing and servicing."[21]

He was referring to T. Vincent Learson, a tall, competitive individual with a degree in mathamatics from Harvard, who had served as sales manager for five years.[22] Watson now appointed him director of Electronic Data Processing (EDP) with the goal of making IBM a leader in electronic computers.

In June 1954, two months after Watson appointed Learson director of EDP, David J. Crawford was transferred from Project High to the commercial development area of IBM to develop magnetic core memories for commercial computer systems.[23] Crawford had not been involved with memory work in Project High, but he had directed the work of fifty engineers in developing SAGE vacuum tube circuits including some of those used in the memory. Previously he had worked for Jerry Haddad on the TPM and the IBM 701 computer. Before joining IBM in 1950, he had worked on digital circuitry in the Army Signal Security Agency and had obtained the master's degree in electrical engineering from MIT.[24]

Crawford recalls the differing views concerning the use of large ferrite core memories for the IBM commercial computers. One segment of management believed an experimental ferrite core memory system should be built in which new techniques for reducing costs could be tried. The success (or failure) of these techniques would then determine whether or not core memory was economically feasible for commercial use. Another group argued that IBM did not have sufficient time for an experimental approach. By the time the results were determined, the 704 and 705 computers would be fully committed to using electrostatic memories. This group believed the feasibility of the more important design techniques for memory cost reduction had already been established by the success of the small 776 tape buffer. They asserted that the price of critical components, such as cores, would come down as soon as large-scale production was achieved.

Dave Crawford (representing memory development) and Richard E. Merwin and Peter K. Spatz (representing memory requirements of the new computers) participated in many of the meetings in which the various points were argued during June and July 1954. As Crawford recalls, "Sometime during July 1954 there was a meeting reviewing the whole situation. Pete Spatz introduced a cost estimate which showed that the ultimate cost of a core memory of about 4000 words would be slightly less than that of the equivalent amount of electrostatic storage. From where I sat, this cost estimate was the final thing that tipped the scales."[23]

The Decision

In June 1954 Pete Spatz was assigned to the 704 computer project.[25] His job was to design a ferrite core memory with superior cost-performance to any memories designed outside IBM. Three engineers who had worked on the Type 776 ferrite core buffer technology in Mike Haynes's group now reported to Dave Crawford, providing important technical expertise and continuity for the commercial memory·development effort.[26] This group believed a low-cost main memory could be achieved if ferrite core specifications were set loose enough that grade B cores could be used and if an anticoincidence switch-core matrix, similar to that used in the Type 776 buffer, could be used to drive the much longer lines of the proposed memory.[23]

Preliminary tests of grade B cores from General Ceramics indicated that about 70 percent would be acceptable. Even with a 30 percent loss, the net cost would be less than half that of grade A cores used in SAGE.[27]

Driving long lines using an array of switch cores appeared to be more difficult. The engineers at International Telemeter had reported that small currents induced throughout the memory array from partially selected switch cores resulted in too much electrical noise to permit detection of the output signals. A discussion with MIT engineers revealed that they also believed this was a very difficult problem.[11] Bench tests conducted that summer, however, convinced Spatz that it was possible to use a switch core matrix to drive the long lines required for the proposed memory.[25] The noise control techniques implemented on the 3D ferrite core tape buffer were critical to this accomplishment.

Additional cost reduction was to be achieved in a variety of ways. Molded plastic frames were to be used instead of machined frames for holding the wired core planes. These molded frames were designed with grooves on the upper surface into which core plane wires could be placed. This was cheaper than threading wires through holes in the frame as was done for SAGE. Circuits were designed to minimize the use of large-sized vacuum tubes and to be tolerant of changes resulting from tube aging.[23] This feature reduced the frequency with which tubes needed to be replaced and was especially important because IBM included the cost of maintenance in the rental price.

That July the new director of EDP, Vin Learson, and IBM's director of engineering, Wally McDowell, toured the Poughkeepsie laboratory, where Spatz "gave them a sales pitch" on the favorable costs and reliability of ferrite core memories.[25] Learson, already convinced that IBM customers wanted more reliability, was quick to act. A product program was initiated under Pete Spatz in July to put ferrite core memories on the IBM 704 computer. During August a similar decision was made for the IBM 705 under the direction of Richard Merwin.[23] Ferrite core memories were subsequently made available for the 701 and 702 computers as well.

Developing Main Memories

On October 1, 1954, one month before Sperry Rand delivered its first ferrite core memory to the National Security Agency on the ERA 1103 computer, IBM announced that ferrite core memories would be available on the 701 and 704 computers beginning early in 1956. The 704 originally had been announced in May 1954, with 2048 words of electrostatic memory for a monthly rental of $2,600 and an optional second memory of the same capacity for an additional rental of $3,500. The new Type 737 magnetic core storage unit with 4096 words of memory was announced at a price of $6,100 per month, identical to the price previously announced for the same amount of electrostatic memory.[28]

The announcement did not mention the anticipated, but unverified, improvement in reliability from ferrite core memories; however, it did indicate there would be an improvement in processing speed: "An advantage of Magnetic Core Memory is that regeneration time is not required. Consequently. . . customers who elect to order Magnetic Core Memory will obtain advantages in processing speed. For example, addition time including access is reduced from 60 microseconds to 36 microseconds."[28]

IBM's announcement was a surprise to Pete Spatz and Dave Crawford who were still trying to solve a number of difficult technical problems in the just-announced magnetic core memory. The public announcement provided additional incentive to accomplish the development effort as quickly as possible. Crawford's group had the task of developing memory drive and sense circuitry that would work with either the 704 or 705 circuit technologies, Spatz's group was to incorporate the various circuits and parts into a memory system compatible with the 704 technology, and Merwin had a similar responsibility for the IBM 705 computer.

The design work was completed toward the end of 1954, and final memory testing was undertaken in mid-1955 by the machine groups.[23] Both memories used 50-80 mil cores and the array wiring pattern of SAGE. Lower performance required of the memory made it possible to use half-select current pulses of about 375 milliamperes, or about ten percent less than those used in SAGE.[29]

The memory used in the IBM 704 scientific computer was called the Type 737. It was housed in its own box, which was 98 inches long, 29 inches wide, 64 inches high, and weighed 1620 pounds.[17] It contained thirty-six planes of 64×64 cores each plus two spare lines of cores to facilitate repair in the field. Each plane therefore had 64×66 cores. The memory was capable of achieving a 9 microsecond cycle although only 12 microseconds was required by the computer.

The memory used in the IBM 705 commercial computer was built into the computer and consisted of thirty-five planes of 50×80 (4000) cores each. The 9 microsecond cycle was used to handle input-output devices of the system and also for transfer of data between locations in memory. The memory was used at a cycle time of 17 microseconds during operations involving the arithmetic section of the processing unit.[30]

Both memories employed anticoincident-current, switch-core drive matrixes similar to those Bloch had used in the Type 776 tape buffer. The switch cores were molybdenum-Permalloy tape cores. Each switch core in the matrix had two primary windings driven by 5998 vacuum tube drivers, the same vacuum tubes as were used in the SAGE drivers.[31] A secondary winding from the selected switch core transmitted the induced current to the corresponding drive line in the memory array. In the case of the IBM 705 computer, for example, 80 switch cores in an 8×10 matrix switch drove the 80 X lines of the memory array and 50 switch cores in a 5×10 matrix switch drove the 50 Y lines. Thus 33 current drivers were required to operate the two matrix switches, about four times fewer drivers than the 130 that would have been required if direct drive of the 80 X lines and 50 Y lines had been used, as was done in SAGE.[30]

By the end of 1954 a serious problem emerged: the average grade B cores from General Ceramics had greater variability from core to core than originally perceived. They could not meet the specifications for the 704 and 705 memories.[27]

By now IBM was producing ferrite cores for SAGE memories that were somewhat better than the grade A cores and far superior to the grade B cores of General Ceramics. Their use in the 704 and 705 memories would quickly solve the problem; however, IBM had recently been selected as a second source of cores for SAGE production memories and had to meet that commitment. Therefore a decision was made in March 1955 to reserve for SAGE all IBM-manufactured cores as well as all grade A cores from General Ceramics.[27, 32]

A degraded specification was established by Dave Crawford's group that could be met by grade B cores. Tolerances on all memory support circuits had to be reconsidered and in some cases tightened to permit the use of the poorer-quality cores. This decision was believed to be essential to the success of SAGE, but it increased substantially IBM's risk in its own commercial memory development.

Less than five months later, in August 1955, Tom Watson highlighted the importance of ferrite core memories when he berated his engineering managers for not developing them more rapidly for commercial machines. As early as spring of 1955, he

Switch core

Pluggable tape core unit used in the matrix of switch cores for driving the Type 775 3D selection ferrite core buffer memory. A portion of the clear plastic potting has been cut away to reveal the vertical copper wire windings wrapped about the horizontally mounted tape core.

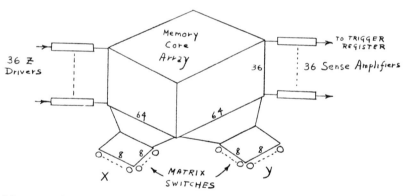

Memory schematic

This hand-drawn figure from an IBM engineering report of March 1955 was referred to as a 704 EDPM core memory layout showing main array, X, Y, and Z drivers, and sense amplifiers. The report described how 8×8 matrixes of switch cores could be used to drive a large memory array of 64×64 words of 36 bits each. The technique was similar to that used in the smaller 3D selection ferrite core buffers already developed for the IBM 702 computer.

asserted, telephone calls to IBM 701 and 702 customers revealed dissatisfaction with the reliability of Williams tube memories. In contrast telephone calls to customers with UNIVAC computers revealed satisfaction with mercury delay line memory. Citing one of many competitive situations lost to a UNIVAC, Watson noted with dismay that the John Hancock account was lost because of bad reports they had received from IBM customers.

Why, Watson demanded, didn't Ralph Palmer alert corporate management to the fact that there would be errors in memory? Why did engineering decide to use Williams tubes on the IBM 702 when they knew Williams tube memories were not reliable? "Our men in the field will fight the battle with whatever we have," Watson said as he pounded on the table, "but they want better tools." Concerning the shift to ferrite core memories he complained, "I had to make the decision."[33] Indeed he had, shortly after Pete Spatz gave his sales pitch to Wally McDowell and Vin Learson during their tour of the Poughkeepsie Laboratory in July 1954. Palmer attempted to respond to Watson by pointing out the high cost of ferrite cores and the improvements anticipated in Williams tube memory costs and reliability. Then realizing this was the wrong tack, he stated simply, "It was a wrong decision."[33]

Shipments of the IBM 704 and 705 to outside customers began in January 1956. That same month, the fourteenth and last IBM 702 was retrofitted with a ferrite core memory in the plant before it was shipped to Ford Motor Company where it replaced a room full of National Cash Register Company mechanical ledger machines.[34]

The customers who most appreciated ferrite core memory were those who had previously worked with an IBM 701 or 702. Problems on the 701 were frequently run twice because, without parity check, there was no other way to know if an error had occurred. On the 702, which had parity check, errors were frequent. A programmer at the Bank of America in San Francisco recalls how impressive it was to see the "banks upon banks of electrostatic storage tubes" on their IBM 702 replaced with a small metallic box with a glass window, revealing the ferrite core memory with twice the storage capacity.[35]

Many problems associated with national defense requirements needed particularly large main memories. Among these problems were cryptography and the simulation of nuclear weapons. Even for typical data-processing applications, the larger memory capacity made it possible to bring more records from magnetic tape into main memory at one time. Sorting of records could thus be done more rapidly, and writing programs was easier. Programmers became willing to entrust larger quantities of data and instructions to ferrite core memory when they learned how reliable it was.[35] Large, reliable main memories made programmers more efficient and made their programs run faster. It was the beginning of a new era in the use of computers, an era in which user requirements for main memory seemed to increase without limit.

Shortly after the announcement of ferrite core memory for the IBM 704 computer, a few customers expressed interest in having even larger memories. Cuthbert Hurd recalls Paul Armer of the Rand Corporation telephoning him to inquire about the possibility of building and attaching a 1 million bit memory to their IBM 704, about eight times the capacity of the announced Type 737 memory. After some preliminary cost estimates, Hurd said that such a memory might be installed for about $500,000. It seemed like a very large sum to Hurd, but Armer responded enthusiastically, "We'll take three."[36]

Once again International Telemeter Corporation offered to build the ferrite core memory units, once again IBM's business planners felt this might be the most economical way to obtain them, and once again IBM engineers believed it did not make sense to contract with an outside vendor for ferrite core memories.[37] When McDowell approached Erich Bloch about designing a larger memory in mid-1955, Bloch quickly agreed and put together a design proposal that management approved. He then approached the Rand Corporation and got a contract to build the memory for them. In the summer of 1955 he established a group to design and build a large memory later called the Type 738 for the IBM 704 computer.

Introducing Transistors

As part of the original assignment, Ralph Palmer urged Erich Bloch to use transistors instead of vacuum tubes in all memory support circuitry.[23] Palmer was eager to capitalize on the experimental work on semiconductor device development for which he had been given responsibility in 1950. By 1954 his semiconductor device development group had developed a family of logic circuits using junction transistors.[38] These circuits were used in the experimental all-transistor version of the IBM 604 electronic calculator, which was demonstrated to the public in October 1954, and they were the basis for circuits used in the first all-transistor calculator to be placed in production, the IBM 608.[39]

The IBM 608, shipped in 1957, is believed to be the world's first fully transistorized, commercial calculator. In 1955, however, IBM was not a leader in transistor technology. Bell Laboratories, RCA, General Electric, Westinghouse, Sylvania, and Raytheon (among others) had significant efforts and stronger patent positions in semiconductors.[40] Palmer had been moving into this field aggressively, capitalizing on Art Samuel's ability to recruit competent people in solid-state physics and electronics and on the pool of skilled engineers already in the company. In 1955 the race was on, and IBM appeared to be behind. The MIT Lincoln Laboratories had maintained an exploratory effort on transistor circuits following Bell Laboratory's demonstration in 1951 of a 16-digit serial multiplier using forty-four transistors and no vacuum tubes.[41] The MIT work did not come to fruition in time to affect the development of SAGE, but the results did lead to a decision to build an experimental computer at Lincoln Laboratories using transistor circuits.

Of even greater interest to the memory group was an optimistic report written in January 1955 by Ken Olsen of MIT, concerning the use of transistor circuits for driving coincident-current ferrite core memories.[42] However, a few months of design effort on the large memory convinced IBM engineers that transistors with sufficient power to drive ferrite core memories economically were not yet available. This attempt to use transistors in the drive circuits delayed the Type 738 memory project by several months.[23]

The delay was not without benefit. Improved core processing and characterization techniques at IBM produced ferrite cores significantly superior to those produced by General Ceramics for SAGE. The excellent process control and greater squareness of the hysteresis loops of the new cores reduced the tolerance requirements on drive circuits and decreased the electrical noise from half-select pulses.[43] These improvements in ferrite cores greatly reduced the difficulty of building large low-cost memory arrays.

Within six months after the Type 738 memory project was started, Erich Bloch turned it over to Ernest Foss who became its program manager, and Ralph S. Partridge became the engineering manager with responsibility for the technical effort. Partridge, who joined IBM in February 1950 with a bachelor's degree, had spent two years as a customer engineer (serviceman) before he was accepted for a development job in Poughkeepsie, designing vacuum tube circuits for the magnetic disk drive on the TPM.[44]

The Type 738 memory was completed using a vacuum tube drive system. Ralph Partridge also chose vacuum tubes for the logic circuits in order to make them compatible with the logic circuits of the IBM 704 and thus easier to service. However, transistors were used in the sense amplifiers, making the Type 738 memory the company's first product containing transistors to be manufactured and shipped to a commercial customer. Leon Wun, a young engineer in Partridge's group, designed the sense amplifier with positive feedback—an unconventional approach that received a lot of criticism but provided the required amplification.[23,44]

The memory array was organized with 128 address lines in the X direction, 256 address lines in the Y direction, and 36 bits per word in the Z direction. Once again Erich Bloch achieved a substantial cost reduction and improved reliability in the memory drive system by using switch core matrix drive. The switch cores were arranged in 8×8 matrixes. Two switch-core matrixes were used to drive the 128 X lines and four to drive the 256 Y lines. Larger matrixes than 8×8 were not used because of the large back voltage (about 100 volts) on the driver circuits. The type 5998 low gain, twin power triode vacuum tube driver first used in the XD-1 memory for SAGE, was selected and incorporated in a current feed-back amplifier similar to that used in the earlier IBM memories.[45]

The large size of the memory array resulted in a delay of 0.2 to 0.3 microsecond between the times of establishing a full half-select current in the first and last cores in a string of 8192 cores. This was simply the time it took an electric current to travel the length of the line. To minimize this effect, the inhibit winding was divided into four independently driven sections. The sense windings were similarly divided. The output signal was rectified before being amplified, as in previous IBM memories. Separate outputs from the four segments of each memory plane were coupled by means of OR circuits so that output signals from a full plane of 32,768 cores were picked up by each of the thirty-six output lines of the memory array.[45]

The Type 738 memory was first shipped on April 29, 1957, to the Rand Corporation for use on an IBM 704 computer, and subsequently was used on the IBM 709. It was the company's first memory with over 1 million bits. Its 32,768 word, 36 bit per word, memory array had 1,179,648 bits—eight times as many ferrite cores as were used in the Type 737 memory shipped on the IBM 704—yet the Type 738 memory occupied a volume only about two and a half times larger and weighed about two and a half times as much.[17]

The original sale price of the Type 738 memory was $1,040,000 or about 88 cents per bit. This price was soon reduced to $940,000 or 80 cents per bit, expensive compared to today's memory prices but cheap compared to $1.31 per bit then charged for the smaller Type 737 memory.[17]

Four months before the first Type 738 megabit ferrite core memory was shipped, Bill Papian's group at MIT announced completion of the megabit memory, which had been defined as the group's major objective at the end of 1954.[46] It had an array of 256×256×19 (1,245,184) ferrite cores and was thus about the same size as the IBM memory. Unlike the memories designed for

Driver frame used in the Type 738 memory
The large Type 5998 vacuum tubes, used for memory drivers, are on the
panels together with standard eight-tube pluggable units for memory
support logic. (From the *IBM Journal of Reserch and Development*, April
1957, p. 102.)

SAGE, it used switch core matrixes to reduce the number of high-powered vacuum tube drivers. Ironically switch core matrix drive was implemented by IBM in its product memories before it was used at MIT even though it was first proposed by Ken Olsen at MIT and Jan Rajchman at RCA.

Like the IBM megabit memory, the MIT memory used transistor sense amplifiers. The MIT memory was attached to the newly completed TX-0 computer, which was built at Lincoln Laboratory to "demonstrate and operationally test 5 megapulse transistor circuitry."[47] Transistor logic circuits were therefore also used in the memory. In contrast the logic functions of the IBM memory were implemented in vacuum tube circuits to be compatible with the logic of the commercial computers to which it was attached. The MIT memory had a 7 microsecond cycle, almost twice the speed of the IBM 738 megabit memory.

The higher performance and greater use of transistors in the MIT memory did not necessarily indicate IBM was behind in memory technology. Erich Bloch's memory was engineered for mass production and attachment to production computers, whereas the MIT memory was a laboratory model. Nevertheless the MIT TX-0 semiconductor computer with its high-speed megabit memory served as a prod to IBM engineers. It was indicative of the progress being made in semiconductor technology and the growing trend toward use of semiconductor transistor circuits in computers.

At about the same time that Erich Bloch began to work on the Type 738 memory, Dave Crawford's group was assigned the task of designing small memories for what was called the Modular Accounting Calculator (MAC) system. The Type 608 calculator with a 40 bit by 38 word 10 microsecond cycle memory was to be the first unit of the MAC system.[48] Larger, compatible calculators were to be designed later. The next larger memory was to have 1000 instead of only 38 words.

In order to provide IBM with practical experience in the use of transistors, Palmer insisted that these systems use only transistors in all the circuits, but partway through the design effort, sufficient problems arose that a shift to vacuum tube drivers was begun. When Palmer learned of this, he adamantly asserted that the

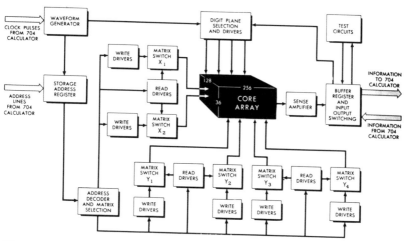

Block diagram of the Type 738 memory

The Type 738 was IBM's first ferrite core memory with more than one million cores. Like its predecessors, it used switch-core matrixes to select the X and Y drive lines. (From the *IBM Journal of Research and Development*, April 1957, p. 104.)

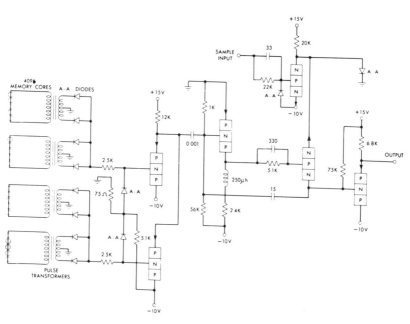

Sense amplifier in the Type 738 memory

Signals are fed through a pulse transformer and rectified before being amplified. One etched-wiring card held four transformers, each of which handled the output of 4096 cores from the memory array. (From the *IBM Journal of Research and Development*, April 1957, p. 108.)

memory for the 608 calculator was not going to use vacuum tubes. There was to be no retreat from the original objective of using only transistor circuits.[23]

To meet this objective and to provide the required current, three transistor drivers were used in parallel to drive each line. The memory array contained the same 50-80 mil ferrite cores as were used in the 737 and 738 memories. It was completed in 1955 and first shipped on the IBM 608 calculator in December 1957. Ultimately thirty-two were produced.

The main memory was very small, but it was IBM's first commercial ferrite core memory to be built using transistors for all the support circuitry. Ralph Palmer had achieved his objective of producing what is believed to be the world's first fully transistorized commercial calculator to be placed into production. Because of changing market requirements and the development of new system designs, the 608 calculator was the only member of the MAC series ever produced.[23]

Ferrite Core Fabrication

The development of ferrite core processing capabilities was instrumental to the success of large, low-cost ferrite core memories. By June 1954 John Gibson's pilot line in Component Research was producing well over 5000 cores per day. In October 1954 facilities were established in the Poughkeepsie plant to manufacture cores for Project High and for the IBM 704 and 705 memories.

Henry A. DiMarco, an electrical engineering graduate from Clarkson College in 1950, was responsible for transferring the process from development to manufacturing. DiMarco had started at IBM in a newly formed Release Engineering Group, whose job it was to ensure that new products were properly designed for manufacture, and in 1953 he participated in Operation Bootstrap, one of several internal educational programs organized to teach engineers about the new solid-state technologies. Following this in June 1954, he was sent to meet John Gibson and Bill Walker and to learn about ferrite cores. He reported back to his management that he believed ferrite cores could be manufactured successfully and was immediately assigned the task.[49]

DiMarco had difficulty convincing manufacturing engineers that detailed process specifications were needed in the documentation for the release of ferrite cores from development to manufacturing. Manufacturing engineers were accustomed to simple instructions, such as cut, bend, drill, or solder. They could not understand why precise temperatures and times had to be included with the otherwise simple instruction to bake the cores.[49]

In July Ernest C. Schuenzel had arrived with a degree in ceramics from Alfred University and a few years of experience at Curtiss Wright. His training in ceramics made him a natural choice for Gibson's ferrite core pilot line. Within months Schuenzel had technical responsibility for ferrite core development, reporting to Gibson and interfacing with DiMarco in manufacturing.[50] By April 1955 he had developed a special core for buffer applications, and DiMarco had helped release it to manufacturing. Thus IBM was able to make cores tailored for buffer memories in addition to those for main memories.

IBM could not use these magnesium-manganese (MgMn) ferrite cores commercially, however, without a license to the Albers-Schönberg patent which was assigned to General Ceramics.[51] General Ceramics appeared to be reluctant to negotiate either a simple royalty-bearing license or a paid-up license as IBM preferred. In addition to royalties on all cores produced by IBM, General Ceramics insisted on supplying a guaranteed percentage of the IBM core requirements, a condition Jim Birkenstock was not willing to accept. When a meeting in July failed to break the impasse, IBM initiated a program to develop an alternative composition. Studies were undertaken by Jim Brownlow under Andy Eschenfelder in Physical Research and by Ernie Schuenzel under John Gibson in Component Research.[52]

Brownlow began working on a copper-manganese (CuMn) ferrite material invented at the Philips Corporation in the Netherlands. He then shifted to a chrome-magnesium manganese (CrMgMn) ferrite material of his own that appeared to be outside the composition range covered by the General Ceramics patent.

While working on this material, he developed a unique two-stage quenching process for ferrite cores.[53] It consisted of cooling the cores from an initial high temperature such as 1300°C to about 950°C where they remained for five to fifteen minutes depending on core size and composition before they were quenched to room temperature. This process caused the formation of small inclusions of a nonmagnetic ferrous oxide (Fe_2O_3) on the core surface, which raised the coercive force at the inner surface of the cores and improved the squareness of the hysteresis loop.[54]

Meanwhile Birkenstock began negotiations with the Philips Company to use their CuMn ferrite composition. The composition did not appear to be as good as the MgMn composition of General Ceramics, but the issue was whether it was good enough.[55] IBM also wanted to reach an agreement with Philips as part of its more general effort to find European suppliers for components.[56] Philips was a leader in solid-state components with world-wide operations including research facilities in Holland, England, France, and Germany. Its business was complementary rather than competitive, and it already supplied some components to IBM World Trade for products released in Europe, typically two years after manufacturing started in the United States. A more comprehensive agreement would help facilitate more rapid release of new products for manufacture in IBM plants in Europe.

The ferrite core impasse with General Ceramics triggered a more rapid negotiation to achieve this broader goal. IBM needed Philips CuMn ferrite core material, and Philips was eager to obtain automatic core handling and core testing knowledge. In May 1956 the companies signed an agreement "to facilitate the interchange of technical information on such circuitry and elements. . . with the objective to expedite progress with respect to their activities, by eliminating duplication of efforts, exchanging information on accomplishments and pooling resources to solve particular problems."[57] In the case of ferrite core material, IBM was to pay royalties to Philips of 1 percent to 7.5 percent of the manufacturing cost.[32]

Later in May Philips supplied IBM with samples of the CuMn ferrite cores, which they were producing with less than 10 percent yields to the IBM core specification. Schuenzel initiated an effort to improve the processing procedures for cores using the Philips CuMn composition.[58] A variety of adjustments to the Philips process were made, including the use of Brownlow's two-stage quenching process. By October 1956 IBM manufacturing was able to produce CuMn ferrite cores for the Type 738 memory with a 60 percent yield, and IBM had supplied Philips with technical information aimed at improving their yield.[32]

By November 1956 Schuenzel had developed CuMn ferrite cores tailored for small buffer memories in addition to cores for large main memories, and in January 1957 the ferrite core development and product engineering activities were transferred to the Poughkeepsie Product Development Laboratory.[32] IBM now had a fully operating ferrite core development and manufacturing facility and had acquired the freedom to manufacture the CuMn ferrite cores for reasonable royalty payments to Philips.

The Philips agreement made negotiations with General Ceramics easier. In April 1957 IBM signed agreements with General Ceramics to purchase 49.5 million cores during 1957-1958 for an average price of 3.4 cents each and an additional 30 million cores (or half of the SAGE requirements, whichever was smaller) for an average price of 2.7 cents each. IBM also agreed to pay $250,000 for the right to manufacture 50 million MgMn cores.[32]

One month later IBM agreed to buy 90 million CuMn ferrite cores from Ferroxcube, a U.S. subsidiary of Philips, during a three-year period for commercial machines at an average price of 1.5 cents each.[32] Although this price seemed to be low at the time, IBM's own cost of manufacturing cores dropped to less than 0.6 cents per core by 1960 and averaged only about 0.8 cents per core during the same three-year period.[59]

The MgMn ferrite cores covered by the General Ceramics patent continued to be used for SAGE, but after 1958 IBM never again manufactured or purchased MgMn ferrite cores for commercial machines. In discussing these events, John Gibson noted that Birkenstock and others believed IBM should use its limited cash resources to develop products and should buy as many components outside as possible. "I really believe that if General Ceramics had been reasonable, we would have bought all our cores from outside," Gibson asserts, "but they so infuriated everyone that we got our backs up and said we are just not going to be blackmailed."[55]

Array Wiring Improvements

The first IBM core planes were wired and assembled completely by hand. The high cost of this tedious work was a major contributor to IBM's reluctance to become committed to the manufacture of large quantities of ferrite core memories. Mechanical designers and engineers were asked to look into ways to reduce the cost. One of these was Hans Peter Luhn, a prolific inventor who had been hired by T. J. Watson, Sr.[60]

Luhn devised a number of clever ways for wiring core arrays. A simple device was a large takeup spool that facilitated the wiring of the long, thin sense wire that ran diagonally through all cores in a core plane. It had to be one continuous wire, and without the takeup spool it was difficult to keep the wire from twisting or breaking.

An even more innovative idea was the use of a comb-shaped structure that held the cores for wiring and became an integral part of the memory structure.[61] The teeth of the comb were far enough apart that each core was positioned between two teeth with its axis perpendicular to the plane of the comb. A wire was caused to zigzag up through one core, then down through the next, until all of the cores mounted between the teeth of the comb were wired. A number of combs were then stacked on top of each other in such a way that one could look down through the holes of the cores. By inserting parallel wires through these holes, an XY wired array of cores was created. Luhn developed methods for implementing this type of core array on the small Type 608 calculator memory, which was completed in 1955 and first shipped in 1957. Larger arrays were experimentally wired but this type of core array wiring was abandoned in favor of better methods.

The most successful core plane wiring method was based on an MIT proposal that a flat plate with cavities regularly spaced on its surface be used to hold the cores in the desired position for wiring. As implemented by IBM, this matrix was a plastic plate with cavities in which individual cores were held by a vacuum applied through a small orifice in the bottom of each cavity. The matrix was mounted on a vacuum manifold affixed to a vibrator. Loose cores were dumped on the surface of the matrix and vibrated until they fell near an empty cavity. The vacuum drew the cores into the cavities, which were shaped to hold each core in the desired orientation for the subsequent threading operations.[62]

Because of the high cost of the plastic matrix and vacuum system, a technique was developed in which a sheet of sticky tape was placed on the array of cores once they were oriented in the plastic matrix. The vacuum system was then turned off, and the array of cores, held in place on the sticky tape, was ready for wiring.

To wire the array, a piece of insulated wire was stripped of insulation on one end and inserted approximately one or two inches into a long piece of hypodermic tubing that was used as a needle to thread a line of cores. Friction between the wire and the interior of the tubing held the wire as it was being pulled through the cores. Once through the cores, the wire was held in place and the needle pulled off and rethreaded for the next row of cores.[62]

This work was done under the direction of Roderick W. Link who had joined IBM in 1947. Fascinated by manufacturing processes, he had worked on tooling for IBM typewriters and key punches before becoming a manager in 1952. By 1954 IBM was primarily using vendors to supply mechanical components, and Link's group became more concerned with complex assemblies than with the traditional metal bending, forming, and cutting.[63]

An important addition to his group in 1954 was Walter P. Shaw who had started his career in 1939 as a shop boy earning $2.80 per day and had spent ten years learning the machinist and tool-maker trade under the demanding tutelage of John Grant, inventor of the M-1 rifle. Assigned to Link's group at IBM, Shaw was asked to find ways to reduce the hand work involved in wiring ferrite core arrays. One of the first things he observed was that

Core threading machine used in 1959
The vacuum matrix and covers at the left hold cores in place ready for
wiring. The 64 needles to the right have been withdrawn, leaving the 64
wires threaded through the cores. After these wires are attached to the
terminals on the edge of the core plane, the needle feeder is indexed to
the left to insert the adjacent group of 64 wires.

Needles passing through cores
Needles of the wiring machine are shown passing through the cores and
over orthogonal wires previously inserted. The cores have an inside
diameter of 30 mil and outside diameter of 50 mil.

no manual guidance of the needle through the cores was required—the cores themselves acted as guides. This caused Shaw to believe the needles could be propelled through the cores in gangs, instead of individually. He soon devised a machine capable of impelling up to eighty hypodermic needles through cores at one time. It used typewriter rollers mounted like old-time washing machine wingers, to drive the needles.[64]

Link liked Shaw's idea but noted that the hypodermic needles had to be rewired each time an array was wired. He proposed that the wires be inserted in the hypodermic needles so that the ends protruded from the front of the needles. The ends of the wires could then be grasped and wrapped around a terminal before the needles were withdrawn back through the array of cores. In this way the needles were rewired automatically as they were withdrawn if the wire through them came from a continuous spool.[64,65] The core threading machine was conceived late in 1955 and implemented in production in 1956.[64] It reduced the time to thread the X and Y wires in a 64×64 plane from 25 hours to 12 minutes.[66]

In August 1956 Shaw was joined by Robert L. Judge who had spent nearly seven years at Fort Sill, Oklahoma, in charge of tool makers, model makers, and draftsmen before coming to IBM. Working together they devised a mechanism which grasped the X and Y wires after they were threaded and wrapped them automatically around terminal posts on the frame of the core plane.[67] The time for this operation was reduced from 2.5 hours to less than a minute.[68]

Wiring the inhibit and sense lines was a particularly difficult problem because they each consisted of a single wire 10 to 30 feet long strung in a zig-zag pattern through the core plane. Pete Luhn's takeup spool and other techniques had only limited success in reducing the problem of wire breaking and kinking. The possibility of cutting the wire into short segments for wiring the plane and then soldering the ends together to create one electrical conductor was considered. This in effect is how each of the X and Y lines was caused to zigzag through the core planes once the planes were stacked in the three-dimensional array. For a variety

Vacuum matrix
The operator is shown pouring ferrite cores onto a vibrating plastic plate with holes shaped to orient cores for wiring. A vacuum applied to the bottom of the plate holds the cores in position.

Core plane for the Type 738 memory
The core planes used in the Type 738 megabit memory contained 64×128 cores each. (From the *IBM Journal of Research and Development*, April 1957.)

of electrical, mechanical, and reliability reasons, however, this solution was not considered attractive in the early core planes, especially for the sense lines.

Shaw solved this problem in 1960 with his invention of the capstan wire handler.[69] His invention provided a powered capstan for each loop in the sense line. The operator threaded the sense line, which was butt welded to the end of a long straight needle, through the first row of cores. Then making a U-turn around the first capstan, the operator threaded the wire back through the next row. As the wire was pulled tight the capstan helped to propel the wire through the first row of cores and into the second. The operator continued this process until all capstans had been used and all the core rows were wired.[64]

Innovations in ferrite core fabrication, memory array wiring, and drive and sense circuitry had made IBM the lowest-cost manufacturer of ferrite core memories in the world. Nevertheless Ralph Palmer and the other engineering managers felt they had little reason to be complacent. External reports suggested IBM was getting behind in the use of semiconductors for logic and for memory support circuits. New memory technologies under development by others had the potential to destroy the company's advantage in only a few years.

6
Project Stretch

In the fall of 1954 a small but increasing portion of IBM's revenue was coming from electronic stored-program computers. The IBM 704 and 705 computers with ferrite core memories had just been announced. The information IBM sales representatives obtained from customers for electronic computers was providing a much better understanding of customer requirements and of design deficiencies in the systems.

A number of engineers sought new solutions. Among these were three young systems designers: Werner Buchholz and Stephen W. Dunwell, who had first worked together designing the experimental Tape Processing Machine (TPM), and Gene Amdahl, who had been the chief designer of the IBM 704 computer.[1] They began to meet several times a week to discuss computer system design, and toward the end of 1954 their discussions resulted in a conceptual computer system, which they christened the Datatron.[2]

They held meetings with representatives from engineering, product planning, and the Applied Science Department, and John von Neumann, as a consultant to IBM, attended several of the meetings.[3] The machine concepts that evolved were intended to combine in one system the scientific computational capabilities of the IBM 701 and 704 with the business-oriented data handling, sorting, and comparing capabilities emphasized in the IBM 702 and 705. They also addressed the problem of having card readers, card punches, and printers for each system, which were all different; there were no standard units or interfaces.[1]

Seeking Government Funds
A business issue of substantial concern at this time was how to respond to several organizations that had requested information on the company's plans for high-speed machines. These

organizations included the Bureau of Ships (for the National
Security Agency), three atomic energy facilities, General Electric,
and United Aircraft.

In a meeting of IBM executives in January 1955, it was noted
that all of these customers for large computers "desire machines
which are as fast as possible, which have large amounts of random
access memory, and which can be made available in 1957 or
earlier.[3,4] The specific applications were unique to each
organization and included cryptography, nuclear weapon
simulation, aircraft design, and weather forecasting. All
applications used large arrays of data that could not be held even
in the megabit memory then scheduled for shipment in 1957 on
the IBM 704 computer.

Problems involving such large arrays of data had to be solved
by bringing parts of the data into main memory from magnetic
tape, performing calculations, returning some data to magnetic
tape, and then bringing in more data. Pieces of the data often had
to be moved in and out of main memory many times to complete
one calculation. The accuracy of a calculation often could be
improved by increasing the number of data points in the array, but
this was done at the expense of increasing the time required to
complete the calculation. In the case of weather forecasting, for
example, there was little interest in improving the accuracy so
much that several days of computer time were required to
calculate the next day's weather. Better weather forecasts
therefore required faster computers with larger memory.

These applications had one other important common feature:
they were related to national security and enjoyed potentially
higher levels of funding than were available from commercial
customers.

The executives attending this meeting decided that IBM should
seek government funds to assist in developing a combined
scientific computer and business data-processing machine. As an
alternative they would seek funds to develop a large high-speed
random-access memory which appeared to be critical to this
objective. Cuthbert Hurd was to visit several Atomic Energy

Commission (AEC) installations to inform officials of the IBM plans and to determine how best to secure funds.[3]

Competition for government funding was expected especially from ERA, which was now part of Sperry Rand. ERA had been very effective in securing government contracts and had just delivered an ERA 1103 computer with one thousand words of ferrite core memory to the National Security Agency (NSA). Furthermore Seymour Cray of ERA was reported to be developing magnetic core logic for a machine to be delivered to NSA in 1957 at a cost of $2 million to $4 million. Competition was also expected from the International Telemeter Corporation, which was reported to have proposed a machine with about the speed of an IBM 704 but with much larger memory.[3]

After being informed of IBM's interests, Edward Teller, associate director of the University of California Lawrence Radiation Laboratory, at Livermore, California, asked IBM to bid on a large two-megapulse computer called LARC (Livermore Automatic Research Computer). A two-megapulse machine was one in which the basic internal clock cycle was 2 million cycles per second. A proposal for this machine by Sperry Rand provided a competitive bid.[1] Teller was convinced that future machines should use transistors instead of vacuum tubes so the use of transistors became an important requirement of the proposal.[5]

A group of about twenty engineers, scientists, and product planners were brought together to formulate IBM's proposal. Gene Amdahl was a chief architect, and many of the advanced concepts from Datatron were included. The system design was well along when a review of IBM's transistor technology revealed that it was neither fast enough nor sufficiently well developed to provide the required circuits. The IBM proposal for LARC, therefore, made use of Philco surface-barrier transistors which appeared to be the fastest available devices.[5] At this time Philco had just entered into a subcontract with the MIT Lincoln Laboratories to obtain Air Force funds to develop their surface-barrier transistors for digital computers.[6]

Ralph Palmer now changed the entire thrust of the proposal. He asserted the LARC proposal was not bold enough. It would tie up two hundred to three hundred people for several years building a state-of-the-art machine with vendor components. IBM would thus help a vendor develop components that others could use. In the meantime the magnitude of the effort would prevent the company from building a superior machine with more advanced technology.[5] Palmer believed that IBM's own transistor technology would be superior to that of Philco if sufficient resources were available to develop it.

Crucial to Palmer's decision was a new transistor structure being developed by Lloyd Hunter and his group of solid-state technologists. Hunter, who had thirteen years' experience in semiconductors and a doctor's degree from Carnegie Tech when he joined IBM in 1951, was in charge of solid-state device work.[7] He and his group spent several years attempting to improve point-contact transistor devices, which were much faster than junction transistors. Then in 1954 he became aware of theoretical papers published in a German scientific journal that proposed a way to increase the speed of junction devices dramatically. The structure required that the impurity concentration in the base region of the transistor decrease from the emitter to the collector. This created an internal electric field that increased the rate of drift of the electric current carriers across the base region. The device therefore became known as the graded-base or drift transistor.[8]

Hunter was distressed that he did not have enough experimental data on these new structures in time to recommend their use in the LARC proposal. However, he and Palmer were both convinced that they could be made to work and that they would be easier to mass produce than the surface-barrier transistors then being developed by Philco.[7]

Palmer therefore redirected the design effort to a more advanced machine using IBM's own transistor technology. There was consternation on the project because the systems designers had spent considerable time designing the two-megapulse LARC using Philco transistors and were eager to build the machine; nevertheless Palmer's orders were carried out.[5] The success ultimately achieved with drift transistors makes this one of the more important technical decisions of this era.

In April 1955 the two-megapulse LARC machine designed by IBM engineers with Philco transistors was described to the Livermore organization. Livermore was advised, however, that IBM wanted to take a more significant step forward and therefore was proposing a five times higher performance ten-megapulse machine. Inasmuch as the higher-performance machine was not yet specified and new technologies were needed, it was estimated that a minimum three-year development effort would be required. The cost was estimated at $3.5 million instead of $2.5 million. Following these discussions, the contract for LARC was awarded, not surprisingly, to Sperry Rand. Sperry Rand had specified a twenty-nine month schedule, and this earlier date was of major importance to Livermore.[9]

The fact that Livermore chose Sperry Rand's LARC spurred on IBM's management. Tom Watson in particular was concerned about the company's position in high-performance computers. IBM engineers continued to define the faster ten megapulse machine while Ralph Palmer and others sought government funding. An informal proposal was made to NSA in June 1955. The bureau responded that the IBM-proposed ten megapulse machine was not technically feasible in the foreseeable future; therefore the agency would not fund its development.[9] One month later the agency indicated that it was interested in funding a technology effort leading to an advanced high-performance system.

Palmer immediately called a number of key technical people back from vacation for a brainstorming session. At that time all IBM employees took their vacation during the same two weeks. The session resulted in two memory device concepts that provided the basis for a proposal made to NSA in September 1955.[1] These concepts were a 2 microsecond cycle megabit memory using small, high-coercive-force cores, and a smaller 0.5 microsecond cycle memory using ferrite cores with three holes instead of one. Three-hole cores had been used experimentally to achieve nondestructive readout, but their use to achieve higher speeds was an entirely new idea. Both memories were to have all-transistor support circuits, using graded-base drift transistors being developed at IBM to provide the required high drive currents and voltages.

The proposal was accepted by NSA, which agreed to contribute $1,100,000 to a memory development program (called Silo) and $250,000 for the design of a computer for their specific purpose. The contract was officially signed in January 1956.[9]

Informal discussions late 1955 revealed that the Los Alamos Scientific Laboratory might be interested in buying a computer in the ten-megapulse range. With this information Ralph Palmer began funding a development effort. The Datatron program provided the basis for early systems design objectives, but the name Datatron was abandoned and replaced by Stretch, meaning simply stretching the technology. As project Stretch evolved, many of the original Datatron objectives were also abandoned in order to meet costs, schedules, and customer requirements.

Steve Dunwell was appointed manager, and Joseph C. Logue, who had managed a semiconductor circuit development group, was given responsibility for hardware design.[10] Gene Amdahl, who had contributed to the system's design, left IBM late in 1955 after finding that the new organization placed him "way down in the innards having essentially very little to say about anything."[11,12]

In March 1956 a formal presentation of IBM's proposed Stretch computer was made to the AEC at Los Alamos. The ten-megapulse speed was to be achieved with five stages of logic per machine cycle and a 0.02 microsecond delay per stage. That November a contract was signed for delivery of the Stretch computer to the AEC within forty-two months.[13] The contract established rather specific design objectives for the system but did not specify the overall processing speed; however, there had been discussions suggesting the system would be approximately 100 times faster than the IBM 704.[9] The performance actually achieved by Stretch became a major issue shortly before it was delivered.

The AEC reluctantly contracted to pay $4.3 million for the proposed machine instead of the originally projected $3.5 million.

It was, nevertheless, expected to be a good buy. IBM planned to spend $13.8 million in its development and construction. Of the $9.3 million not paid by the AEC, the company hoped to recover only about $5.5 million through additional government contracts and by selling the engineering model.[14] To avoid a loss on the program, IBM needed to benefit from the technologies developed in the Stretch project. This was accomplished by obtaining free use or ownership of all patents developed on the project.[13]

By this time the Project Silo memory development effort was well underway. Dave Crawford in Phil Fox's area had the primary responsibility, but substantial support was received from other groups.[15] Semiconductor circuits with enough power and speed to drive the memories were a major concern.

Problems at Two Microseconds

Gregory Constantine, Jr., joined IBM and Project Silo in March 1956 immediately after receiving the master's degree in electrical engineering from MIT. There were only six people in Crawford's group when Constantine arrived, but during June it swelled to twelve as more graduating engineers were hired. By September Constantine was already a senior member of the group with responsibility for designing the semiconductor drive circuits for the proposed 2 microsecond memory.[16]

The magnitude of this problem was not fully appreciated at the time nor were the limitations of semiconductor devices well understood. The very long drive lines, threading through 4096 cores of the Z line or through 9216 cores of the X or Y planes, experienced heavy inductive loads, creating large back voltages. Even today it would be difficult to obtain transistors capable of meeting the requirements for the semiconductor drivers for the 2 microsecond memory.[17]

Constantine says, "We were working with IBM transistors that were much better than those on the market, but they still were not what was needed to drive the memory. It was December 1956 that the progress report for transistor drivers was very discouraging. I had been thinking about some crazy ways of adding currents and cancelling currents with transformers. I suggested it might be possible to use these concepts to drive the memory even with the available transistor drivers. I remember being laughed at. Several of the managers who laughed at my idea had to go to a conference immediately following that meeting. By the time they came back, we had such a device wired and working."[16]

By January 1957 Constantine had written a report describing the new matrix switch design that combined the input power from many transistors into one larger output pulse. The first version provided sixteen output lines from a 4×4 array of switch cores.[18] At first there was not much interest in the device; however, as it became evident that the required currents and voltages could not be supplied by individual transistors, Constantine was asked if he really could make switches good enough to be used in a product. He responded positively and was soon given the job.[16]

By the end of the summer he had designed and fabricated a matrix switch similar to the ones ultimately used in the Type 7302 Stretch memory.[19] He called it a load-sharing matrix switch. It consisted of sixteen magnetic switch cores used as transformers. The output from thirty-two separate transistor drivers drove thirty-two primary windings, which were coupled positively and negatively to the sixteen switch cores in such a way that only one core experienced the positive input from all sixteen drivers when an appropriate sixteen drivers were activated. The positive and negative orientations of the selected primary windings were such that each of the other fifteen cores experienced exactly eight negative and eight positive input pulses. Proper selection of sixteen out of thirty-two drivers permitted any one of the sixteen cores to be so activated. In this way the output power of sixteen transistor drivers could be combined to drive any one selected line in the memory array.

For the planned 2 microsecond main memory of Stretch, 125-250 mil ferrite switch cores, 1.8 inches long, were used. Drive line currents of 0.585 ampere at 100 volts were required from these switch cores. This was 58.5 watts of power. Assuming a 90 percent efficiency in the load-sharing matrix switch, the sixteen input transistors had to supply a total of 65 watts or only

about 4.1 watts each, well within the state of the art. The
transistors finally selected were capable of furnishing 0.37 ampere
at 11 volt and with an 0.5 microsecond pulse.[20] The most difficult
problem of all—providing the required large currents and high
voltages with transistors—had been solved.

Only when Constantine wrote an article for publication did he
become aware of the related work reported by others. He may
have heard of some of these ideas in discussions with fellow
engineers at IBM, but by now there were so many alternative ways
of driving memories and so many variations on each alternative
that the original source of ideas was unclear. In his article he
cited a load-sharing matrix switch proposed by Jan Rajchman of
RCA in June 1953.[21] Constantine asserted, however, that
Rajchman's design would result in spurious output signals and
erroneously switch unselected memory cores.[20]

The remaining problems in the 2 microsecond memory also
were not trivial, as Edwin D. Councill quickly learned. Councill
had joined the Silo project two months before Constantine. His
first assignment, ferrite core characterization for Stretch, revealed
that even small changes in temperature altered the ferrite core
characteristics so that the memory would not work.[22]

It was necessary to stabilize the core temperatures. Councill
tried many things: talcum powder, grease, oil, and Freon. Only
complete immersion in a liquid was satisfactory. Ultimately the
entire core array was immersed in transformer oil. The oil was
cooled or heated under thermostatic control to maintain the
temperature of the cores to within a few degrees of the nominal
temperature at which they were designed to operate.[22]

One of the hardest problems was detecting the output signal.
Leon Wun, who had designed the transistor sense circuits used on
the Type 738 memory, designed an improved version for the
higher-performance Type 7302 Stretch memory. At first it could
not detect the desired output signals because the electrical noise in
the memory array was too high. Never before had the memory
group been faced with such fast rise-time pulses in such long lines.

To solve this problem, the sense line was wired not in the
traditional diagonal pattern. Instead it was wired parallel to the

Load-sharing matrix switch

The switch cores used to drive the 2.18 microsecond cycle memory in Stretch were 1.8 inches long with a 125 mil inside diameter and 250 mil outside diameter.   The unit standing on end in the center of the photograph held two rows (or matrixes) of 16 cores. Four of these units were packaged on the sides of a modified ferrite core plane as shown. Eight load-sharing switches, packaged in this manner, were used for each address selection coordinate of the memory.   Each switch has 32 single-turn input windings and 16 nine-turn output windings.

drive lines with a cross-over in the center so that the drive pulse pickup would cancel over the length of the sense line.[23] The sense lines were treated as long transmission lines and terminated by resistors of the correct characteristic value.[24] This increased the peak power required to drive the memory array lines by nearly a factor of ten, and the rise and fall times of the drive pulses had to be shortened.

To satisfy these requirements, IBM technologists developed a medium-power, graded-base transistor that produced 60 volt, 0.6 ampere pulses with rise times of 0.1 microsecond.[25,26] This transistor was so good that it could be used to drive the inhibit lines without the help of the load-sharing switch, but load-sharing switches continued to be essential for the X and Y lines.

To reduce noise pickup from the inhibit line, the sense lines on each plane of 128×128 cores were divided into four segments of 32×128 cores each, and the inhibit lines were divided into four orthogonal segments. Thus only one-sixteenth of the cores in a given plane coupled their inhibit noise into the sense lines. Numerous other methods were devised to reduce the noise.[22]

One of the most difficult things to accomplish was creating a figure eight pattern in the sense lines so that drive-line noise coupled into the sense line would be cancelled. Bob Judge, who had earlier helped Walt Shaw devise a wire-wrap machine for ferrite core arrays, devised a jig to solve this new problem. The jig split the core plane in half so that the two halves could be moved relative to each other. By shifting the two halves by one core row, a long, straight needle could be used to wire one row of cores halfway across the plane and the adjacent row for the rest of the way.[27]

Staggered read, which had been rejected for the 6 microsecond cycle SAGE memories because it lengthened the cycle time, was adopted for the three-times faster Stretch memory. With smaller ferrite cores to provide an output signal and with more cores per line to contribute electrical noise, staggered read was essential. It helped to keep the noise low enough that the signal could be detected reliably.

The correct technical decision at one point in time was not necessarily the correct decision at a later time. As ferrite core memory technology matured, it was becoming less important to create new solutions than it was to select the most effective combination of old solutions, including some that previously had been rejected.

Program Management

At the same time that critical technical problems were being solved for the 2 microsecond memory, major changes in direction were occurring in project Stretch. In May 1957 it had been decided to derive three different computers from the Stretch technologies. Known as the three-in-one approach, the plan called for a small serial computer with three to four times the speed of the IBM 704, the Stretch computer with up to 100 times the performance of the IBM 704, and finally Stretch with a streaming unit for performing special statistical operations desired by NSA. Less than one year later the small serial processor effort was eliminated because it was not achieving a satisfactory cost and performance for the market and because its requirements were adversely affecting the design of Stretch.[9]

The possibility of using magnetic core logic in place of semiconductor logic in the input-output devices of Stretch was also carefully considered. Erich Bloch, who had designed IBM's first commercial ferrite core memory products, got the job of doing the same for magnetic logic. This time he was not successful. He was defeated by the technical strength and conviction of Joe Logue's semiconductor device group and by the fact that magnetic core logic was technically less attractive than magnetic core memories. Magnetic cores were excellent for storing information but were less well suited to the dynamic switching of logic circuits. A fundamental problem, highlighted by Bloch's effort, was that almost as many vacuum tube or semiconductor devices were needed to drive magnetic core logic as were required to perform the same logical functions without any magnetic cores at all. In November 1957 the decision was made to reject magnetic core logic and to use transistor circuits for all logic functions in Stretch.[9]

Although Haynes and others continued to explore novel forms of magnetic logic, the decision not to use it in Stretch was the last serious consideration of magnetic logic for IBM products. It was the end of Mike Haynes's dream that magnetic core logic, which he pioneered first at the University of Illinois and then at IBM, would have significant commercial use. Soon after this decision, Erich Bloch was put in charge of all hardware development for Stretch, and Joe Logue, who had previously held this job, was given responsibility for developing semiconductor circuits for all computers including Stretch.[28] This assignment led to the development of a standardized circuit and packaging technology known as Standard Modular System (SMS).

During 1958 the uses for Stretch technologies broadened as a result of the company's winning a contract to supply a transistorized version of the IBM 709 computer for the Ballistic Missile Early Warning System (BMEWS). Two transistorized 709s, later called IBM 7090s, were to be used to collect and process data at each of the three early warning sites in Alaska, Greenland, and Scotland.[29] Information from these sites was then transmitted to the SAGE air defense system. The 7090 used the architecture of the 709 and the semiconductor circuits and magnetic core memories originally designed for Stretch.

RCA was the prime contractor for BMEWS and Sylvania was the subcontractor for the computer and programming. Sylvania rejected using its own computer for BMEWS partly because of concern over its reliability. The decision to use the proposed 7090 computer was heavily influenced by the possibility of using an existing vacuum tube 709 for software and system development and by the availability of solid-state technology in IBM for making the conversion to transistors.[29]

With these decisions made concerning the 7090, the company decided to design and market a transistorized version of the business-oriented IBM 705, which was later designated the IBM 7080. By the end of 1958 the 2 microsecond memory designed for Stretch was slated for use in four systems: Stretch for the

AEC; Harvest, a special-purpose computer for NSA that combined a Stretch computer with an array processor and a high-speed magnetic tape unit; the IBM 7090 scientific computer, required for BMEWS; and the IBM 7080 business computer.

In December 1958 Ralph Partridge, who had previously served as engineering manager for IBM's first million-bit Type 738 memory, was designated program manager for the 2 microsecond Type 7302 memory for these systems.   He quickly became embroiled in disputes among the systems managers who were to use the Type 7302 memory.   "They all wanted the memory," Partridge recalls, "without anything they didn't need for their own system.   It took quite a bit of doing to get this to be one memory in production with only simple modifications for the different users."   The memory unit finally developed was manufactured identically for the three systems; however, a modification installed in the field was required to permit the memory to appear on Stretch as 16,384 words of 72 bits per word, on the 7090 as 32,768 words of 36 bits each, and on the 7080 as 160,000 characters of 7 bits each.[17]

The first engineering models were to be operational by late in the summer of 1959, less than nine months after Ralph Partridge joined the project.   Production memories were needed by October in order to meet the contracted schedule of shipping four IBM 7090 computers for BMEWS by the end of the year.   By early fall they still did not have the first three engineering models operating, but the production schedule for the 7090 memories was so tight that twenty production units were already being assembled.   This was a high-risk decision.   Major changes might have to be made in the engineering models, and if they were, these changes would also have to be made in all the production models, at a very high cost.   Fortunately only minor changes were required.

The first Type 7302 memory was shipped on an IBM 7090 computer in December 1959 to Sylvania in Needham, Massachusetts, for use in BMEWS.   Its actual cycle time was 2.18 microseconds as compared to 12 microseconds for the earlier Type 738 memory.   The 7302 used all semiconductor circuits and smaller 30-50 mil ferrite cores.[31]   It was housed in one box, 30

IBM 7302 memory

The 2.18 microsecond cycle, Type 7302, memory used on Stretch had a 128K byte core array submersed in oil to maintain a nearly fixed temperature. The oil-filled tank housing the array is in the center. The swinging gates, to either side, house electronic support circuits and can be swung against the array, making a compact unit.

inches wide, 56 inches long, and 69 inches high; whereas its vacuum-tube-driven predecessor, the 738, had used a T-shaped structure that was three times longer and wider.[32]

Moe Every

At the beginning of the Silo project, there had been a lot of enthusiasm for ferrite cores with three or more holes because of their faster switching speeds. Consideration was even given to using three-hole cores for the 2 microsecond as well as for the 0.5 microsecond Silo memory.[17,33] Lloyd Hunter, who had originally suggested three-hole cores for high-speed memories at the brainstorming session in July 1955, described the basis for fast switching in these devices as follows:

A coincident summation of magnetic flux causes the element to switch, and the magnitudes of the currents inducing the flux are not critical. This allows the switching time to be freed of the current-selection-ratio limitation typical of the coincident-current selection systems. In the coincident-flux system, one may use selecting flux densities representing fields very much greater than the coercive field, giving very fast switching times.[34,35]

Enthusiasm for three-hole cores gradually faded as an increasing number of technical problems were discovered. One problem was the large back voltage induced in the drive lines. This was reduced somewhat by use of an extra bias winding through the core that prevented flux switching in partially selected cores; however, the need for more than one wire per hole was a deterrent to improvements in packaging. Cores with five and six holes (using fewer wires per hole) were developed and tested, but these presented even more problems.[36]

Ed Councill found the cooling and wiring problems to be more severe than with the 2 microsecond memory. Eventually the three-hole core array was immersed in Freon (CCl_3F) for temperature stability. Using evaporative cooling in a closed tank, the cores were held in a temperature range between the 20°C bath temperature and the 23.8°C boiling point of the Freon. The low-temperature boiling characteristic of Freon helped to cool the ferrite cores effectively but made packaging difficult.[37]

Toward the end of 1958, it was clear that it would be very difficult to achieve the objectives of the three-hole-core memory project. Nevertheless the program schedule required that an engineering model be built preparatory to producing a production unit.

At this stage Maurice A. (Moe) Every, was put in charge of the project. With a bachelor's degree in power engineering and six years' experience at IBM in magnetic tape storage, logic design, and manager of design and drafting services, Moe Every had already earned a reputation as a person who got difficult jobs done. More a student of people and organizations than of technologies, Every nevertheless had a quick grasp of essential issues and could hold his own in arguments with the best engineers. A man of earthy humor and saltier language, he was unflappable and confidently stubborn in his decisions. One otherwise calm engineer recalls standing on Moe Every's desk, shouting down at him, in an effort to get his attention and convince him to change a decision.[38]

After a year in charge of the three-hole core memory project, Every found the problems were more clearly identified but no closer to solution. Failing to solve the technical problems, he helped work out an agreement with the AEC in July 1959 to eliminate the 0.5 microsecond memory from the Stretch computer, a decision that took a lot of pressure off the development effort.[39]

The small, high-speed memory was not sufficiently critical to the Stretch computer performance to risk dependence on a technology that might not be developed on time. The 0.5 microsecond memory did remain a part of NSA's Harvest machine, which had unique systems requirements. More important NSA did not want to admit failure in a technology its funds had helped to develop.[38]

In December 1959 William H. Rhodes replaced Moe Every as manager of the 0.5 microsecond memory program, and Every was promoted to the manager for all nonmechanical memory development.[40] Rhodes, who had previously worked with Erich Bloch on the first 3D ferrite core buffer memory product, soon presented Every with a list of all the technical problems that

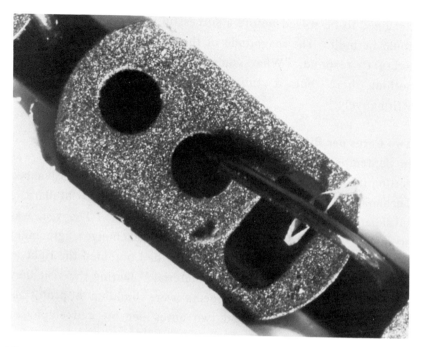

Three-hole core

A partially wired three-hole core of the type developed for Stretch and
Harvest. The hole for the sense winding was made larger than the other
two holes to improve the performance.

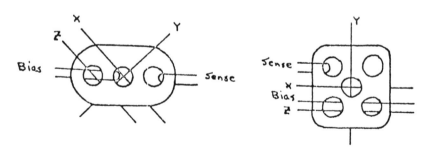

Multihole cores

The three-hole and five-hole core wiring schematics are from an internal
IBM report of June 25, 1957. An advantage suggested for the five-hole
core was that no more than two wires threaded any one hole.

remained to be solved before a successful three-hole core memory could be built. The magnitude of the remaining problems caused Every to respond, "What you're telling me is that you've got nothing here but a tub of mush." Rhodes responded affirmatively.[41]

Two Cores per Bit

In September 1959 as the three-hole core memory project was getting into deeper difficulty, Robert M. Whalen of the Advanced Technology Group joined Dave Crawford in a visit to Mullard, a subsidiary of the Philips Corporation in England. The visit was arranged as part of the information exchange agreement negotiated three years earlier when IBM had obtained the right to use the Philips CuMg ferrite core material.[42] During the visit they learned that the Mullard engineers were building a prototype high-speed memory that used two cores per bit and employed three primary features:

First, the memory array was wired in a 2D manner in which all cores on a given word line were read simultaneously. Because no other cores were coupled by the selected word line, a large drive current could be used to produce fast switching.

Second, two cores per bit were wired so that the sense amplifier detected the difference in signal between them, resulting in better noise rejection.

Third, cores were written by pulses too short to saturate them, resulting in a partial-switching mode that was faster than a full switching mode. The information stored in partially switched cores was more sensitive to disturb pulses than fully switched cores, but this difficulty was overcome by use of a 2D selection mode in which bit line pulses were kept much smaller than half-select pulses.[43,44]

When Whalen and Crawford returned to IBM they immediately began work on "a variety of two core per bit schemes." Four months later, January 1960, they were seriously considering two cores per bit as an alternative to the three-hole core memory for Harvest. By clever modification of the Mullard scheme to match their own needs, they were able to devise a one-to-one replacement for the three-hole core memory that made use of circuit technologies already developed for the three-hole-core memory. Whalen optimistically predicted that a prototype memory could be completed in a few more weeks, thus permitting IBM to meet its schedule for Harvest.[42]

By May 1960 Moe Every had convinced the Bureau of Ships to authorize this change in the high-speed memory for Harvest. But the bureau, which had funded the three-hole core development for NSA, was eager to retain some of this technology in the computer. Every agreed to try, and finally one plane of three-hole cores was retained to perform a special bit map function—not because it was the best technical solution but because it satisfied the customer's desire for some success from a development effort it had supported.[38]

The two core per bit memory proposal adopted for Harvest in May 1960 was for a 73,728 bit memory organized in a 2D array of 1024 words of 72 bits each with a cycle as close to 0.5 microsecond as possible. Each bit consisted of a pair of ferrite cores 30-50 mil diameter and 11 mil high. The information in all 72 bits on a word line was read out simultaneously by sending a large current pulse through the selected word line. The readout current in this line could be made as large as needed to switch the cores rapidly because it was not limited by half-select requirements of coincident-current selection. In the proposal there was a separate write and read line, and the readout line was wired twice through the cores so that twice the ampere turns could be achieved with the same current. In this way the same load-sharing matrix switch could be used to drive both the read and write lines.[45]

The write lines were pulsed coincidently with the bit lines to store information. There were two bit lines for each bit—that is, a separate line for each of the two cores in the bit. Prior to writing, all of the cores on the word line were saturated by the large read pulse. The opposite polarity write pulse on the singly-wound word line alone caused little flux reversal, but when combined with a bit pulse, the core was partially switched—not to

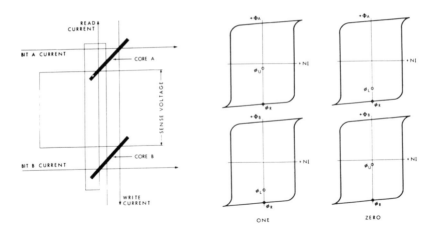

Two core per bit storage cell

The manner in which two cores of a single bit are threaded by drive and sense windings and the respective current and voltage polarities are indicated at left. The approximate flux states to which the pair of cores are driven for the storage of a 1 or 0 are shown at right. The read current is conducted through a two-turn winding in order to halve the drive-current requirements. This drive is applied to both cores with a polarity that switches them to the negative flux state. On removal of the read drive, both cores relax to the states indicated by Φ_R on the hysteresis loops. The cores may now be switched to the appropriate states corresponding to the information to be stored. (From the *IBM Journal of Research and Development*, July 1961, p. 175.)

the opposite direction saturation state but rather to a nearly demagnetized state.[45] In contrast the Mullard scheme had driven the two bit lines with simultaneous pulses of opposite polarity, which could not have been provided by the semiconductor circuits previously designed at IBM to drive the three-hole core memory.

In less than a month, just as Whalen had predicted, the first prototype memory was assembled; but it took all summer to debug it.[42] One of the last problems to be overcome was a magnetostrictive ringing of the ferrite cores: when an electrical drive pulse was applied to the cores, they began a mechanical oscillation that lasted several cycles. Undesirable electrical noise was induced, and there was concern that the cores would wear out mechanically as they vibrated on the lines. These effects were caused by the well-known phenomenon of magnetostriction, but the two core per bit memory was the first to be plagued by it because of its high speed.

There was no time for basic studies or analyses. A solution was needed quickly. The engineers placed a large tub out on the lawn, held the wired core arrays over it, and poured a polyurethane material over the cores, hoping the liquid would dry into a soft coating and damp out the mechanical vibration. "It was kind of a gamble," Whalen recalled. "We were afraid it might change their switching characteristics, and we had no solvent to remove the material from the cores."[42] The technique worked and was used in later core memories as well.

Soon the first two core per bit memory was operating, and work began on the second of the two memories needed for Harvest. These two memories were completed and shipped to Harvest in December 1960.[41] The cycle time achieved was 0.7 microsecond instead of the targeted 0.5 microsecond. Nevertheless it was the fastest full-sized memory built to that time.[45] Because of the system design, the two core per bit memory was actually used at a cycle of only 0.9 microsecond instead of 0.7 microsecond. The Harvest system was shipped to NSA in January 1962.

IBM had achieved two major technical successes with ferrite core memories. The 2.18 and the 0.7 microsecond memories were

Moe Every with Bill Rhodes
Moe Every (right) holds a two core per bit plane of the type used in the Harvest 0.7 microsecond memory. The completed memory is housed in the large cabinet behind them. A standard pluggable circuit module lies on the table close to Every and a load-sharing matrix switch is on the table to the far right.

the fastest memories of their sizes in the industry. However, many of the engineers felt the end of the line had been reached. Memories immersed in liquid were difficult to handle. Transistor drive and sense circuitry had been pushed to the limit. Cores smaller than 30-50 mil would be hard to fabricate, test, and wire, and two cores per bit was an expensive way to build a memory. It appeared that substantially different memory technologies would be needed in the future.

The Stretch Problem
The Stretch effort had been long and costly. The system delivery date had slipped by almost a year from its originally contracted date. Personnel on Stretch exceeded 300 by 1959, and the total program cost over $25 million, almost twice the cost estimated in February 1956. Government development contracts plus the purchase price for the system covered little more than half of this.[9,14]

IBM management had taken these problems in stride, convinced that new technologies developed for Stretch could be used on future IBM commercial products. Indeed the 7080 and 7090 computers had already used Stretch technologies, and in April 1960 Tom Watson advised stockholders that IBM planned to offer Stretch-like machines to other customers.[46]

Watson believed that the real significance of Stretch-class machines was the ability to solve problems so large and complex that they might otherwise be incapable of solution.[47] Business firms and government agencies were contacted to buy Stretch-like systems with a performance Watson described as seventy-five times that of an IBM 704. By May 1961 seven machines had been ordered by six customers.[48]

Although Stretch was nearly completed, one serious problem remained. Stretch had been tested on several customer problems and found to take about twice as long as projected. With so many improtant customers committed to Stretch, Watson was concerned, and demanded "frequent reports on the Stretch problem until it is solved."[49] The credibility of the company was far more important to Watson than the profit or loss on any one sale. Although no specific performance figure had been cited in the development contract with the AEC, people had talked about performances of as much as 100 times the IBM 704 and customers had come to expect a performance of about 75 times the 704. Watson believed IBM had a moral commitment to supply this performance or to adjust the price.

A difficult aspect of the problem was that the typical performance of Stretch was hard to measure. The relative performance of Stretch to the IBM 704 could vary by as much as one hundred on different problems. Watson arranged for two independent consultants to review the situation.[50] When they concurred with IBM engineering estimates that Stretch was only about thirty-five to forty times faster than the IBM 704 on typical customer jobs, he relieved Steve Dunwell of further responsibility for Stretch and reduced the price of a typical Stretch system from about $13.5 million to about $7.8 million, saying, "We will make delivery of these machines because we do not want to break our promise to our customers. We are going to take a good, fat loss on Stretch. . . ."[51]

Although Stretch was not as fast as expected, it was the fastest and most powerful machine in the market for at least two years before the Atlas computer, built by the Ferranti Company in Great Britain, became operational and matched the Stretch performance in a number of aspects.[52] Sperry Rand's LARC computer built under contract to the AEC suffered a two-year slippage in its delivery schedule, but was shipped about one year before Stretch. Its surface-barrier transistor circuits had about half the performance of IBM's internally developed graded-base drift transistors, and the cycle time of the main memory in LARC was 4 microseconds or nearly two times slower than the 2.18 microseconds of the memory in Stretch.

From a commercial point of view, the IBM memory probably had an even more significant advantage in cost. The main memory in LARC was divided into independent modular units, each with a ferrite core array of 2500 words of 60 bits each or 150,000 bits per unit. Up to thirty-nine of these units could be attached.[53] The IBM engineers in contrast had managed to drive a seven times larger array of 1,079,648 ferrite cores in the 3D mode, causing the costly semiconductor support circuits and packaging to be shared by more cores. This was facilitated by the load-sharing matrix switch, improved semiconductor devices, an improved ferrite core composition and process, and automatic wiring and packaging technologies developed at IBM.

The use of Stretch technology in the IBM 7090 computer also provided IBM with the first fully transistorized large-scale computer to be placed in production.[54]

Nevertheless the public concessions about the lower than projected performance of Stretch came at a particularly embarrassing time. Two months earlier William Norris, president of Control Data Corporation (CDC) had advised his stockholders that CDC was developing a Stretch-class computer, called the 6600. The CDC 6600 was to have 20 megacycle circuits throughout—two times faster than those in Stretch—and a 1 microsecond main memory.[55] Its technical specifications and shipment date were not at first announced, but the success of earlier CDC computers left little doubt that Stretch and other high-performance computers would soon have stiff competition.

Three years after Stretch was shipped, Steve Dunwell was still fighting the battle for recognition of the contributions of Stretch and of the engineers who had worked on the project. In a memo to Watson he wrote, "The new System/360 is in many respects the image of Stretch. It is important to me that you know this, for I hope that in time you will look upon the Stretch contribution to our technical heritage as an excellent bargain."[56] Watson replied, "There has never been any question in my mind but that the money we spent on Stretch has been a good investment from the standpoint of technological fall-out of the project. I do believe, however, that our customers and the top management of this corporation were led to believe that the performance objective was being achieved when, in fact, we were falling short of it."[57]

As the success of System/360 became more evident, however, Watson's view changed. Early in 1965 he wrote to Albert L. Williams, then president of IBM, "Poor Dunwell took all the lumps on Stretch. In retrospect, Stretch proved to be an excellent move for IBM."[58] One year later Watson appointed Dunwell an IBM Fellow and acknowledged that Stretch was "the lead machine at that time in the whole world and maintained that position of leadership for a fairly substantial period of years. Also from this machine derived. . . literally billions of dollars of revenue and growth for the IBM Company."[59]

The recognition that Stretch had been successful did not occur until four years after it was shipped to the AEC. In the meantime the perception of top managers that Stretch represented a problem requiring a solution was a driving force behind IBM's engineering efforts. It confirmed the view held by many engineers that radically new memory technologies were needed before more advanced computer systems could be developed.

7
The Road to System/360

By 1960 the problems of noncompatibility, diversity, and complexity of IBM data-processing products had become severe. The Stretch project provided insight to these problems, but schedules, costs, and technical uncertainties had prevented it from achieving many of the early objectives. Meanwhile the pressures of the marketplace and the organizational and geographical separation of IBM's development laboratories had worked to compound the problems.

Competitive Chaos in IBM
During the 1950s while the IBM Poughkeepsie Laboratory worked on computer designs and technologies, the Endicott Laboratory was looking for ways to apply electronics to conventional electromechanical accounting machines.[1] Electronics were much faster than cams and relays, but economic solutions were elusive. Then Francis O. Underwood, a systems planner in the Endicott Laboratory, came up with a novel solution; he proposed that a very low-cost stored-program computer be used to handle the work of accounting machines. He arrived at this solution when his cost analysis revealed that almost half the cost of existing electromechanical accounting machines was in the plugboard control panel and associated electronics.[2] If this costly item was replaced by instructions stored in the main memory of a small computer, nearly half of the cost of the accounting machine could be devoted to the stored-program computer function. A critical requirement was that the stored-program computer costs be kept as low as possible.

The development project was headed by Charles E. Branscomb, a young mechanical engineer who resisted pressures to add extra features and kept the computer very spartan. The resulting machine was sold as the IBM 1401 and transformed the market for accounting machines into a market for small stored-program computers.[1] The 1401 used the sms semiconductor circuits and packaging developed in Project Stretch and an 11.5 microsecond cycle ferrite core memory. The first 1401 was installed in September 1960. The number of installations passed 2000 by 1962 and ultimately exceeded 10,000.[3]

At the same time as the 1401 project was being formulated in Endicott, there were discussions as to the appropriate architecture for a transistorized follow-on to the IBM 705 commercial stored-program computer in Poughkeepsie. Palmer believed that it should not be a simple transistorized extension of the vacuum tube 705, so he let the Endicott and Poughkeepsie Laboratories compete with each other for this machine. The Poughkeepsie group based their designs on the 705 with ferrite core memory, and the Endicott group based their designs on their successful 650 stored-program magnetic drum machine. Reacting to the Poughkeepsie proposal, the creative Endicott group added some ferrite core memory and subsequently removed the mechanical drum storage altogether. The two groups competed vigorously during 1956 and 1957. Then in 1958 Palmer gave the project to Endicott.[1] The resultant machine was announced in September 1958 as the IBM 7070.[4]

Before the 7070 was completed, however, a company-wide reorganization occurred. In June 1959 the Data Processing Group was divided into three product divisions: the Data Systems Division with large system responsibility, the General Products Division with small system responsibility, and the Data Processing Division with sales and service responsibility. Learson became the group executive responsible for the three divisions and Palmer became director of engineering with staff rather than line responsibility. The new organization was successful in placing more responsibility at lower levels and in reducing the day-to-day work load of top executives, but it also introduced new centers of responsibility and new sources of contention.

Because the 7070 was a large system, the reorganization placed responsibility for its development in the Data Systems

Division in Poughkeepsie—in the hands of its original opponents. Steve Dunwell thought he could stop the 7070 project before it went any further, and told his group to design a replacement that was twice the speed and half the cost and that would fit in one standard hardware frame. He got excellent engineers from the Stretch project to work on the 7070 replacement, which they called the 70AB.[5] When Palmer and Learson became aware of Dunwell's decision, they ordered that maximum effort be placed back on the 7070, which was closer to completion than the 70AB and was urgently needed in the market to compete with the RCA 501.[1]

Thwarted in that effort, the 70AB group began to target their machine for the lower performance region just above the 1401. The General Products Division engineers in Endicott then countered with the 1401-compatible 1410 processor, announced in October 1960, which was more powerful than the 1401 and could grow on its well-established base. Once again the 70AB project was blocked.

Following this defeat, the Data Systems Division engineers in Poughkeepsie used the SMS circuit technology and the 2.18 microsecond cycle Type 7302 ferrite core memory developed for Stretch to build an improved version of their IBM 705 computer. The resulting IBM 7080 computer was announced in January 1960 with three times the performance of the already upgraded 705s and ten times the performance of the original 705 computers.[6] The Poughkeepsie engineers also began to consider expanding the 70AB into a family of computers, soon called the 8000 series, to serve across the marketplace.

The central version of the 8000 series was like the 70AB but renamed the 8106. It was a bit more powerful than the 7070. The engineers were under pressure to have a product in the performance range between the IBM 1620 and 7090 computers where the Control Data Corporation 1604 computer was doing very well. So they planned a high-speed scientific feature to add to the 8106 called the 8108. They also had a much bigger scientific machine to replace Stretch called the 8112, a small data-processing version to serve as an I/O computer called the

8103, and a small scientific version called the 8104. These machines made up the 8000 series being formulated by the Poughkeepsie group.[1]

As a result of the reorganization, the General Products Division had also developed a market plan. It had marketed the 1401 and expanded it into the 1410. It brought out the 1620 at the same time as the 1401 and was developing a faster version called the 1620 Model 2. These computers were in competition with the 8000 series.

Matters were further complicated by the desire of the IBM World Trade Laboratories to produce their own products. They rationalized that products developed by the domestic laboratories were not appropriate for their marketplace and began work on a small scientific machine called the Scientific Computer and Modular Processor (SCAMP).[7] When they learned that more sales volume was required to reduce costs, they began to plan a larger scientific version of SCAMP, as well as a modified version for business data-processing applications.

By the end of 1960 IBM thus had three organizations running in divergent directions: the Data Systems Division with its 8000 series, World Trade with its SCAMP series, and the General Products Division with its 1400 and 1600 series. Additionally the Data Processing Group was already supporting machines in the market with as many as seven different architectures and design philosophies.[8]

A Plan Evolves

The June 1959 reorganization, which divided the Data Processing Group into three divisions, had been accompanied by the formation of Group Staff, a small staff organization under Donald T. Spaulding that was responsible for coordinating the activities of the three divisions. Spaulding, who had previously served as director of systems in Endicott, was immediately skeptical about the 8000 series proposed in Poughkeepsie. He felt it was based too much on the large system architectures of Stretch and the 709 and 705 computers. To be successful across the whole product spectrum, he believed the needs of low-cost, high-volume systems would have to be carefully considered. To ensure this, he arranged to have Bob O. Evans transferred from Endicott to Poughkeepsie where Evans would head up the planning and development work in the Data Systems Division.[9]

In Endicott Evans had served as a systems manager for the 7070 and 1410 and had worked on special assignment to transfer the 7070 from Endicott to Poughkeepsie and get it released to manufacturing. In his new assignment in Poughkeepsie, he was instructed "to verify that the 8000 series is a meaningful course, or to change to the proper direction." After spending two to three months examining the 8000 series, Evans decided that the 8000 series was "dead wrong. Incompatible machines with no architectural relationship, depending upon programming to tie these things together at the customer level (something we now know would have been absolutely impossible to achieve). . . . More important, the plan did not recognize General Product Division's direction, nor the World Trade direction."[8]

A study initiated early in 1961 also had considerable impact on Evan's thinking and IBM's future direction. Erich Bloch was put in charge of a task force, the Advanced Technology Study Committee, "to consider alternatives and to recommend what logic component technology should be used in future EDP equipment manufactured by IBM." The component technologies considered quickly reduced to three alternatives:

1. Improve the SMS technology developed for Stretch and used in many IBM products such as the 7090 and 1401.

2. Finish development of a hybrid technology in which several silicon chips were mounted on a 0.5 inch square ceramic module on the surface of which conductors and resistors were silk-screened. Each silicon chip would have one transistor or a few diodes processed on it. The chips were thus functionally very similar to chips mounted individually in small metal cans on the SMS cards. This hybrid technology was called SLT for Solid Logic Technology.

3. Initiate a more advanced technology effort in which several transistors and resisters were fabricated on a single silicon chip and interconnected by fine conducting lines on the chip itself.

Referred to as monolithics, this resulted in a single silicon chip, perhaps 0.03 to 0.05 inches square, having as much logical function as an SLT module which was 0.5 inches square.[10]

The task force rejected the first alternative because it did not offer sufficient improvement over the existing SMS technology. Indeed the primary candidate almost from the beginning was SLT. At the time it was referred to as Compact, having been under development at IBM for eighteen months in the Compact Program.[10] With this technology, up to nine 0.5 inch square SLT modules could be mounted on the proposed 1.5 inch square SLT card, making the SLT card about the logical equivalent of an SMS twin card of 5.5 inches by 4 inches. The area density improvement of SLT over SMS was thus about a factor of ten.

A minority of task force members believed SLT was too conservative and recommended the third alternative, but even the most optimistic could not have envisioned thousands of logic circuits on one silicon chip as has been accomplished in the 1980s. What they could envision was several complete circuits on a single chip instead of using several chips per circuits as was planned for SLT. The pros and cons of SLT versus the more aggressive monolithic alternative were vigorously debated before the report of the Advanced Technology Study Committee was formally presented in April 1961. They recommended the use of Compact (SLT) in future stored-program computers because successful completion of SLT was reasonably assured. In contrast the development of monolithics was judged to have very high risk and would require much more time. The plan to develop and use SLT thus had little opposition in April 1961 when the task force report was given.

Bloch's task force recommendation took on more significance in August 1961 when IBM formed the Components Division under John Gibson. Previously the company had developed many of its own semiconductor devices and manufacturing techniques but usually had made these devices and techniques available to outside vendors (such as Texas Instruments) for volume production.[11]

Birkenstock and others encouraged this arrangement because component manufacturing tended to have a lower profit margin than IBM's other businesses. It was also expected that outside vendors would have greater experience and greater production volumes than IBM and thus should be more cost effective in the component business.

This traditional wisdom concerning the manufacture of components had been under review by Emanuel R. Piore, IBM's director of research, and others since the fall of 1959. Piore, who as Chief Scientist for the Office of Naval Research had helped guide government funding for basic and applied research before joining IBM, was keenly aware of the importance of component development to the success of advanced electronic systems. He and the rest of management concluded that the creation of a Components Division would provide better control of vendor prices, more incentive for IBM component engineers, better knowledge of the component business, and better control of proprietary technologies.[11]

The decision to develop and manufacture SLT in IBM's new Components Division provided further reason to redesign the 8000 series of computers. Redesigning the entire series would enable the use of the new SLT instead of the older SMS technology. If the job could be done quickly, it would give IBM leadership both in systems architecture and in circuit technology.

Making a change in plan was not easy. One of the 8000 series, the 8106, had already been built, and product announcement was planned for that August.[12] No replacement for this series could be developed and announced so quickly. Delays in bringing out systems with improved cost and performance could be especially harmful because most of the company's revenue came from the rental of products. If competition had superior products, customers could return their IBM products with only one month's notice and replace them with those of a competitor.

Frederick P. Brooks, who had worked as a designer of the Stretch and Harvest systems and subsequently was assigned to design the 70AB that led to the 8000 series, became the chief proponent of the 8000 series.[13] He enlisted considerable support for the 8000 series and took the case to the Corporate Management Committee, which included Tom Watson, chairman of the board, A. K. Watson, head of World Trade, Al Williams, President, and Vin Learson, the group executive responsible for executing whatever plan was adopted. Evans countered with his plan to stop work on the 8000 series and to develop a product plan for the entire company using more advanced technologies. It was a six months' battle Brooks recalls, "fought bitterly with two separate armies against and for the 8000 series."[14]

By May 1961 the battle was over. Management had decided to leapfrog the 8000 series and to go directly to more advanced technologies and systems. The key workers on the 8000 project were brought together for a meeting at which Bob Evans announced that the project was dead, all of them would be reassigned to new projects. The reactions included dejection, bitterness, and rage.[12] Management now had the problems of soothing those who had worked so hard on projects just terminated and of defining, developing, manufacturing, and marketing an as yet undefined series of computers. It also had the task of developing interim products to hold IBM's position in the market until more advanced systems could be defined and developed.

Evans asked one group of engineers to design a scientific system with performance just above the very successful 7090. This resulted in the 7094 I and II. He asked another group to design a scientific machine to compete with the CDC 1604 and the Bendix G-20 in the performance range just under the 7090. This resulted in the 7040/44 systems. The commercial computing market was to be covered by extensions of the 1401 and 1410 computers.[12]

The SPREAD Report

In the fall of 1961 Don Spaulding, head of Group Staff, formed a task force "to establish an over-all IBM plan for data processor products." It was to encompass all stored-program processor developments and to provide development and product direction extending to 1970. Named SPREAD (an acronym for Systems Programming, Research, Engineering, And Development), the task force had technical representatives from the Data Systems

Division, the General Products Division, and World Trade, and was chaired by John W. Haanstra, Director of Development in the General Products Division, with Bob Evans as vice-chairman.[15]

Progress at the task force meetings was slow. Technical decisions were difficult to reach, and there was no well-defined common view of future systems. Haanstra believed the small-computer segment of the market would be served best by enhancements of the highly successful 1401 architecture, whereas Evans was committed to a compatible line across the entire computer market.[16] In November Haanstra was promoted to president of the General Products Division, and Evans became in practice the chairman of SPREAD. The conflict among the task force members was greatly reduced. Increasingly Fred Brooks, the twenty-nine-year-old proponent of the terminated 8000 series, emerged as the person shaping the direction of the new series.[7]

In December 1961 the task force report was completed.[15] The system it proposed was called the NPL (New Product Line) or the SLT Series. Ultimately it was marketed as the IBM System/360. A fundamental assumption of the report was that a compound annual growth rate of 20 percent should be achieved by processors in the United States. An even larger growth rate was projected for peripheral equipment and for all of World Trade. Some of the major recommendations to achieve this growth objective were summarized as follows:

It is recommended that the processor product line comprise five compatible CPU's. The internal performance ratio between successive entries should be between three and five, with the low end entries having smaller spacing ratios.

The line of CPU's must each be software supported and equipped with a selection of other devices which affect system performance: input-output channels of various data rates and various degrees of memory interference, memories of various sizes, and various complements of I/O devices.

Specialization in design for each customer must be achievable through the ability to couple any number and combination of CPU's into a single stored-program-controlled system.

Each processor is to be capable of operating correctly all valid machine-language programs of all processors with the same or smaller I/O and memory configuration.

Each processor is to be economically competitive at the time it is introduced.[15]

The task group believed that upward compatibility could be achieved—that is, programs written on the smaller systems could be run on the larger systems. They were less sanguine about downward compatibility but urged that "the design requirement for downward compatibility be stated as a firm ground rule and that the development proceed on this basis until the Phase I review. Compatibility was expected to offer numerous advantages: greater effectiveness of the IBM sales force, protection of the customer's investment in applications programming, and easier education of users and service personnel. Compatibility, the report correctly predicted, would also create numerous problems:

Once committed to compatibility, it will be difficult to change to another approach.

Every product or support announcement may affect all of our customers instead of a few and, therefore, must be more thoroughly pre-tested.

Compatibility increases the market potential for others in the Service Bureau or Data-Center business.

IBM compatibility may encourage competition to be compatible with us in order to tap our support efforts.

The family concept will allow competition to better anticipate our product line and to react more effectively.

Compatibility will make competitive salesmen more productive since their knowledge of IBM processor logic, applied programming languages, and knock-offs will apply to the entire family.[15]

Concerning the timing of the product announcement, the report proposed an *earliest* desirable announcement based on forecasted sales decline and the *latest* desirable announcement based on declining installations. It suggested that the second and fifth processors in the series be announced in the first and third quarter, respectively, of 1964. Announcement of the first and fourth processors in the series was projected for 1965, with the mid-range processor to be announced in 1966.[15]

The company's top executives were generally enthusiastic about having a fully compatible line of computers in which each processor could handle commercial and scientific data processing and was supported by a software operating system capable of providing easy use of I/O and peripheral equipment. They were, however, greatly concerned by the magnitude of the proposed development effort. Many believed the proposal was too grandiose. The potential payoff was great, but the problems to be encountered were hard to assess. Delays or failures in development would affect the entire line of computers instead of a single unit. The executives wished for a less risky alternative, but the 8000 series had already been rejected and no other alternatives were offered. Hesitantly they endorsed the effort to develop what became the IBM System/360. Formal approval was given by the Corporate Management Committee in May 1962.[17]

Getting support of the Poughkeepsie engineers was not difficult. The disappointment of losing the 8000 series of computers had largely worn off during the three months of the SPREAD committee's deliberations, and some of the engineers had already begun analyzing and defining objectives for the new system. When Fred Brooks was given engineering design control of the entire System/360 project, any lingering reluctance of the Poughkeepsie engineers vanished.[14]

The situation in the IBM Laboratory in Hursley, England, was more difficult. The engineers who had developed the SCAMP computer architecture for the World Trade market believed its success was essential to demonstrate that they and their new laboratory were essential parts of the corporation. They had little knowledge of the SPREAD committee deliberations or of the broader implications of the new plan. What they primarily knew was that SCAMP had been terminated to make way for some other approach.[7]

Redirecting the efforts in Hursley became the assignment of John W. Fairclough, a British citizen and 1954 graduate of Manchester University who had worked on Stretch and managed the SCAMP project. Fairclough had played an important role in the SPREAD task force as an advocate for the use of read-only memory as a computer control store for System/360 computers. The first use of a computer control store in IBM had been in the Hursley Laboratory.[7]

During the negotiations that resulted in cancellation of SCAMP, it was agreed that the IBM Hursley Laboratory would be given the opportunity to develop one of the computers of the new system. Fairclough was chosen to lead this effort using the same team of engineers who had worked on SCAMP. It was a major concession to the Hursley Laboratory and a significant corporate risk. Never before had such an important part of a development effort been given to a laboratory outside the United States. The important new mission plus the planned use of control stores in the new system mitigated the sense of loss of the Hursley engineers. Nevertheless Fairclough recalls, "It took some time to get across to them that termination of the SCAMP project was the right thing to do."[7]

Convincing John Haanstra and most of the engineers in Endicott was even more difficult. More than a thousand of their very successful 1401 computers were already installed and thousands more were on order. Haanstra expressed the Endicott Laboratory view when he indicated he was willing to support the new line of computers only if it did not compete directly with the 1401 class of computers. In this environment Jack E. Greene, who had been responsible for file attachment and other functions of the 7070 computer, was chosen to take on System/360 engineering responsiblity in Endicott. His manager was Ernest S. Hughes, who also had engineering responsibility for the 1401-compatible 1410 computer.[18]

In his new role Greene had good support from Hughes, but John Haanstra continued to resist any attempt to make the new system compete with the 1401 class of computers. Greene and Hughes frequently had to go around their line management, working directly with Fred Brooks to obtain the support of IBM Vice President, Vin Learson. This created strained relations in Endicott.[18] Only Learson's vigorous management plus an unexpected and surprisingly successful use of computer control stores in System/360 caused Haanstra and the General Products Division to support the new system.

Computer Control Stores

The use of read-only control stores in the IBM/Systems 360 computers was based on ideas first presented in July 1951 by M. V. Wilkes of the University of Cambridge. Wilkes observed that basic machine instructions of a typical digital computer, such as addition, subtraction, and multiplication, were constructed from a number of more elementary operations which he called microoperations. He proposed an orderly approach to the creation of machine instructions using a sequence of microopertions and coined the term microprogramming to describe this process, which he likened to that of writing a larger software program using machine instructions. For microprogramming to be applicable, Wilkes asserted, "it is necessary that the machine should contain a suitable permanent rapid-access storage device in which the microprogram can be held."[19]

Conceptually the function of the control store is quite simple. The computer consists of a collection of registers, adders, and other functional units interconnected by a network of switches to control the transfer of information among the various units. All of the logical work of the computer is carried out by opening or closing the switches in the proper sequence. The control store is constructed so that each bit of a stored word is associated with a control line to one of these switches. When a particular word of control store is addressed, the pattern of 1s and 0s in the word automatically sets the switches in the computer in a predetermined manner to execute one microoperation during the next machine cycle.

Control stores were selected as a key hardware feature of IBM System/360 computers because they made it possible for computers with very different hardware implementations to appear identical to the user, except for different costs and speeds. Each computer of System/360, no matter how its internal data paths were structured, was able to respond to the same set of instructions defined for the machine language. There were approximately 150 of these instructions, including such simple ones as "load," "store," and "add." When the proper word in control store was accessed, its prestored pattern of 1s and 0s caused switches in the data path to be set to begin the execution of the desired instruction.[20]

The patterns of 1s and 0s required for a given instruction were different for each computer because the internal data paths were different. Even the lengths of the control words were different. However, these differences were transparent to the user. Only the designer needed to understand the internal data paths and the manner in which the machine was microprogrammed to provide the required instruction set.

In order to achieve a series of computers of differing performance capabilities, simple instructions that were executed with a single access to the control store of large computers were implemented with several accesses to control store for smaller computers. This was made transparent to the user by having the first word in a sequence automatically address the next word until the full System/360 instruction was completed. The smallest System/360 computer, the Model 30, had a data path that was only one byte (8 bits) wide, whereas a word in System/360 was four bytes wide. Thus the Model 30 computer required a minimum of four machine cycles to process a word of data that was processed by a larger machine in one cycle.[21]

The person responsible for the control-store and systems design of SCAMP was Antony Peacock, who had joined IBM in 1957 with two years of military service and a bachelor's degree in mathematics from Imperial College. He says a company-wide

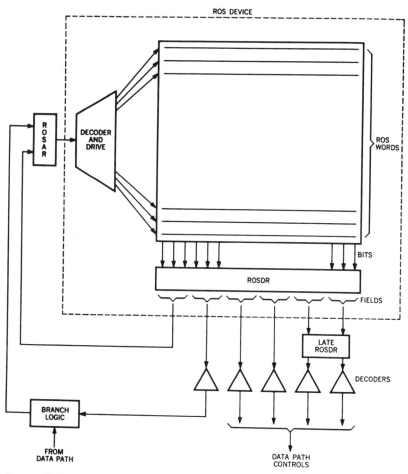

System/360 microprogram control

The unit within the dotted lines represents a read-only store (ROS) containing a few thousand words of from 56 to 100 bits each. The longer words are used on the larger System/360 computers. In all cases the ROS cycle time is the same as the basic machine cycle time, but the ROS access times are somewhat less. On each cycle a word is read out of the ROS array into the read-only store data register (ROSDR), where it is held for the duration of the cycle. (From the *IBM Systems Journal* 6, 1967, p. 226.)

edict that transistors, rather than vacuum tubes, must be used in all future machines precipitated the Hursley work on control stores. Transistors were very expensive in England, and control stores were viewed as a way to reduce the number of transistors in a machine. He credits a fellow engineer, Matthew Taub, with making this observation and initiating the work in 1958. Several preliminary designs of control-store-operated machines were made before the design of SCAMP was begun. Work on one of the early designs, intended to replace the Type 604 calculator, reached the model-build stage before it was stopped because it was not sufficiently cost-effective.[22]

The SCAMP computer was significant to IBM not only because it pioneered computer design using a control store but also because it implemented the control store in a technology with good cost-performance capabilities. The existence of control-store technology and system design experience in the Hursley Laboratory facilitated an important achievement in IBM System/360: first use of read-only control stores in a series of commercial computers.

It is somewhat surprising that there was no significant commercial use of computer control stores until IBM introduced them in System/360 more than ten years after Wilkes's proposal. This can be attributed partly to the lack of suitable memory technology but even more to the lack of a recognized market requirement for a line of compatible computers. In IBM it was the forced interaction among technologists, systems designers, and market-oriented individuals in the SPREAD task force that led to an appreciation of this requirement and to the identification of read-only control stores as the best way to achieve this objective.

A significant benefit of the control store was that it also enabled System/360 computers to run software programs written for computers of quite different architectures. That is, an additional control store or enlarged control store could hold instructions unique to computers not in the IBM System/360 line.

This capability of control stores had been studied in the SCAMP project even before the System/360 effort was initiated. Responding to criticism of the Poughkeepsie engineers that SCAMP was a new architecture that would not provide natural growth for customers with IBM 704, 709, or 7090 computers, the Hursley engineers had designed a preliminary set of control-store instructions to make SCAMP operate as an IBM 704 computer. The performance of SCAMP when operating as a 704 was not very attractive because of major differences in their internal data paths; but the use of a control store to make one computer operate as another had been demonstrated. Years later the term emulation was adopted to describe this feature.[22]

The importance of control stores for emulating other computers did not become evident to corporate management, however, until after Honeywell announced its H-200 computer in late 1963 with deliveries to begin by July 1964. The H-200 architecture was similar to that of the popular IBM 1401 computer. In addition it was equipped with a software program, called the "liberator," which translated machine language programs written for the IBM 1401 so that they could be run on the H-200. It permitted IBM customers to be "liberated" from their equipment by installing the Honeywell H-200.[23]

The Endicott Laboratory's response to this competitive announcement was to undertake development of an enhanced and cost-reduced 1401, tentatively called the 1401S. The engineers were convinced that they would lose many of their 1401 customers unless they extended the popular 1401 design. Haanstra and the other General Products Division managers were therefore more reluctant than ever to embrace the entirely new System/360 line.

About this time Karl K. Womack, who had already been assigned the task of using as much of the Model 30 hardware as possible to build a 1401-like machine, showed that the instructions in the control store of the Model 30 could be modified to make the Model 30 operate like a 1401. Instead of using much of the Model 30 hardware, he had used all of it, without change, to create a 1401-like machine—and it had a performance four times that of the 1401.[18] John Haanstra had expected Womack to devise a way to make two separate products out of substantially similar hardware. Instead Womack had made it possible for the small System/360 computer to be sold as a 1401 replacement.[24]

Emulation of a 1401 by the System/360 Model 30 threatened to remove cost control of small computers from Endicott and place it in Poughkeepsie. This is not what the Endicott managers wanted. Haanstra stubbornly held out for the 1401S until the end of 1963, asserting that the cost-performance of the Model 30, operating in 1401 mode, was not as good as that of the specially designed 1401S.[25] However, the benefits of compatibility of the Model 30 with the rest of the System/360 line and strong management pressure from Vin Learson ultimately forced a change in this position.

Growing Requirements for Memory
Main memory, which was fundamental to any stored-program computer, had added importance in System/360. In addition to the data and instructions of user programs, it was needed to hold many modules of the new operating system.

The operating system was termed second generation because it was to handle either batch jobs or real-time applications. For traditional batch jobs, the entire computer was dedicated to one job; for real-time applications the operating system interrupted jobs in process in order to handle requests from terminals and other I/O. The supervisor portion of the operating system, for example, allocated main memory, managed the loading of programs into memory, controlled the concurrent execution of tasks, logged in any errors, and issued and monitored input/output operations.[21] Language translators were also provided so that users could write application programs in a variety of languages such as FORTRAN, COBOL, RPG, and a new generalized language, PL/1, to be offered by IBM. These features were intended to provide ease of use, increased throughput, and improved response time, but to accomplish them was much more difficult than anticipated. During the development of System/360, it was learned that the operating system required far more bits of main memory than was initially planned.

In addition to main memory, which was intrinsic to any stored-program computer, there were numerous other uses for memory. There were small high-speed registers to help improve computation speed, small buffers for I/O, tiny memory-protect memories to store information to protect memory contents against unauthorized use, a very large capacity memory (LCM) to serve as an extension to main memory, and read-only control stores to translate the machine-language instructions—identical for all System/360 computers—into the unique logical steps required by each of the computers in the line.

The five computers of the New Product Line (NPL) were specified early in 1962 as having performances, respectively, of 0.5, 1.2, 4.5, 12, and 48 times the IBM 709 computer on scientific applications and the same amount faster than the IBM 7070 on commercial applications.[26] Fred Brooks, of the Data Systems Division in Poughkeepsie, had corporate responsibility for controlling the design of all computers in the line. Processor 1 (later called Model 30) was to be designed by the General Products Division in Endicott, processor 2 (Model 40) by World Trade in Hursley, England, and Processors 3, 4, and 5 (Models 50, 60, and 70) by the Data Systems Division in Poughkeepsie. Before System/360 was announced, a higher-performance Model 60, called the Model 62, was added to the line, and before any systems were shipped, Models 60, 62, and 70 were replaced by Models 65 and 75 with improved performance.

Because the SLT circuit technology and the ferrite core memory technology developed for System/360 had a very limited range of speeds, the one-hundred-fold difference in performance between the slowest and fastest computers was achieved by greater parallelism in the larger computers. The smallest processor (Model 30) operated on one byte (8 bits) at a time, whereas the largest processors operated on eight bytes at a time. A variety of other design features were used to increase the difference in cost and performance among the computers in the series.

A review of hardware and software development in July 1962 indicated the progress was about as expected. The total cost of the development and manufacturing effort was estimated at

$675 million. Of this $35 million was to be spent on software development.[27] Two hundred to three hundred programmers were expected to be required, and they were rapidly being recruited. In the first three months of 1963 alone, thirty-three experienced professional programmers and forty-four college trainee programmers had been hired. Another twenty-three programmers had been transferred into the Data Systems Division from other IBM divisions.[28]

As the size of the programming staff increased, the perceived size of the total programming job also increased. More programmers were needed to write the code, and more main memory was required on each computer to hold modules of the operating system.

Meanwhile management was beginning to consider announcing at one time the entire line of computers instead of just two as originally planned. The Honeywell H-200 was a major threat at the low end, so announcement of the smallest System/360 computer had already been moved up one year to early 1964. Numerous customers for medium to large computers had requested IBM to supply special hardware or software to satisfy their requirements.[29] If the company responded to these requests with special hardware, it would tend to perpetuate noncompatible systems and also place additional strain on the already overextended development forces. Because the features planned for System/360 would satisfy many of these requests, the special customer requests increased the need for an early announcement. Finally the trade press was providing increasingly accurate accounts of IBM's plans, and it was becoming difficult to prevent salesmen from trying to hold customers by leaking information about new systems under development.[30,31]

Giving vent to his frustration over top management's refusal to commit to an earlier announcement of System/360 (then called NPL), Evans wrote to the president of the Data Systems Division in September 1963 saying, "I am certainly baffled by executive management's failure to champion NPL. . . . there have been established checks and balances, reviews, audits, etc. which have only kept the company moving in circles. . . . NPL is good—it is

simple and powerful—it is ready enough—proven enough. IBM
should go forward with. . . full announcement in the 1st or 2nd
quarter of 1964."[29]

On April 7, 1964, the entire IBM System/360 line was
announced.[32] The announcement included six processor models
and nineteen processor-memory configurations. Special operating
system support was announced for systems with only 8K bytes of
memory. By then it had been determined that the full operating
system, OS/360, would not be able to operate on computers with
less than 16K bytes of memory. (The letter K represents the
binary number $2^{10}=1024$ and is frequently referred to simply as a
thousand.)

The public announcement of System/360 caused increased
concern among the IBM software development personnel.
Individuals vocalized problems they had previously kept to
themselves. More people were hired. Fred Brooks was put in
charge of the software support effort for systems with more than
16K bytes of memory. By September 1964 the minimum memory
size to be supported by OS/360 was again increased, this time
from 16K to 32K bytes. The cost of developing the software was
now estimated at $60 million, almost twice the original estimate.[34]
But even this estimate was low. By the end of 1965 there were
two thousand programmers working on System/360 software at a
cost of over $60 million per year, causing Brooks in frustration to
assert, "Adding manpower to a late software project only makes it
later."[35,36]

Pressure was again mounting to increase the minimum memory
configuration for OS/360, this time from 32K to 64K bytes. With
such large requirements for main memory on the System/360
computers, it was urgent that IBM have reliable, low-cost memory
technology in production to meet the anticipated demand.
Freedom to use all necessary patents was essential to the
production of ferrite core memories, but the status of the
all-important Forrester patent was still being argued in the courts.

The Forrester Patent Settlement

The Board of Patent Interference had awarded the ten broadest claims of the Forrester patent to Rajchman of RCA in October 1960. Civil action to recover the claims was initiated by Research Corporation, assignee of the Forrester patent because of a long-standing relationship with MIT in which they handled business negotiations for patents of MIT employees. RCA countered with a civil action to obtain those claims that it had not been awarded by the board. IBM had already entered into a cross-licensing agreement with RCA in 1957, obtaining rights to use all claims awarded to Rajchman, but patent negotiations with MIT had moved more slowly.

Only a few months before the IBM System/360 was to be announced, there was still no settlement between IBM and MIT on the critical Forrester patent. Negotiations had begun in March 1956, with an offer by representatives of Research Corporation to discuss the terms of a license.[37] An initial amicable atmosphere gradually deteriorated as the parties failed to agree on license fees. There were innuendos that MIT had entrapped IBM and the rest of the computer industry by urging the use of ferrite core memories without advising them of the MIT patent application.[38] There was concern that IBM might withdraw its traditional support of MIT in order to achieve a better settlement. At one point Tom Watson privately complained to Jim Birkenstock, head of Commercial Development and IBM's chief negotiator, that the company had given laboratory equipment and hundreds of thousands of dollars to MIT, and now MIT was demanding a million dollars for one of its patents.[39]

Watson was mistaken, however, about paying $1 million for the Forrester patent. IBM did not get it so cheaply. IBM, in fact, paid a larger fee than was on record at that time for any other patent.[40] The patent licensing negotiation led to the resignations in May 1962 of Tom Watson as a member of the corporation of MIT and of James R. Killian (chairman of the MIT Corporation) as a member of the IBM board of directors.[41] Lawsuits over the patent also broke the long-standing relationship between MIT and Research Corporation.[42]

In assessing the value of the Forrester patent, IBM initially estimated that its own manufacturing cost for ferrite core memories through 1961 would be about $53 million.[43] Assuming a license fee of 5 percent of manufacturing cost, which was on the high side of license fees paid by or to IBM, a fee of $2.65 million was estimated. However, Forrester was the junior party (having the later filing date) in a patent interference with Rajchman of RCA. Results of past interference proceedings indicated that, as junior party, he had only a 20 percent chance of winning. Thus the value of a license to Forrester's patent was estimated at $530,000.

An offer of this amount was not pursued, however, because Research Corporation negotiators indicated they preferred "to derive their royalties on the basis of the usage of their patents."[44] Furthermore, it would place IBM at a competitive disadvantage if the Forrester patent was found to be invalid and others paid nothing. Meanwhile Research Corporation was arguing that 5 percent of sales price rather than of manufacturing cost was a fairer basis for patent royalties. The Research Corporation estimated this would result in about a three times higher payment.[43]

In November 1959 Research Corporation formally offered IBM and others a license at a fixed rate of two cents per core. Jim Birkenstock rejected this offer, noting that "in our core storage units we employ seven of our own patents, as well as having acquired licenses under five patents of outsiders, which were necessary to make the Forrester patent usable." If IBM paid a two cents per bit royalty on each of these other patents as well as Forrester's, the cost per bit would be twenty-six cents, making core storage economically infeasible. He concluded that two cents per bit was ten to twenty times too much. Research Corporation indicated it had already rejected an offer of one cent per bit, so an impasse resulted.[45]

IBM negotiators were concerned by the increasing importance engineering managers were attaching to ferrite core memories. Cryogenic computer technology, which in 1956 was considered to be a likely replacement for semiconductor logic and ferrite core memories, had run into serious difficulties.[46] It was no longer regarded as a likely replacement for ferrite cores in the near future. The use of ferrite cores in memories was estimated by IBM in August 1959 to total 1.9 billion cores through 1970, and the manufacturing cost of these memories at $166 million. At a license fee of two cents per core, the company would pay over $33 million for use of the Forrester patent. Even at 5 percent of manufacturing cost, the projected fee was a staggering $8.3 million.[47] Nine months later IBM's internal estimate of its core use was increased by 140 percent, raising the projected royalty payments even higher.

In contrast Research Corporation indicated it expected to receive only $10 million to $12 million at a two cent per core license over the life of the patent, based on estimates of IBM's installed base plus market and cost projections from the rest of the industry. Research Corporation was unaware of how cheap memory manufacture had become in IBM and how large the future sales might be.[49]

To break the deadlock, IBM initiated two activities: (1) a study of prior art to show that Forrester's contribution was relatively minor and that several more important patents had been obtained for only a few million dollars total and (2) a study of alternative memory technologies was undertaken to develop memory devices not covered by the Forrester patent.[50] The most promising of these alternatives in 1960 appeared to be the use of two cores per bit as developed for Harvest.[51]

By February 1962 IBM's patent licensing position was bolstered by a plausible alternative technology, an analysis of prior art, and the fact that the U.S. Patent Office Board of Interferences had awarded most of the claims in Forrester's patent to Jan Rajchman of RCA.[52] It appeared to be a good time to propose a settlement. Accordingly Birkenstock proposed that IBM pay one-quarter cent per core for memories installed before December 1960 and one-seventh cent per core after that if Forrester won the court case, but only half of those amounts if Rajchman's position was upheld. IBM would have the option of making a one-time payment of $3.5 million or $1.75 million, respectively, in lieu of per-bit royalties.[53] Sensitive to the fact that the settlement would affect the rest of the industry, Birkenstock insisted that the settlement must be above criticism, that IBM wanted "no better than equal treatment as compared to others needing a license under MIT's patents."[54]

By June MIT had made a counter proposal of one-quarter cent per bit for memories installed before January 1966 and one-ninth cent until the expiration of the patent in February 1973. These fees were to be independent of the outcome of the RCA versus MIT litigation.[49]

Birkenstock no sooner had advised MIT that their counter proposal fees were too high than he received a letter from Research Corporation saying the fees proposed by MIT were too low. MIT had apparently not consulted Research Corporation before making its counter proposal.[55] One week later, apparently without prior consultation with MIT, Research Corporation brought suit against IBM for patent infringement.[56]

As the attorneys prepared for the court case, MIT decided that its interests were not properly represented by Research Corporation. Research Corporation wanted patent fees paid over time, based on use, so that a predictable revenue stream would permit orderly operation of its business. MIT preferred a single payment to help cover the costs of a building program. Even more important MIT was concerned about its long-term relationship with IBM and the rest of the computer industry.[57] In December 1962 MIT's President J. A. Stratton advised Research Corporation that MIT was exercising its right to terminate the contract with Research Corporation. By April 1963 the Forrester patent was formally assigned to MIT.[58]

That October Tom Watson and Al Williams discussed with Stratton and Killian of MIT a settlement based on a license fee per bit that was similar to those proposed by Birkenstock for IBM and rejected by MIT early in 1962. There was, however, a significant difference: IBM's estimate of its core usage to February 1973 now exceeded 12 billion cores. The formula would result in estimated license fees of more than $16 million over a ten-year period.[59] MIT subsequently agreed to accept a single payment of $13 million in lieu of royalties.[60] In February 1964 a contract was signed by which IBM agreed to pay MIT $2,784,000 unconditionally. The rest of the $13 million was to be paid within thirty days after MIT settled its suit with RCA, so long as the settlement upheld at least one of Forrester's patent claims.[61]

At the end of March 1964 the suit between MIT and RCA was settled. The settlement specified that RCA acknowledged the validity of the Forrester patent. RCA was granted a royalty-free license for all claims in the interference but agreed to pay MIT one-seventh cent per bit for memories sold after January 1964 that made use of the other Forrester claims.[62] A month after this settlement between MIT and RCA was completed, MIT received a check from IBM for the remainder of the $13 million.[63]

The total payment was $4 million more than any patent license agreement then on record. Yet based on IBM's 1963 estimate of future production, it would cost an average of less than one-tenth cent per bit—only one-twentieth of Research Corporation's two cent per bit proposal. As the sales of IBM System/360 computers skyrocketed well beyond the 1963 projections, the actual cost per bit dropped further, making the $13 million settlement cheap.

But was it? As early as 1959 IBM's ferrite core memories employed seven patents of IBM engineers as well as five patents licensed from others. The large market for ferrite core memories resulted from the development efforts of many individuals and organizations.[51] From 1954 to 1963 IBM alone had spent over $26 million to develop commercial memory products and many times this amount to develop the computer systems that made Forrester's patent so valuable.[64]

8
System/360 Memories

More than half a billion ferrite cores were produced by IBM in 1961, five times the number produced two years earlier and fifty times the number produced six years earlier when the first full year of production was completed.[1] Economies of scale and automated production techniques had reduced manufacturing costs for tested ferrite cores in 1961 to 0.3 cents each, one hundred times less than the price paid to General Ceramics only eight years earlier.[2] Fully assembled ferrite core memories with all necessary electronic support circuitry cost five to ten cents per bit, about ten times less than the Williams tube memory used on the IBM 701.[3] The large reduction in manufacturing cost came much more rapidly than anticipated, making ferrite core memories one of the most profitable segments of the company's business.

A dozen different memory types had been developed and shipped to customers, and many more designs were in preparation.[4] Each laboratory had its own memory development group designing memories for its own products. A chaotic situation would soon exist unless control and standardization was imposed.

Management Pressures

Into this situation stepped Moe Every, who had been promoted to manager of Nonmechanical Memory Development in 1959 after resolutely pushing the three-hole core memory for Stretch to the brink of disaster. Following this promotion he had managed a successful last-minute shift to the new two core per bit memory. Now in January 1961 he was given responsibility for Solid-State Memory Development in the Data Processing Group: including the Data Systems Division, the General Products Division, and the newly formed Components Division.[5] Every's responsibility encompassed product engineering of current products, the development of memories for committed products, and work on advanced technologies in the Poughkeepsie, Endicott, and San Jose laboratories. He had a staff of 125 and a budget of $3.5 million in 1961. Within three years the manpower of the solid-state memory development effort doubled as Every sought to deal with the ever-increasing problems and requirements.[6] In addition to traditional engineering problems, Every had to overcome parochial interests of geographically separated engineering groups and to contend with a corporate-wide perception that radically different memory technologies were needed. This perceived requirement resulted from three factors:

1. The unrealistically high royalty demanded for the Forrester patent had convinced corporate management that new memory technologies must be found.

2. Experience from Project Stretch suggested memory performance requirements for future computers exceeded the capabilities of ferrite core memories.

3. Many IBM engineers agreed with Jan Rajchman's view that fabrication, testing, and wiring of individual cores was too expensive. A batch-fabricated device was needed in which many storage cells, preferably prewired, were created in one process.

The pressure on Every was unusually strong because corporate managers, right up to Tom Watson, attached great importance to memory and because of the workings of the new organization. In his staff role as director of engineering, Ralph Palmer no longer had direct development responsibility. It was his function to influence others and to view with alarm actions which did not meet the corporate needs as he saw them.

Also, Mannie Piore, hired as director of research late in 1956, had been given a relatively free hand for five years to develop a strong research division. Now Al Williams, who succeeded Watson in 1961 as president of IBM, and other executives were asking what they had gotten from Research. Success of one of the exploratory memory projects in Research would be a welcome answer, and Piore, with his easy access to Watson, was prepared to apply pressure to be sure Research's technologies were not overlooked. In this environment Every spent considerable time on issues of advanced technologies.

The most promising patent-avoidance technology in 1960 appeared to be the high-speed, two core per bit memory used on Harvest. Its rapid implementation as a replacement for the unsuccessful three-hole core memory suggested that further refinements would not be difficult. Although it was more expensive than memories using one core per bit, its superior performance might make it acceptable for many applications. It was not, however, viewed as a long-term solution to future memory requirements.

A technology developed at the Research Laboratory late in 1962 appeared to offer a long-term solution. It was based on a proposal of Robert F. Elfant who had received the Ph.D. in electrical engineering from Purdue University only the previous year. Called the Flute because of its appearance, tubes of ferrite material were formed about wire conductors and then fired to create the desired magnetic properties. The memory was organized in a 2D array, and it operated in a manner that IBM patent attorneys believed was not covered by the teachings of the Forrester patent.[7]

A patent application was filed immediately, and Research was encouraged to develop this technology rapidly. Gene Brosseau, who had constructed IBM's first automatic core testers for commercial products, was brought in from development to manage an elaborate twenty-five-man yield study.[8] Promising results were at first reported, causing the Flute to be one of the projects shown to MIT engineers to convince them that IBM could circumvent the Forrester patent if necessary. But by the end of the year, a serious technical problem was encountered: the signal attenuation on the lines was so large that full-sized memory arrays were not operable. "The results were just staggering," Elfant recalls, "we didn't find any electrical pulses when they were supposed to come out. . . . If I had been ten years older and had spent more time in the memory business, we would have built a couple of arrays and tried to drive them instead of doing the yield study."[7]

IBM employed even more resources beginning late in 1956 to develop a cryogenic logic and memory technology. Some early funding was provided by the government as part of an effort to improve SAGE. Intended as replacements for vacuum tube logic and ferrite core memories, cryogenic logic and memory devices made use of persistent currents in superconducting lines. Dudley A. Buck of MIT had proposed the basic device and the name Cryotron, and an improved device, named the Crowe Cell after its IBM inventor, was the basis for much of IBM's development effort. The logic and memory devices were batch fabricated on flat substrates and then immersed in liquid helium (about 290°C below room temperature) for operation. The devices were expected to provide high performance, and although they were difficult to fabricate, they were projected to have a low cost because many devices were to be fabricated together.[9]

In retrospect the effort to develop this technology appears to have been naive even with the information available at the time. By 1962 the cryogenic logic effort had been terminated. All that remained was an effort to develop cryogenic main memories with a 1 microsecond cycle and a cost of one cent per bit.[8] Most of this work was carried out in the Research Division.

Toward the end of 1962 the group in Research claimed they had solved most of the fundamental problems. What was needed, they asserted, was a process development effort of the type more appropriate in a development division. Under pressure from the Research Division and corporate management, Every agreed to take responsibility for the project. Key personnel were transferred from Research to the Data Systems Division where a large process effort was initiated.[8]

By May 1963 the problems in this and other advanced memory programs had become severe. Every arranged to have the cryogenic memory project reduced in size and transferred to the new Components Division where work on device processing was emphasized. The project was continued as a small technology effort until continuing technical problems led to its termination in early 1965.[8]

Of all the advanced memory technologies, flat magnetic films provided the greatest promise—and the greatest problems. Like cryogenics the flat magnetic film effort was initiated late in 1956 to provide improved memories for SAGE. Like cryogenics its technical challenges were greater than anticipated. By 1960 the flat magnetic film effort was reduced to a relatively small project in the Research Division.[10]

Successes reported by the project in Research combined with competitive announcements, especially by Sperry Rand, caused IBM to increase its effort once again. In October 1961 Sperry Rand announced that the UNIVAC 1107, due to be delivered in April 1962, would be equipped with a 128×36 bit flat magnetic film memory with a cycle of 0.6 microseconds.[10] The UNIVAC film memory was not as fast or large as rumors had suggested, but it was an indication of product feasibility and of future directions in memory technology. IBM technical managers generally believed that the first company to develop high-speed magnetic film memories would have a major advantage in the development of super computers.

In September 1962 the IBM Components Division and Systems Development Division, under pressure from Research and the corporate technology staffs, initiated a product-development program for flat magnetic film memories. To obtain adequate resources for this, they terminated their own plated core project, which was targeted toward a 0.5 microsecond cycle memory using toroidal-shaped glass cores onto which a ferromagnetic metal was plated. Q. William Simkins, who had managed the plated core project, was given responsibility for the flat film memory. This helped contain the frustration and bitterness within the development organization. Nevertheless a number of engineers left the project. Some of these initiated another high-speed memory development project using a device conceived in the Research Division.[11] Called the chain store, it consisted of ferromagnetic metal plated on a chain-shaped copper conductor.[12]

Thus by 1963 there were three projects aimed at achieving main memories with cycle times under 1 microsecond: two cores per bit, the chain store, and flat magnetic films. Of the three, flat magnetic films were expected to provide the highest-speed memories, perhaps as fast as 0.1 microsecond cycle. When progress by May 1963 failed to make commitment to a System/360 computer feasible, corporate management urged increased effort. In a memorandum to Data Systems Division managers, Bob Evans announced this decision saying, "The payoff for flat films is so great when one considers the magnitude of its potential impact on large systems that it was concluded we cannot afford to fail in this area."[11] Moe Every responded by assuming direct management of the effort, while retaining his responsibility for all solid-state memory development.

Additional resources and Every's boundless energies were applied, but by the fall of 1963 the technical situation was little changed. With announcement of System/360 under consideration for the coming spring, all computer development managers placed their commitments on less-risky memory technologies. Development of high-speed flat magnetic film memories for super computers would have to wait.

Moe Every had lost his gamble to create a much desired high-performance, batch-fabricated memory technology for System/360. Meanwhile his other memory development responsibilities had suffered, both from his absence and from an organizational flaw over which he had little control: lack of an adequate effort on semiconductor support circuits required for memories. This organizational flaw was corrected, and Every was replaced as manager of Solid-State Memory Development late in 1963, but these changes did not occur until after he had left his mark on the main memory and control-store technologies used in the IBM System/360 computers.

TROS versus CCROS
The read-only control memories needed for the smaller System/360 computers presented no fundamental technical problems, but the requirement did highlight a limitation of ferrite

core memories, which were unable to provide the required high performance at a reasonable cost. Many alternative technologies for read-only memories were described in the literature; at least eighteen different types were considered by IBM engineers.[13]

Engineers at the IBM Hursley Laboratory, whose early work had contributed to the decision to use control stores, also played a leading role in designing the control stores used in System/360. Antony Proudman, a 1954 graduate of the University of Cambridge with two years' military service and three years' experience at Standard Telephones and Cables Limited prior to joining IBM in 1959, was responsible for memory development in the Hursley Laboratory. Not surprisingly, his engineering group decided to build an improved version of the Transformer Read-Only Store (TROS), which they had previously used on SCAMP. The TROS on SCAMP provided 1280 words of 64 bits each with an access time of 0.5 microsecond. Its design was inspired by a TROS used in the Bell Laboratories' Model 6 computer and reported in 1951.[14]

The design of the TROS used in SCAMP can best be understood by considering a 2D magnetic core memory array. Because the information stored in a control store is not changed once the computer is designed, electronic circuits are not needed for writing information. Instead of using the direction of magnetization in each core to define a 1 or a 0, information can be stored simply by placing a core where a 1 is wanted and no core at all for a 0. The cores in this case operate much like conventional transformers, coupling the input line to the output line. A cost reduction can be achieved by having only one row of cores instead of separate rows for each word line; 1s and 0s are then defined by passing the word line through or around a given core in the row. To permit one hundred or more word lines to pass through each core of the single row, much larger cores are used than in conventional ferrite core memories.

The Hursley design facilitated the change of stored information during development and for engineering changes in the field using a word line structure printed on a long thin strip of Mylar.[15] The word line was given a ladder shape with a hole

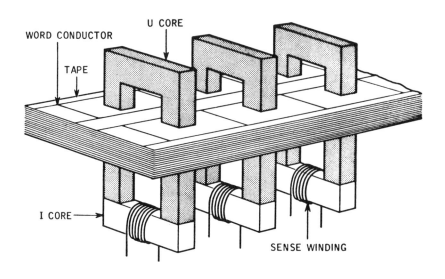

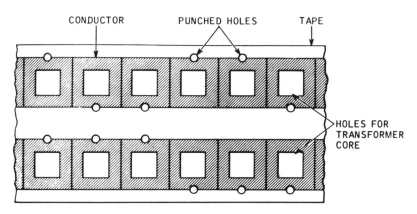

Transformer Read-Only Store (TROS)

Mylar tapes with ladder-shaped printed conductors (above) are shown with U-shaped portions of three magnetic transformer loops passing through the holes between the rungs. The view of a single mylar tape (below) shows how small circular punched holes can be used to force the word line current to pass either through the transformer loop or outside it. (From the *IBM Journal of Research and Development*, September 1964, pp. 444-445.)

between each rung large enough to permit one leg of a U-shaped portion of a magnetic loop (transformer) to be inserted. One of the two long parallel sides of each word line thus passed through the U-shaped loops and the other side passed outside. By punching a small hole in the tape to break the continuity of one or the other side of these parallel lines at each U-shaped loop, a series of 1s and 0s was coded into the word line on each Mylar strip. Stored information could be changed by removing the Mylar word strip and replacing it with a new one with appropriately punched holes. The U-shaped loops were magnetically closed with ferromagnetic bars to which sense windings were attached.

The read-only memory for the Model 40 was implemented with 16 TROS modules containing 256 words each. Each module had 128 Mylar word tapes with two ladder-shaped word lines. These tapes passed through a series of 56 magnetic loops, creating a read-only memory of 256 words of 56 bits. The cycle time was 0.625 microseconds with an access time of 0.24 microseconds including address decoding and delays through the sense amplifier.[14]

The Hursley-developed TROS was planned for use on the Model 30 as well as the Model 40, but in October 1963 Jack Greene, the engineering manager of the Mod 30 in Endicott, advised John Fairclough, manager of the Mod 40 in Hursley, that he was considering the use of an Endicott-developed Card Capacitor Read-Only Memory (CCROM).[16] Originally known as CCROM, the name was changed to CCROS (pronounced sea-cross) when the use of this read-only memory as a control store made the name CCROS more appropriate. The genesis of the program dated back to 1959 when the advance technology group in Endicott began considering the use of read-only memories for a variety of applications. Late in 1962 John W. Haskell, who had responsibility for this one-to-three man project since 1960, initiated a serious effort to build a CCROS that would be cheaper and functionally superior to TROS.[17]

Information in CCROS was stored on cards shaped like IBM punch cards, and indeed information was coded into them by a

standard IBM card punch machine.[18]   Each card had twelve
copper word lines corresponding to the twelve rows on the
standard eighty-column card.   These copper word lines had
rectangular enlargements at regular intervals corresponding to the
hole spacing of the punched card.   The word-line cards were
mated flat against a board of orthogonal copper bit lines so that
the bit lines crossed the word lines at the rectangular
enlargements.   A voltage applied to one of the twelve word lines
induced a voltage on each of the intersecting bit lines.   This
voltage could be greatly reduced by removing the rectangular
enlargements on the word line by punching out that region with a
standard card punch machine.   Punched-out holes provided little
signal and were interpreted as 0s whereas unpunched intersections
were read as 1s.   Data in the memory could be changed simply by
inserting new punched cards, and this capability was believed to
be very important for the Model 30, which had to be compatible
with thousands of IBM 1401s in the field.[18]

John Fairclough believed changing technologies so late in the
development cycle was risky, and Ralph Partridge, on special
assignment in Hursley from the memory development group in
Poughkeepsie, also objected.[19]   But an audit of the situation in
December 1963 concluded the risk was not great.[20]   Group Staff
acquiesced, and it was agreed that development of CCROS would
be moved from Endicott to the Hursley Laboratory, which had
development responsibility for all read-only memories for
System/360.   This decision was expected to provide a fairer
comparison between TROS and CCROS.   If successful, CCROS was to
replace TROS in the Model 40 as well as the Model 30 in order to
achieve the desirable economy of scale in manufacturing.

In February 1964 an engineer, who had worked closely with
John Haskell during the previous year, transferred to the Hursley
Laboratory to serve as a consultant on their CCROS development
effort.   He was distressed that the Hursley engineers were
reanalyzing everything and making design changes he considered
undesirable.   The schedule was tight, and problems were
compounded by the fact that CCROS was to be released to
manufacture in plants in Vermont and Scotland.[17]

(a)

(b)

DETAIL OF CARD

DETAIL OF BOARD

Card Capacitor Read-Only Store (CCROS)

The photograph shows (a) the basic structure of an 8 card storage board with 4 cards per side. The vertical conducting bit lines of the board are shown in the "detail of board" at the lower right. One of the 8 information documents with its horizontal word lines and punched-hole information pattern is also shown (b). A detail of the conducting pattern with capacitor pads (some punched out) is shown in "detail of card." (From the *IBM Journal of Research and Development*, March 1966, p. 143.)

By September 1964 CCROS was in trouble. Unexpectedly high electrical noise in the memory indicated major design changes were necessary, but the project was already behind schedule. Fairclough decided the only solution was to stop work on CCROS and put all control-store work in Hursley back on TROS. The Model 40 engineering group in Hursley reinstated TROS as its control store and so did a small processor project in IBM Germany and the 2841 file control unit.[21] Manufacturing engineering in Poughkeepsie responded with a frantic effort to set up assembly lines to satisfy the newly defined TROS manufacturing requirement. The effort was successful, and TROS performed well in the Model 40 and other products.[22]

Fairclough's decision to stop work on CCROS in the Hursley Laboratory would have ended that read-only memory if the Endicott Laboratory had not previously initiated a project to make CCROS engineering models. These engineering models were to be used to assist in the timely development of the Model 30 processor and were not originally intended to be released to manufacture. However as soon as they learned that the Hursley effort was in trouble, the Endicott engineers changed the objectives to a product development program and successfully released their CCROS to manufacturing. These control stores were shipped on the Model 30, the highest volume processor in the System/360 line.[23]

As finally assembled the 0.75 microsecond cycle CCROS memory array was structured with circuit boards with four capacitor punch cards on each side. Each punch card had 12×60 bits, resulting in 96×60 bits per board. Forty-two boards were used in each Model 30 to provide 4032 words of 60 bits each.[18]

Its reliability was not as good as TROS. In spite of extensive testing in the laboratory, the electrostatic shielding and fittings of the memory were not satisfactory. Service personnel used the expedient of spraying customer carpets with an antielectrostatic fluid to reduce machine errors until engineering changes were made. Information change in the CCROS was also not as easy as predicted. Air bags used to hold the cards in place were cumbersome, and reliability problems were increased by changes in the field.

Neither TROS nor CCROS had the full benefit of high-volume production potentially available, and the cost savings of a common control-store technology in the field were lost. Internal technical entrepreneurship and competition had not served IBM well this time.

A Fast Control Store

Finding a control-store technology for the higher-performance computers in the System/360 line was a significant technical challenge. Each cycle of the control store corresponded to one machine cycle of the processor. The higher-performance computers required memory cycle times shorter than the best projected for TROS or CCROS. By spring 1962 the Model 50 still had no suitable control-store technology, and decisions had been made to build the Models 60 and 70 without control stores.[24]

Fernando (Fred) Neves learned about these issues and decisions while he was on Moe Every's planning staff, a function that had been expanded to include Every's corporate-wide memory responsibility. Neves, who had joined IBM in 1957 with a bachelor's degree in electrical engineering, had prevously been assigned to the debugging and product engineering of the 7302 oil-cooled memories on the 7090 computers. He had spent several weeks in Thule, Greenland, helping to install these computers for the Ballistic Missile Early Warning System (BMEWS).[25]

Concerning the use of control stores on the proposed Model 50, Neves recalls that there was quite a divided camp, "a handful of people who strongly believed in it and a majority that didn't think it was worth a damn." During the annual planning cycle, he learned about the work of Proudman's group in the IBM Hursley Laboratory. In addition to TROS they had done some exploratory work on a higher-speed Balanced Capacitor Read-Only Store (BCROS). Invented by Proudman "while sick in bed with a fever of 103°F. . . calculating signal levels with a slide rule," BCROS (pronounced bee-cross) was called a balanced-capacitor memory because each bit position consisted of two capacitors whose

output signals were balanced against each other to create either a
1 or a 0.[26] To accomplish this, each bit position consisted of the
intersection of four lines: two address lines (one driven positive
and the other driven negative) and two sense lines running
perpendicular to the bit lines. Each address line had a large tab to
create capacitive coupling with one or the other of the two sense
lines. The positioning of the two tabs determined whether a 1 or
0 was stored.[27]

As the fall plan approached, it became clear that the BCROS
project in Hursley would be terminated in order to put more effort
on TROS for the Models 30 and 40. Neves, however, was
becoming interested in developing an improved BCROS for use as a
control store on the Mod 50. A memory cycle of about 0.35
microsecond was required, somewhat faster than projected for
BCROS; but Neves soon had a paper design to achieve this
performance. When Neves showed his design to Moe Every, he
was told, "If you are so interested in the Balanced Capacitor
Read-Only Memory, you should go out and sell it."[25] Neves did.
He described the proposal to a number of people before
presenting it to the engineering manager responsible for
System/360 processors and to the engineering manager for the
Model 50. They offered to fund $350,000 of exploratory work to
develop a BCROS for use on the Mod 50 according to Neves,
"contingent upon my meeting certain checkpoints that I had
helped to set. I felt that was quite a contract since I was a
nonmanagerial staff engineer."[25]

When Neves told Every he had the money and wanted to staff
the project, Every advised him that there were no people. Neves
responded by locating a logic designer and mechanical engineer to
work on the project. He then went to Hursley to see the BCROS
work first hand. While there he reached an understanding with
Proudman that three of the engineers who had worked on the
project in Hursley could come to the United States to continue the
work. Following this, Neves became a manager.[25]

The project was established in the laboratory in Kingston,
New York, to make use of manpower and facilities no longer
needed by Project SAGE. In April 1963, three months after the

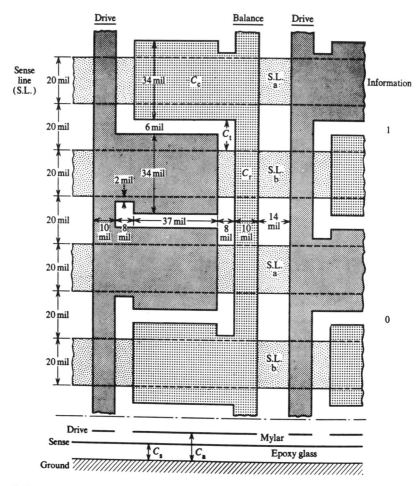

Balanced Capacitor Read–Only Store (BCROS)
This schematic shows the flag configuration for two bits of read-only
memory used in the System/360, Model 65. (From the *IBM Journal of
Research and Development,* July 1968, p. 308.)

project was started, they met their first check point. A small
feasibility cross-section model ran at about a 0.30 microsecond
cycle, easily meeting the speed required by the Model 50. They
now began work on a prototype for the Model 50. Neves named
the memory C-9, where C stood for capacitive or control-store
and 9 was the sum of the digits of the code name, 315, which was
still used to identify the Model 50. By December 1963 the
prototype was running. It was placed in product A-test where it
performed quite well.[25]

At about this time the Model 60 program was having difficulty
meeting its cost-performance targets; its projected sales
accordingly were low. Joseph L. Brown took over as manager of
the project and immediately reconsidered the use of control stores,
which he believed would make the machine less expensive and
easier to design. Neves indicated his confidence that the higher
performance required by the Model 60 could be achieved with an
improved BCROS and proposed a design that could be used for both
the Model 50 and the Model 60. He called it the C-13 where 13
was the sum of the digits of the Model 50 (then known as the
315) and the Model 60 (then known as the 400).[25]

To handle the increased effort in Kingston, Every appointed a
second-level manager, previously with the SAGE project in
Kingston, to take over the BCROS effort. Neves and his group
were to report to the new manager and be responsible for
completing the C-9 memory. Three new groups took over Fred
Neves's C-13 memory effort.

Neves was able to contain his disappointment in the new
organization until he says, "the changes being proposed began to
eat away at me. The mechanical group was reinventing the wheel
and the critical sense-amplifier design was being changed when all
that was needed were changes in the mechanical design, which we
had already proposed." Only the direct intercession of Erich
Bloch kept Neves with the project until the C-13 entered product
test.[25]

As implemented the C-13 was a word-organized storage
system with 2816 words of 100 bits each. It consisted of two
information planes, each mounted in a machine gate. Each

information plane had two sets of printed circuit sense lines, one on each side. These lines were photo etched on a circuit board about 3 feet by 1.5 feet in size. Four bit planes were mounted on each sense board with their bit lines perpendicular to the sense lines. The bit planes were photo etched on copper-clad epoxy glass laminate, approximately 18 inches by 8 inches. A 1 mil Mylar dielectric was sandwiched between the bit plane and the sense plane and held in that position by means of a pressure plate system.[27]

The C-13 had a cycle of 0.25 microsecond and an access time of 0.1 microsecond as required by the Model 60 and 62 processors.[28] Before these computers were shipped, however, changes in the BCROS array terminating resistors permitted the performance of C-13 to be improved. The improved version, renamed C-90, had a cycle of 0.20 microsecond and an access of 0.09 microsecond. The improved performance of the BCROS plus innovations in main memory led to a business decision to replace the Models 60 and 62 with the very successful Model 65.[29]

Although Fred Neves did not have the pleasure of managing the C-13 project, he did have the satisfaction of seeing many of his ideas work. He was particularly pleased when Erich Bloch introduced him to others as "Mister Read-only Memory."[25]

Joe Brown's decision to use read-only control store on the Model 65 made the computer easier to design, as expected, but it also facilitated the development of a compatibility feature that permitted the Model 65 to function like the older IBM 7070 computer. This feature, known as the *7070 emulator*, was important to customers who wanted the greater power of IBM System/360 but had a large investment in software written for the 7070. The word *emulator* was subsequently used for the compatibility feature that permitted the Model 30 to function as an IBM 1401, and in a few years *emulator* was adopted by the industry to describe this feature on any computer.[24]

Memories from Mecca
Early in 1961, about a year after the first Type 7302 oil-cooled memory was shipped on a 7090 computer, Moe Every asked Del

Elder to look into making an air-cooled version of the memory.[30] There had been a number of oil leaks in the field, and servicing the oil-cooled memories was disagreeable, time-consuming, and expensive.

The solution was found not in superior air circulation techniques but rather in changing the ferrite core itself from the 30-50 mil to a smaller 19-32 mil size. This change increased the area-to-volume ratio of the core so that cooling was automatically improved. The resulting memory had the same number of cores as its predecessor, but it was physically smaller and easily achieved the targeted 2.0 microsecond cycle, about 10 percent faster than the oil-cooled version. It was shipped on the IBM 7090, 7080, and 7030 computers beginning in 1962. Subsequently its cycle was reduced to 1.4 microsecond for use on the IBM 7094-II, first shipped in April 1964.[4]

In November 1961, some months after work on the air-cooled 7302 memory began, Every organized the Mecca task force, so named to symbolize the religious fervor with which it was to seek ways to provide memories "at the lowest entry, development, and manufacturing cost consistent with IBM engineering standards."[31] Robert J. Flaherty, hired with a bachelor's degree in physics to work on Stretch in 1956, was in charge. The eight members of the task force represented such skills as memory design, circuit design, packaging, and array wiring. Their main objective was to achieve fully functional megabit memories at a cost of less than one cent per bit. Secondary objectives included cycle times as short as 4 microseconds, less than 2 cubic feet volume (including power supplies), power under 750 watts, an operating temperature range from 50°F to 100°F, and improved reliability and serviceability.[31]

The task force study provided numerous ideas that gave IBM cost-performance leadership in memory technology during the 1960s. The most important of these was an array wiring pattern that permitted the same wire to be used for both the sense and the inhibit functions. Previously this had been impossible because of electrical noise induced in the sense line by the inhibit pulse as well as by the coupling between the sense line and X drive lines.

The wiring pattern that made the combined inhibit-sense line possible was the invention of six members of the Mecca task force.[33] Their discussions at first centered on the figure-eight sense line pattern as originated on the Stretch memories. In this pattern a current pulse on an X line, parallel to a figure-eight sense line, induced one polarity noise in the sense line before the figure-eight crossover and an opposite polarity (cancelling) noise after the crossover. This feature of the figure-eight sense winding prevented its use as an inhibit line because the polarity of drive currents on the inhibit and X-drive lines had to be the same for the entire length.

The problem facing the group was how to circumvent this fundamental geometric problem. The solution was provided by a clever wiring pattern in which noise cancellation took place between two core planes in the 3D array, instead of entirely on one plane. This new wiring pattern required a sense-inhibit line that shifted by two rows in the center of the core plane instead of by one row as had been done for the figure-eight sense line of Stretch.[31]

The mechanism for implementing the wiring pattern in a manufacturable way was invented by Bob Judge, who previously had designed the wiring mechanism for the Stretch memories. Judge's patent describes the wiring mechanism this way: "Two of the three sets of wires are wound in the same dimension of the core plane with the wires of one of these two sets offset at the midpoint of each row from one row to a different row. The offset is formed by first threading the wires in straight rows and then shifting one half of the core plane with respect to the other half."[34]

Using the small 19-32 mil core as planned, there was not enough room for a hollow needle to carry the third wire through the cores. Even the first two wires were a problem, for which Judge had another unique solution. Stretching the end of each wire until it broke, he caused the leading end of the wire to become work hardened and shaped like a miniature bullet able to serve as its own needle.[34]

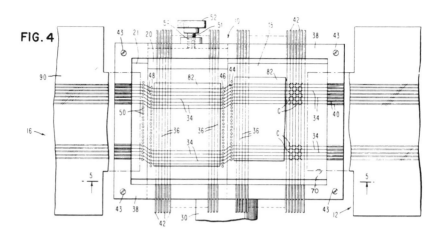

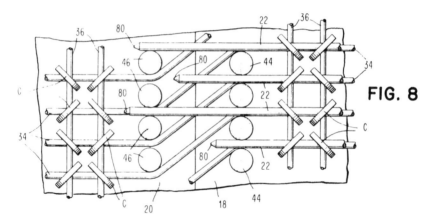

Wire threading with offset

Judge's patent (3,314,131) shows how the two parts of the wiring jig are displaced relative to each other (Fig. 4 above). How this displacement is used to create an offset of two rows for the second set of wires threaded through the cores is shown in Fig. 8 below.

To reduce further the cost of array stringing, large planar core frames of 12.2 inches by 6.5 inches were proposed, capable of holding 256 X wires and 128 Y wires or a total of 32,768 ferrite cores per frame.[31] Such large arrays were possible because improvements in core processing and testing resulted in fewer than one bad core out of 8000 tested cores. Thus an average of only four cores per wired array would have to be replaced by the laborious process of cutting and replacing the wires through the defective cores, and this was judged to be an economically acceptable number of replacements per core array.

To facilitate use of such large frames in various sized memories, each frame was wired so that it was divided into eight segments of 32 by 128 cores. For small memories, each segment could be treated logically as a single core plane, whereas for the large 1.2 million bit memory, 36 of these frames were stacked into one 3D array.

Another important improvement was elimination of jumper wires, which had been used to interconnect the X and Y lines from one plane to the next in 3D core arrays. To accomplish this, the conducting terminals at the edges of the core planes were modified so that they touched the appropriate terminals on the planes stacked above and below them. These terminals were then soldered or welded together to form a rigid, fully interconnected array.[35]

The use of 19-32 mil cores and a relatively low-performance objective permitted direct drive of each line by semiconductor devices. This was cheaper than using the load-sharing matrix switch required in Stretch. The Mecca task force report proposed that the higher-power drive circuits be mounted on SMS cards, whereas the logic circuits needed for the memory were to be implemented in the new SLT. It also recommended that Judge carry out a twenty-six-week study of the proposed wire feeder and indexing matrix and that an additional man-year be devoted to demonstrating feasibility of the entire array wiring concept.[31]

While Judge was developing the methods and tooling for wiring the Mecca arrays, Flaherty undertook development of the 2.5 microsecond cycle megabit memory to be used on the

System/360 Model 40 and also the 2.0 microsecond cycle memory to be used on the Model 50.[32] Smaller 2 microsecond main memories were designed in Endicott for the Model 30, making use of Mecca technologies developed in Poughkeepsie.[36] After the first 1000 were shipped, an improved 1.5 microsecond memory was introduced on the Model 30, using improved Mecca technology.

Just before the IBM System/360 was announced, engineering management estimated that the Models 30, 40, and 50 would be ready for first customer shipment by June, May, and September 1965, respectively. These predicted first shipment dates were either met or bettered.[37] The main memories shipped with these computers were two times faster than had been projected by the Mecca task force study.

These statements, of schedules met and memory performance objectives surpassed, fail to reflect the substantial difficulties and state of panic that accompanied each project. Flaherty recalls working around the clock toward the end of 1963 trying to solve a noise problem in the memories. One morning, following a night-time effort, Flaherty recalls Ed Councill coming in "wearing a black outfit because he believed we would kill Mecca that day. But at three o'clock in the morning, we found the problem and put in a fix." The fix worked. Rather than being a fundamental problem caused by the common sense-inhibit wire as feared, the noise was caused by the manner in which the drive circuit bias voltage was activated. Once identified, this problem was easily corrected.[32]

A Fast Main Memory
The large high-speed memory required by the Models 62 and 70 was designed to use the same 19-32 mil cores and direct transistor drive through a transformer as the slower memories. Four wires through each core, instead of three, were used to achieve the lowest possible noise level.

Edward R. Hee was the first line manager responsible for this M-4 memory. He reported to Ed Councill who now headed much of the memory development work. Councill and Hee both had gained early memory engineering experience on Stretch. After project Stretch, Councill managed an exploratory memory project which attempted to achieve a 0.75 microsecond memory using two cores per bit and Hee had worked on the air-cooled 2 microsecond memory.[38]

In his new assignment, Councill became concerned about the the M-4 memory status. So he assigned himself "to the second shift and spent three weeks working with the guys on the project to see what the problems were." The major problem was the inability of transistor drivers to supply the required 60 volts. The solution seemed obvious to Councill: use a load-sharing matrix switch to reduce the power required from the transistors. But Every refused to make the change because he believed a load-sharing matrix switch would be cumbersome and expensive. Councill was equally adamant and requested a technical audit. The audit supported Councill's view, but still Every did not not relent. Instead he removed Councill from the project and urged Ed Hee to try a new drive circuit conceived at the IBM San Jose Laboratory. This circuit failed to function properly, and problems continued to persist.[39]

By the fall of 1963 pressure was mounting to announce the entire System/360 line early in the next year, causing development managers for the Model 62 and 70 computers to demand models of the promised 1 microsecond cycle M-4 memory. But there were no models. Every's approach to solving the M-4 memory problem had failed. His reputation as a technical manager was already tarnished by failure to achieve the goals established for the cryogenic and flat magnetic film memory projects. More important, solid-state memory development was beset by many other problems arising from the lack of adequate semiconductor circuit and packing support from the Components Division.

In the fall of 1963 a series of engineering management changes were made in an effort to strengthen the company's ability to produce System/360. Moe Every became manager of the laboratory in Kingston, New York, to which Ed Hee also transferred to work on memory projects. Andy Eschenfelder was brought in from Research to replace John Gibson as head of the

Components Division; Gibson was promoted to group executive responsible for the three major development divisions; and Solid-State Memory Development was moved from the Systems Development Division to the Components Division where it was to be be managed by Erich Bloch.[40]

Bloch refused to relinquish management of SLT development when he took on the memory development assignment.[41] This gave him responsibility for the development of SLT as well as solid-state memories. By retaining direct responsibility for SLT, Bloch had only to negotiate with himself to acquire the semiconductor circuit support required for memory development.

Even before the organizational change was announced, Bloch established a task force to study the possibility of replacing memory drive circuits, implemented in modified SMS technology, with the newer SLT technologies.[40] After the announcement, he called Ralph Partridge back from England to review the M-4 memory project with Ed Councill, Greg Constantine, and others. Not surprisingly, the group recommended use of a load-sharing matrix switch of the type invented by Constantine and previously recommended by Councill. They also recommended changing to a much smaller 13-21 mil core from the 19-32 mil core. In doing this Partridge believes he was following Moe Every's long-established practice: any time something had to be reworked because of technical problems, Every took advantage of the opportunity to make it a better product than originally planned.[30]

The decision to use the smaller cores was made in January 1964. In April they had their first fully-wired core planes and by July a memory operating at the desired 1 microsecond cycle. The electrical design was very conservative so that by August 1964 an improved cycle of only 0.75 microsecond was achieved.[39] Bob Judge's invention—creating work-hardened bullet-shaped ends to the wires so they served as their own needles—was critical to the economic implementation of arrays using these very small cores.

The availability of this faster memory, now called M-4I (I stood for "improved") was a major factor in the decision to withdraw the System/360 Models 60, 62, and 70 from the market and to replace them with faster processors using the 0.75

microsecond memory. On April 22, 1965, the Model 60 with its 2 microsecond cycle memory and the Model 62 with its announced 1 microsecond memory were officially withdrawn and replaced by the Model 65 with its faster 0.75 microsecond cycle memory. The same announcement replaced the Model 70 with the faster Model 75. John R. Opel, vice president for marketing asserted, "today's announcements greatly exceed our past achievements. Significant technical improvements have resulted in unprecedented price/performance, making System/360 better than ever."[29] Announced for delivery beginning March 1966, the first Model 65 was shipped in November 1965, four months ahead of schedule. The first Model 65 was, in fact, shipped only three months later than had originally been announced for the lower-performance Models 60 and 62.

Progress in Manufacturing

IBM's early entry into ferrite core memory technology and its initiation of mass production techniques for SAGE had paid off. Good tested cores from General Ceramics cost 33 cents in 1953. One year later IBM was producing tested cores of superior quality for only 5 cents each. The manufacturing cost in IBM was less than 0.2 cent per core when System/360 was announced in 1964, and by 1970 fully tested cores were costing IBM an average of only 0.03 cent each.[1]

These cost reductions were the result of improved core compositions and processing methods plus dramatic improvements in tools for automated core pressing and testing. Ernie Schuenzel, who was now responsible for manufacturing engineering for memory products, reported that during 1963 twelve new core types were developed, sintering yields of the 30-50 mil and 19-32 mil cores were increased from 5 percent to 85 percent, press tool life was increased by a factor of two, and test handler speeds were doubled. In 1964 a third continuous furnace was installed, seventeen 16-station rotary presses were converted to 32-station presses, and core tester handler rates were again increased.[42]

By 1964 the manufacture of ferrite cores had become the show piece of automated production in IBM. The mechanical

Mixing ferrite powder
Dry ferrite powder is mixed with a binder, a lubricant, and distilled water. The binder provides cohesion between ferrite granules during pressing, and the lubricant prevents excessive wear of the punch from abrasion by the powder. Photograph was taken in the IBM plant in 1964.

design skills, which provided IBM with product leadership in punched-card equipment in the 1940s and 1950s, had been applied to automate the production of ferrite cores, ferrite core planes, and complete memory units. Typical of the individuals who contributed to memory production automation was Leopold P. Schab, who graduated from Poughkeepsie Technical High as an apprentice tool maker in 1941. After serving briefly in the military he "knocked about in a number of jobs before joining IBM in 1948 as a tool and model maker on the second shift at the Poughkeepsie plant." Working on electric typewriters and punched-card equipment until these projects were transferred out of Poughkeepsie, he was assigned to memory core manufacturing engineering in 1957. His job was to design and build improved core presses for manufacturing.[43]

In this assignment he worked closely with Bill Walker of the Component Research Department who had built the first single-station core press for IBM in 1954 under the direction of John Gibson. By 1957 the presses produced 320 cores per minute using eight rotating stations instead of one.[44] Most cores were now 30-50 mil, small enough to fit inside the hole of the cores Walker first pressed for project SAGE. Schab and Walker worked together on numerous improvements, including the 16-station presses for 19-30 mil cores, introduced in June 1961.

By 1963 annual core production forecasts had climbed into the billions. Leo Schab was by then a senior associate manufacturing engineer in tooling and equipment, not a manager but an engineer with a lot of responsibility. After noting how many more presses and operators would be required to meet production requirements, he began to work on a double press with 32 stations in which two pressings occurred simultaneously as the stations rotated. These presses were first used for production of 30-50 mil cores in December 1964. They pressed 42 cores per second and required one operator per press. "We got the machines out," Schab recalled, "and then the schedule zoomed again, so we introduced a quadruple press with 48 stations." The 48-station presses required one operator and were first used in October 1966 to manufacture 13-21 mil cores at a rate of 102 cores per second.[44]

Rotary presses with 32 punches
Rotary presses producing ferrite cores for IBM System/360 in the spring
of 1964. A 32-punch rotary press with outer case removed to reveal the
punches is shown below.

"This was by far the most exciting time for me in IBM," Schab asserts. "We were constantly aware of new memory technologies that were expected to replace ferrite cores. There were plated glass cores, the chain store, and flat films. But we had a lot of our own work in cores that we didn't want to lose, so we worked hard to reduce costs and meet schedules."[43]

A similar story is told by Leon Novakowski concerning the development of high-speed ferrite core testers. Coming to the United States from Poland in 1949, he joined IBM in February 1957 after spending seven years working for the Homelite Corporation on manufacturing systems for chain saws and pumps and and getting his master's degree in mechanical engineering at Columbia University. At IBM he was immediately assigned to making high-speed test equipment for ferrite cores.[45]

Novakowski decided the reciprocating motion of the solenoid-operated probe was not suitable for high-speed operation. He replaced it with a rotating drum equipped with electrical probes sticking out radially from the surface. Cores were fed into a vibratory bowl that spiraled the cores to the outside edge where they were picked up one at a time by the electrical probes as the rotating drum was indexed past the pick-up position. A vacuum system in the rotating drum helped to pull the core onto the probe and hold it. As the drum rotated, the core came to a test station where electrical contact was made to the end of the probe, and a series of electrical tests were made. The results of these tests determined whether the vacuum mechanism should release the core into the accept or reject bin.[45]

Novakowski, like Schab, had considerable responsibility but was not a manager. From 1958 to 1960 he was technically responsible for about twenty people working in the design and construction of test handlers. Because of the urgency of the work, ten to fifteen of these people were under contract, rather than IBM employees. Twelve-hour days were frequently worked to meet the schedules. When Novakowski was transferred to semiconductor manufacturing in 1960, these core handlers were operating at a speed of 12 cores per second, and there were two handlers per tester.

Core testing speeds were improved year by year until by 1968 a speed of 180 cores per second was accomplished.[46] A significant improvement was the creation of small indented cylindrical nests on the surface of the drum into which cores were pulled and held by the vacuum. When the nested core reached the test station, the electrical probe was inserted through the hole in the core and engaged with multiple electrical contacts.[47] Reciprocating motion, rejected earlier by Novakowski, had returned, but now it was used with Novakowski's rotating drum handler. Improvements to the drum handler were patented, but Novakowski had been unsuccessful in patenting his basic invention. Inventions by individuals at Philips and elsewhere were judged to be too similar. Viewing this philosophically Novakowski concluded, "If the physical problems are similar, creative human minds will come up with similar solutions even if they are 3000 miles apart."[45]

The cost of core production and testing was kept low enough that it was a small fraction of the total cost of ferrite core memories. Memory costs therefore were determined primarily by the cost of the electronic support circuits and the cost of wiring the core array. The results of improvements in these technologies were dramatic.

IBM's Type 737 commercial ferrite core memory first used on the 701, 704, and 709 computers in 1956 had an average product cost of 14 cents per bit, and IBM's first megabit memory, the Type 738, cost 8 cents per bit. This was five to ten times less than the 70 cents per bit cost of the Williams tube memory used on the IBM 701 in 1953. The average manufacturing cost of the 2.5 microsecond cycle M-7 memories used on the System 360/40 computers was just under 1 cent per bit, and even the higher-performance 0.75 microsecond M-4I memory enjoyed an average manufacturing cost of less than 3 cents per bit.[3]

A Successful Technology

Large quantities of reliable, low-cost main memory were essential to the success of System/360. The small operating systems called BPS and BOS required 2K to 5K bytes of ferrite core memory just to hold instructions that permanently resided in main memory.

Other operating system instructions were brought in from magnetic disk storage as needed. This left little space for user programs in a Model 30 computer equipped with the minimum 8K bytes of memory. The large operating system, OS/360, required 13K bytes just to hold instructions permanently resident in main memory for a processor doing batch jobs with a minimum I/O configuration. For systems handling concurrent jobs and with a more complex I/O configuration, 64K bytes of main memory was required to hold the permanent instructions and to provide space for transient instructions and data.[48]

The convenience and improved systems performance provided by operating systems were desired by the customers who paid for them by the rental or purchase of more main memory. As a result more bytes of main memory were installed per system than originally expected. This effect, coupled with much larger sales of System/360 computers than originally forecasted, resulted in unexpectedly large demands for memory.

The production of ferrite cores in IBM had just reached 1 billion per year in 1964 when System/360 was announced. By 1970 it exceeded 20 billion cores per year, almost all being attached to IBM System/360 computers. Most of the System/360 equipment, including memory, was placed on rental. But if all the ferrite core memories produced by IBM in 1970 had been sold, they alone would have accounted for a revenue in excess of $3 billion. IBM's leadership in core fabrication and testing, automated array wiring, and mass production methods combined with unexpectedly large sales volumes to create a very high profit margin.

Cost–Performance Limits

The announcement of System/360 in April 1964 featured a low-cost, large-capacity memory. Primarily intended for use with the Model 70 but also available with the Models 60, 62, and 50, it was attached to the storage bus to provide up to 8 million bytes of directly addressable main memory.[28] It was to provide the cheapest possible random access memory so that high-use items typically stored on magnetic disks could be kept in the higher-performance memory.

The Type 2361 memory used for this purpose was available in 1 million and 2 million byte units and had a cycle of 8 microseconds. A cost of about 0.5 cents per bit was to be achieved by using very large core planes with 256×1152 (294,912) cores each. A so-called 2 1/2 D memory organization plus an IBM invention that permitted one wire to serve both as the sense and bit drive lines facilitated a low-cost memory design with only two wires threaded through each core.[46] These were the largest ferrite core arrays ever made and were wired automatically using bullet-tipped wire feeding. It was quite an impressive sight to watch 64 wires being fed in parallel, down the four-foot length of a core plane.[35]

The actual cost achieved was almost twice as high as projected. It was only slightly lower than that of the 2.5 microsecond memory because of fundamental limits of ferrite core memory technology and because poor customer acceptance kept production volumes much lower than expected. Poor customer acceptance was induced by IBM's inadvertently poor software support and by the introduction of a stand-alone channel and control unit that moved information more efficiently between main memory and electromechanical disk storage units, reducing the need for very large memories. These large ferrite core memories nevertheless did play an important role in special applications such as the first Apollo moon mission.[35]

The dominant main memories for System/360 ranged in cost and performance from the 1 cent per bit, 2.5 microsecond cycle memory used on the Model 40 to the 3 cents per bit, 0.75 microsecond cycle memory used on the Models 65 and 75.[3] With less than a factor of four in memory performance, system designers had managed to develop computers with almost a factor of one hundred difference in performance between the Model 30 and the Model 65.

A variety of techniques were employed. Most important was increasing the amount of information used for each memory cycle. The Model 30 computer used one byte per memory cycle, the

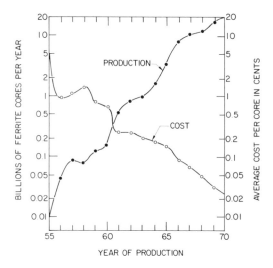

YEAR OF PRODUCTION

Ferrite core production
The production of ferrite cores in IBM is shown in billions of cores per year from 1955 to 1970 (left ordinate) and the average manufacturing cost per core, in cents per core (right ordinate). The dramatic 2000-fold increase in production quantity and 200-fold reduction in cost, during this 20-year period, require the use of a logarithmic scale.

Repairing a ferrite core plane
One of IBM's core plane wiring and repair experts repairs a Large Capacity Memory plane. These core planes were four feet long, contained 294,912 cores each, and were used in the Type 2361 memories available on System/360.

Model 40 used two, the Model 50 used four, and the Models 65 and 75 used eight bytes (equivalent to two System/360 words) per memory cycle. The Models 65 and 75 were also designed with two-way and four-way memory interleaving, respectively. Interleaving meant that one or more of the individual memory units of the main memory could be accessed before a previously addressed memory unit had completed its full cycle.[48]

Another important design technique related to the manner in which internal registers or scratch-pad memories were implemented. In the Model 30 all of these registers were physically part of the main memory, reducing the cost of the computer. This also reduced the effective speed of main memory because many memory cycles were used for register or buffer functions. For this reason a faster memory was needed on the Model 30 processor than on the higher-performance Models 40 and 50. The Models 40 and 50 implemented I/O buffers with the main memory and CPU registers with small, separate ferrite core memories. Finally, the Models 65 and 75 did not use the main memory for any buffers or registers. Registers for these computers were implemented separately to achieve the desired high performance.[48]

Clever systems design techniques permitted IBM to use low-cost ferrite core technology in all its System/360 computers, but they also highlighted a fundamental problem: ferrite core memories had a limited cost-performance range. Very fast memories were prohibitively expensive, and substantially lower-cost memories could not be achieved simply by making them larger or slower. Ferrite core memories were also unable to provide the high-speed read-only control store function, which was such a critical part of System/360 computers.

Even before the difficult problems of meeting System/360 commitments were past, IBM turned its attention once again to advanced memory technologies. An immediate requirement was to select one of the high-performance memory alternatives for use in the super computer promised by the original System/360 announcement. In the long run, however, it was even more important to find a new memory technology for the next generation of computers.

9
Managing Technological Change

Fortune magazine called IBM's decision to produce System/360 "the most crucial and portentous—as well as the riskiest—business judgement of recent times."[1] Hundreds of millions of dollars had been spent to develop the hardware, software, and systems. Billions of dollars were committed to its manufacture before market acceptance was assured. But customer demand was even greater than anticipated. To meet this demand, new plants were built and existing ones expanded. Whole areas of the company were reorganized, and in 1965 four technical executives were temporarily relieved of their normal responsibilities in order to devote full time to the task of identifying and solving all problems contributing to delays in manufacturing and shipping. The effort to develop, manufacture, and install System/360 strained IBM's resources. It reshaped the company and indeed the entire data-processing industry.

For the first time a full line of computers covering a wide range of performances had been made compatible, a user with increasing computer requirements could move up from one machine to the next without discarding or rewriting the software. System/360 was equipped with the largest and most versatile operating system ever devised. The I/O equipment had standard interfaces so that they could be connected to systems of differing performance. The hardware used entirely new semiconductor circuitry developed by IBM, and the central processing units had the lowest-cost main memories ever produced. Without these large, reliable memories, OS/360 and the many functions it provided users would not have been possible. To achieve the desired function and performance, customers ordered even more main memory capacity per system than anticipated.

The Manufacturing Buildup

Ernest Karl Friedli, who had transferred to the IBM Kingston Plant in 1962 as new products coordinator for Project Stretch after holding a variety of positions in manufacturing, was given corporate responsibility for all memory manufacturing for System/360. There had been difficulty finding sufficient work for the Kingston plant ever since the termination of the SAGE program. Now this problem was to be solved by having the Kingston plant manufacture the large Model 65 and Model 75 computers, as well as ferrite core memories for all systems. Pressing, firing, and testing individual cores would continue to be done in Poughkeepsie, but core plane wiring, memory array assembly, and complete memory box assembly and test were to be done in Kingston. This assignment was within the capability of the Kingston plant until the projected requirements for memory on System/360 started to grow.[2]

The buildup achieved in producing and testing ferrite cores helps to quantify the problem. The new 13-21 mil core introduced on the M4I memory for System/360 was placed into production early in 1964. By the end of the year, over 46 million of these cores had been produced.[3] IBM's production of all core types was 933 million in 1963, 1671 million in 1964, and the staggering number of 8755 million cores in 1966.[4] Each core had to be fabricated, tested, wired into memory arrays, tested, assembled into operational memories, tested, attached to a computer, and tested again before it was shipped.

So many automatic wire feeders were needed for wiring core arrays that an entire department and a production line were established in Kingston to produce them. As quickly as wire feeders were produced, they were placed in the manufacturing lines for making the memories. But the demand for memory increased more rapidly, making it increasingly difficult to produce wire feeders fast enough. By the end of 1964 a new problem emerged: even if the wire feeders were produced fast enough to permit the required number of core planes to be wired on schedule, there would not be sufficient floor space in the plant to assemble the core planes into 3D arrays and the arrays into memory boxes.[2]

"We were just beginning to get this message to corporate," Friedli recalls, "when I was summoned to a meeting in Dick Watson's office." The focus of the meeting, to which a number of manufacturing managers had been summoned, was the Components Division. The SLT modules newly developed for System/360 had been produced at the rate of 45,000 in 1962, 550,000 in 1963, and 6 million in 1964. More than 50 million were needed in 1965.[5] Critical technical and logistical problems had been solved to meet this buildup before an unexpected problem surfaced. IBM's requirements for relatively mundane RC packs, combining resistors and capacitors, were beginning to exceed the total capacity of all suppliers.

In the midst of this discussion Dick Watson turned to Ernie Friedli and said, "And what is your problem?" Friedli responded that the Kingston plant did not have sufficient people or space to produce the memories now required by the sales force. Others in the meeting agreed that more manufacturing space was desperately needed. Watson responded quickly. Within two weeks plans were announced to build new plants in Raleigh, North Carolina, and Boulder, Colorado.[2] The land had been acquired previously but building plans had to be developed.[6] The Boulder plant was to off-load Poughkeepsie in magnetic tape drive manufacturing and Kingston in memory manufacturing. Increased demand for magnetic tape drives and startup problems in Boulder, however, prevented the relief in memory manufacture from being as large as required.

The situation was becoming desperate when George Tamke was appointed general manager of the Kingston plant. He had spent several years in Japan as director of manufacturing for IBM in the Far East. From this experience, he was convinced that people in the Orient had sufficient manual dexterity and patience to wire core arrays by hand. He took a few bags of cores, rolls of wire, and some core frames to Japan. In ten days he returned with hand-wired core planes as good as those that had been wired by the automatic wire feeders in the Kingston plant.[2]

An organization was quickly established in Japan to find vendors to do this work. Soon the work expanded to Taiwan, where a few thousand people were employed wiring core frames by hand. It was slow, tedious, meticulous work, stringing wires in just the right manner through each of the thousands of tiny cores in each core plane. But the cost of labor there was so low that it was actually a few dollars per plane cheaper than with full automation in Kingston. With much of IBM's core stringing work moved to the Orient, the Kingston plant now was able to concentrate on assembling core frames into 3D arrays and arrays into memory units.[2]

Competitors also established core plane wiring operations in the Orient, causing IBM to lose some of its competitive advantage because companies without automatic wire-threading equipment could now perform this operation just as cheaply. IBM nevertheless maintained a substantial overall cost advantage. It had superior automation of core production and unique designs for memory arrays, circuits, and packaging that reduced the number of circuits and facilitated automated mass production of the entire memory unit.

Not Good Enough

Soon after System/360 was announced, IBM managers began to concern themselves more with its shortcomings than its strengths. The systems design was not adequate to provide the time-sharing multiterminal support desired by a number of customers, and software development was plagued by enormous problems. Managers of software development projects were replaced and a number of individuals were dismissed for failing to meet schedules. Manufacturing managers who did not meet the ever accelerating schedules were replaced by others who found the problems to be no more tractable.

Within four weeks after announcement, orders had been received for more than one thousand System/360 computers plus associated peripheral equipment.[7] The large number of orders exacerbated the problems in manufacturing and software development, but they failed to assure market success because orders were easily cancelled and systems on rental could be returned with one month's notice.

The limitations of ferrite core memory technology were addressed with added emphasis on advanced technology efforts such as the magnetic film memory and the chain store projects. Development or research contracts were given to outside organizations that claimed they could provide memories superior to those available inside IBM. Ampex was contracted to make a large capacity memory, Toko to provide plated wire memory technology, and Fabritek to make high-speed ferrite core memories. Texas Instruments was approached about its reportedly faster and more compact thin magnetic film memories.[8]

The promises and projections of these companies concerning their proposed new memory technologies were often as unrealistic as were IBM's own perceived future requirements. Nevertheless corporate management used these promises and projections to demonstrate the inadequacies of internal projects and to stimulate renewed effort and more aggressive objectives.[8]

Even Solid Logic Technology (SLT), newly developed for System/360, was criticized for being obsolete before it was delivered. Outside organizations had reported on laboratory demonstrations and products in limited production which used semiconductor devices with several circuits per chip. IBM's SLT, in contrast, required several chips to make one circuit.

John Haanstra, who had been removed as president of the General Products Division following his failure to support System/360, wrote a report in September 1964 documenting how far behind he believed the company was in monolithic circuit technology. His report, "Monolithics and IBM," played on the fears of corporate managers. It urged immediate development of monolithic semiconductor technology with ten to one hundred circuits per chip. Such devices were projected to be so inexpensive and so reliable that they could replace ferrite core memories as well as SLT logic.[9]

Driven by an insatiable thirst for excellence, IBM management did not recognize the success of System/360 and the wisdom of the technological decisions that had made it possible until several years after it was announced. In the meantime it seemed as though no technical effort was good enough.

By January 1965 IBM had reorganized its development activities so that the Data Systems, General Products, and Components divisions were combined into one division. Manufacturing was placed in a separate division. One purpose of the new organization was to put system and circuit designers and component technologists into the same division where they could work together to learn how to put more circuits and function on each chip. It was an organization geared to bring IBM into the world of monolithics, and John Haanstra was appointed president of the new Systems Development Division.[10]

The frantic efforts to upgrade the company's presumably inadequate technology resulted in a period of uncertainty and frustration. Development objectives, unrealistically aggressive in retrospect, were rejected for not being aggressive enough. Some development groups became so confused that they did virtually nothing. Others continued their own projects while ignoring the rapidly changing objectives established by higher levels of management. Gradually as the needs and capabilities of the organization were better understood, some of these efforts were focused on more realistic goals.

In January 1968 IBM terminated its primary program to develop advanced ferrite core memories in order to concentrate its resources on the development of monolithic semiconductor memories, a daring decision for several reasons. First, the reliability and speed of ferrite core memories had made the stored-program computer a practical reality. Second, ferrite core memories had successfully coexisted with electronic vacuum tube machines and transistorized machines for fourteen years, and they had consistently provided an above-average profit margin. Finally, monolithic semiconductor memories had not yet come close to achieving the cost and reliability of ferrite core memories already in production, and greatly improved ferrite core memories, with improved automatic production techniques, were being developed.[11]

Many criticized the decision to stop development of improved ferrite core memories because it jeopardized unnecessarily the company's highly profitable leadership in this well-established field. The decision was partially vindicated, however, in June 1971 when the world's first commercial computer with an all-semiconductor main memory, the IBM System/370 Model 145, was introduced. The multimegabit memory was composed of bipolar semiconductor chips less than one-eighth of an inch (3.1mm) on a side, each with 128 bits.[12] Its cost, performance, and reliability were competitive with those expected for improved ferrite core memories whose development had been stopped, and the superiority of semiconductor memories was shown during the ensuing years as monolithic semiconductor memories became the dominant computer memory technology throughout the industry.

Ferrite core memories had played their role. They had displaced all other electronic memory technologies during the 1950s. Their speed and reliability had made stored-program computers a practical reality. Ferrite core memories had contributed to the success of the IBM System/360 and to the dramatic growth of the computer industry during the 1960s. During the 1970s, however, their ascendancy was challenged by monolithic semiconductor memories. By the end of the 1970s the memory market, dominated for two decades by ferrite cores, was now dominated by monolithic semiconductors.

In 1979 IBM began shipping its 4331 computer with a memory composed of semiconductor chips less than one-quarter inch on a side and containing 65,536 bits each, the largest number of memory bits per chip achieved in any system to that time. A very high packaging density was achieved by placing eight of these silicon chips, with a total of more than half a million bits, on a double-layer, one-inch square ceramic module. This resulted in memory units 170 times denser and using 100 times less power per bit than the best that had been achieved by ferrite core memories in the IBM System/360.[12] The wisdom of the decision to shift from ferrite core to semiconductor memory development had been confirmed.

Memory chip on core array
A 128-bit bipolar chip of the type used in the first all-semiconductor
main memory announced on the IBM System/370, Model 145, in
September 1970. The core plane supporting it has 30-50 mil cores; the
smallest cores used by IBM in a product were 13-21 mil. (From the
IBM Journal of Research and Development, September 1981, p. 592.)

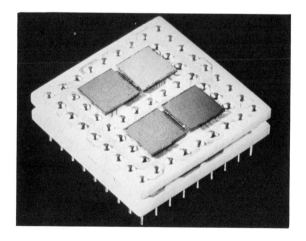

Semiconductor memory module
The double-layer, one-inch ceramic module holds eight semiconductor
chips, each containing 65,536 bits. These modules, each containing
524,288 bits, were first shipped on the IBM 4331 computer in 1979.
(From the *IBM Journal of Research and Development*, September 1981,
p. 595.)

Innovation and Risk

Time and again, technical managers supported by corporate managers, had undertaken development programs with substantial risk. Time and again, technical problems encountered during the development process placed customer commitments in jeopardy. Time and again, all the resources of the corporation were put behind an effort to meet these commitments. Massive expenditures had been devoted to ferrite core processing and memory development for SAGE. There was the push for the ultimate performance for Stretch. Finally, there was the effort to achieve large, high-performance, low-cost memories for System/360.

The different roles of technical versus corporate managers resulted in friction at all stages of the development process but especially when customer commitments were jeopardized. Corporate managers were responsible for meeting these commitments, but they were dependent on technical managers for solving the problems.

John Gibson, who built IBM's first ferrite core pilot-line production facility, served as the first general manager of the Components Division, and advanced to group executive responsible for three development divisions observed: "An engineer has a threshhold of panic on problems. He is a problem solver. As long as he doesn't see fundamental limits, he is basically an optimist who believes he can solve the problems. People without that training have a lower threshhold of panic. They don't have the perspective to separate the fundamental show stoppers from normal startup problems."[13]

Top technical management, therefore, must have the confidence of corporate management. Technical managers have to convince corporate managers that the risks are worth taking, and they must be able to sustain corporate support throughout the development process. Ralph Palmer played that role effectively. He had won corporate management's respect through his highly successful Type 604 electronic calculating punch, and he had maintained it reasonably well through the difficult times of SAGE and Stretch. However, the strains of System/360 were more severe; the entire IBM product line had been placed in jeopardy.

Andy Eschenfelder, who made the first ferrite cores in IBM and who followed John Gibson as head of the Components Division, spoke of the stresses of System/360 saying, "There was too much panic when there was a technical crisis." Then recalling the advanced technology programs initiated shortly after the announcement of System/360, Eschenfelder asserts, "There was too much push on future technology on an unrealistic schedule." Business executives had begun to look to their growing staff of technical advisers for guidance. These technically trained advisers should have provided stability and helped to keep the businessmen from getting too unrealistic in their demands, but according to Eschenfelder, "they were just as unrealistic as anyone."[5] It was a painful recognition that people with technical training are also unable to predict the future. When faced with market forces and internal political pressures similar to those faced by nontechnically trained executives, they respond in much the same way.

In spite of these problems, the system repeatedly had undertaken major technological risks and by and large succeeded. There was a strong belief that superiority in the market required superior products and technologies. To achieve these, one had to have committed development efforts and one had to take risks.

"We were highly successful in memory," Erich Bloch asserts. "We succeeded by foresight and risk taking. We realized that we had to be in the total game, not just one aspect of it. One couldn't depend on the industry as it existed at the time for the guts part of our business."[14] Moe Every reinforces this view saying, "We had a vision of what memory meant in the product line. We felt our role was to be the best."[15]

Management Precepts

When pressed to describe the process by which IBM and its managers had achieved the needed foresight, leadership, wisdom, and risk-taking ability, most of the technical people viewed these as characteristics of individuals rather than of the system itself. Ralph Palmer is particularly cited for his leadership. Edwards describes him as "the Henry Ford of computers whose goal was to mass-produce electronic computers on an assembly line."[16] Birkenstock says, "Probably the key credit goes to Ralph," Gibson calls him a "fantastic guy" who "got us into the modern electronic age," and Haynes describes him as having "good technical taste and judgement and the ability to make things happen."[13,17,18]

The story of memory development, however, reveals characteristics sufficiently pervasive that they should be ascribed to the management system rather than to individuals. Six management precepts appear to account for much of IBM's success. Four of these date back to Watson, Sr., but the last two evolved after World War II in response to the needs of increasingly complex product technologies.

Well defined goals and beliefs — Watson, Jr., attributed much of IBM's success to having goals and beliefs on which it premised all its policies and actions. The three beliefs he identified with his father were respect for the individual, service to the customer, and excellence in all activities.[19] Before the mid-1950s, many engineers acquired direct knowledge of service to the customer by spending their first few years servicing equipment prior to becoming development engineers. This experience beneficially affected many development decisions. Respect for the individual was occasionally overlooked in the highly competitive engineering environment, but the quest for excellence never was. The phrase "not good enough" was applied frequently, even to projects as successful as Stretch and System/360. Key goals of the 1950s and 1960s were to achieve independence from others in all aspects of electronic computer technology, to develop equipment with good performance and reliability, and to devise products and manufacturing methods concurrently so that economies of scale could be realized as markets grew.

Investment in the future — The struggle for increased revenue and profits was ever present. But it did not prevent the company from supporting the early use of punched-card equipment for scientific calculations, building the ASCC and SSEC super machines, hiring people trained in electronics in the early 1950s, and developing electronic computers and technologies even when the market for electromechanical punched-card equipment could have used all of the engineering and sales resources of the company.

Commitment — Hank DiMarco says he became a manager because he was willing to make a commitment to achieve specific objectives, and subsequently he insisted that those working for him make a similar commitment.[20] Fred Neves did not become a manager of the BCROS project until he had obtained a commitment of funds from the user by making his own commitment to meet mutually established check points.[21]

Success in meeting commitments was quickly rewarded. Ernie Schuenzel, who developed the first successful production process for CuMn ferrite cores in the fall of 1955 became the manager of a newly formed ferrite core development group in January 1957; and Hank DiMarco, who was a lone engineer responsible for transferring core processing from development to manufacturing in 1954, found himself only six years later in charge of all ferrite core memory product manufacturing. Erich Bloch, who made the first ferrite core memory products in IBM, was head of development for STL and all memories for System/360 by 1963; and John Gibson, who established the company's first pilot line for making and testing ferrite cores, was head of the Components Division by 1959 and a group executive in charge of three development divisions four years later.

Punishment, in the form of reduced responsibility or removal from a project, was equally swift even though failure to meet objectives was frequently the result of technical difficulties that could not have been anticipated. Quick punishment served to remind all technical people that they were responsible for achieving objectives. Apologies by management for excessive reaction could come later, and sometimes they did.

Competition — External competition, real or imagined, was a driving force behind IBM's emergence in electronic computers. Watson, Jr., says he "was absolutely panicked" when he first learned that Remington Rand had two UNIVACs installed at the Census Bureau.[22] More than anything else, this convinced him to move vigorously to develop commercial electronic computers. The fear that management would buy ferrite core memories from outside suppliers drove IBM engineers to design memories superior to anything that could be purchased outside.

Internal competition was also important. Watson, Sr., had frequently given more than one inventor the same assignment, often in secret. This practice was followed more openly by Palmer to determine which of many alternative technologies was best. Addressing this subject, Watson, Jr., said, "I encouraged competitive attitudes and established competitive situations down through the business so that the laboratories would be competing, factories would be competing. . . . there was a lot of discipline that came from that."[22] Engineers working on alternative memory technologies were goaded to increased effort by Moe Every's assertion that improvements in ferrite core memories made alternatives unnecessary. Simultaneously, Every held up the specter of advanced technologies to those working on ferrite cores. Leo Schab recalls the reaction in manufacturing engineering to the competitive threat of advanced memory technologies, saying, "We had a lot of our own work in cores that we didn't want to lose. . . . We just said, 'By God, we can beat those guys.' And we did."[23]

Free flow of information — Both Watsons maintained direct contacts with customers and with innovative organizations and individuals outside the company. This was an important cause of IBM's success, according to Jay Forrester, who observed that "information channels to IBM's very top management went directly to the top from outside. . . information wasn't being filtered through all of the prejudices of a chain of command within the company.[24] Both Watsons and the engineering executives reporting to them also maintained contacts throughout the company that circumvented the internal filtering process.

Changing social values following World War II and the increasing dependence of the company on the expertise of engineers led to greater freedom of individual expression. Wild ducks and whistle blowers were tolerated and even encouraged. There is always reluctance to bring bad news to the top, but the fluidity of the organization, respect for the individual, and sense of common purpose created a freer flow of information than in many organizations.

Collective decision making — Perhaps the biggest change in management practice during this era was the shift from top-down decision making to a bottom-up approach. Collective decision making was necessitated by the complexity of the product line and the technologies of which it was composed. But even in collective decision making, authority to endorse the decision must ultimately reside with one organizationally responsible person.

Frequently task forces were used as a means of involving many groups in the decision process. They were used for solving problems, identifying new directions, and creating unity of purpose among the participants in development projects. The Mecca task force provided a crucial beginning to the development of memories for System/360, and the entire System/360 program was initiated as the result of recommendations made by the SPREAD task force. Inclusion of people from manufacturing as well as from development in the Mecca task force was significant.

The difficult process of responsibility diffusion was evidenced in August 1955 when Watson, Jr., complained that he had to make the decision to use ferrite core memories in commercial products, a decision he believed should have been made by engineering. In truth Watson made no decision until his engineers had provided the necessary technical information and he had obtained an informal consensus of the sales, service, and engineering management. The actual decision could only have been made by him.

H. A. Simon has described decision making by individuals in the face of limited information and finite intellectual resources as a process of sufficing rather than one of optimization.[25] Faced with large uncertainties, people tend toward a decision of known outcome that suffices rather than seeking an optimum solution with potentially greater risk. Extending Simon's terminology, the IBM postwar decision-making process may well be described as one of *sufficing by consensus*.

Sufficing by consensus was particularly successful at IBM for several reasons. First, the participants viewed the process as one of seeking an optimum decision for IBM even if, for their own areas, the decision was merely one that sufficed. Second, the well known goals and beliefs of the company provided guidance for decisions. Third, the social, management, and monetary rewards were structured to induce a team effort. Finally, the participants had good knowledge of each other and were able to anticipate and interpret each others' responses in the consensus-forming process.

Successful managers were those who stimulated interaction among all participants and created an environment conducive to the formation of an informed consensus and, like Tom Watson, were quick to recognize the consensus, make a management decision, and support the decision.

The IBM Team

In attempting to explain IBM's success, outside analysts have often cited the company's ability to react quickly. An article in *Datamation*, for example says, "The reason that IBM was not further behind [Remington Rand] than about one year was that it kept the development time on the 701 down to a remarkably small period."[26] Fast response in this case was possible because of the unity of purpose of corporate management, teamwork within the development organization, and established projects in relevant technologies. Work on Williams tube main memory, magnetic drums, and magnetic tapes was already underway, and the vacuum tube circuitry manufactured for the Type 604 electronic calculating punch provided an excellent base for design and manufacture of the IBM 701.

The decision to join MIT on Project SAGE was probably the most important decision management made during this period. It gave IBM an inside track to the most advanced computer technologies in the world and propelled the company into a leading position in ferrite core memories. The memory technologies developed for SAGE were modified and refined for commercial products and then pushed to the limit in Project Stretch. By the time decisions for System/360 were made, IBM was already the world leader in ferrite core memory technologies. It had produced some of the fastest, largest, and most reliable memories in the industry, and its accomplishments in reducing manufacturing costs were unmatched.

The company had moved successfully from electromechanical technology to modern electronics. It had moved from a business in which response to customer needs and desires was sufficient to a business in which technical innovations resulted in products and applications unanticipated by customers. IBM had also moved from products created and refined by single inventors to products so complex that teams of technologists were required to develop each of the many component elements.

The simple organization of a beneficent autocracy, under Thomas J. Watson, Sr., had evolved to one in which responsibility and authority were more broadly distributed. The reorganizations in 1956 and 1959 created a formal structure more consistent with this reality, but in engineering at least, the diffusion of responsibility began when Ralph Palmer and other engineers returned from wartime assignments in electronics. Able to use their knowledge of classified wartime developments to formulate judgments, they were not able to communicate the basis for their judgments to their own management. This might have been a transient effect, with full decision responsibility reverting back to corporate management once the wartime advances in electronics were implemented. Instead it was the beginning of a continuing trend, driven by the increasing complexity and diversity of products.

Fewer than ten people were involved in designing and building IBM's first tape buffer memory. By contrast, the ideas proposed by the Mecca task force were implemented for the different System/360 processors by several engineering teams. Circuits were provided by separate groups, and so were many engineering support services. Hundreds of engineers were involved. Many felt remote from the final product, causing the company to establish a system for rewarding inventors in 1961 and people with nonpatentable outstanding technical contributions in 1962.[27]

Increasing company size caused numerous other changes. When Mike Haynes became a manager in 1951, he complained that he had been "put in the position of managing other people" but "there was no help from anybody in IBM for handling this kind of problem."[28] Less than ten years later managers complained about the managers' manual, management training classes, and all the paperwork associated with personnel policies and practices.

Size and rapid growth also added a new measure of success. For many engineers, the game of advancing in the organization had become more challenging than was the job of advancing technology. With many technical people feeling remote from product objectives and their managers jockeying for improved positions in the organization, it became increasingly difficult to define critical technical issues, to organize to solve them, and to maintain the traditional IBM team spirit.

The massive, company-wide gamble on System/360 once again brought the team together. This single project required all of the company's resources and placed the entire product line in jeopardy. The decisions of the SPREAD task force created a development effort that required and received a team effort, and IBM System/360 provided the ultimate opportunity for refining magnetic core memory technology and profiting from an established position of technical leadership.

References and Notes

References include articles published in the technical and popular literature, books, patents, interviews, and internal IBM and MIT documents. Internal IBM documents were obtained from individual employees, trial testimony and exhibits, the IBM Technical Information Retrieval Center, and the IBM Archives. Many references relating to Project Whirlwind and Project SAGE are labeled (*) or (**), indicating they were obtained from the MITRE Corporation Archives, Bedford, Massachusetts, or from the Magnetic Core Memory Collection (MC-140) of the Institute Archives and Special Collections, MIT Libraries, Cambridge, Massachusetts, respectively.

Chapter 1

1. T. G. Belden and M. R. Belden, *The Lengthening Shadow* (Boston: Little, Brown, 1962): pp. 190-217.

2. *IBM Yesterday and Today*, IBM Form G520-3140-2 (January 1981); "Pages from the Past," (Poughkeepsie: IBM, October, 1976).

3. Belden and Belden: pp. 209-210.

4. Belden and Belden: pp. 218-225.

5. G. D. Austrian, *Herman Hollerith, Forgotten Giant of Information Processing* (New York: Columbia University Press, 1982).

6. Belden and Belden: pp. 289-295; "Comparative Statement of Operations of International Business Machines Corporation for the Past Twenty Years," *Business Machines* (May 1959): pp. 8-9.

7. J. F. Brennan, "The IBM Watson Laboratory at Columbia University: A History" (February 1971). Benjamin D. Wood was the head of Columbia University's Bureau of Collegiate Educational Research who convinced Watson to support studies of automatic test scoring and analysis in 1928.

8.   W. J. Eckert, "The IBM Department of Pure Science and the Watson Scientific Computing Laboratory," Educational Research Forum Proceedings, August 1947, pp. 31-36.

9.   H. Aiken Prospectus: "Proposed Automatic Calculating Machine" dated November 1937 and printed in *IEEE Spectrum* (August 1964): pp. 62-69.

10. C. J. Bashe, "The SSEC in Historical Perspective," *Annals of the History of Computing* 4 (1982): pp. 296-312.

11. C. D. Lake, H. H. Aiken, F. E. Hamilton, and B. M. Durfee, U.S. Patent 2,616,626 (filed February 8, 1945); C. D. Lake, F. E. Hamilton, and B. M. Durfee, U.S. Patent 2,616,624 (filed February 8, 1945).

12. "IBM Automatic Sequence Controlled Calculator," IBM Corporation brochure (1945).

13. Saul Rosen, "Electronic Computers: A Historical Survey," *Computing Survey* 1 (1969): pp. 7-39.

14. J. W. Bryce to H. Aiken, October 3, 1944.

15. "Calculator Is IBM's Latest Scientific Development," *Business Machines*, March 15, 1948.

16. J. C. McPherson, F. E. Hamilton, and R. R. Seeber, "A Large-Scale, General-Purpose Electronic Digital Calculator — The SSEC," *Annals of the History of Computing* 4 (1982): pp. 313-326.

17. A. K. Bhattacharya, "The IBM Selective Sequence Electronic Calculator," IBM Research Report RC9225, (January 22, 1982).

18. IBM Selective Sequence Electronic Calculator, IBM brochure (1948).

19. F. E. Hamilton, R. R. Seeber, R. A. Rowley, and E. S. Hughes, "Selective Sequence Electronic Calculator," U.S. Patent 2,636,672 (issued April 28, 1953).

20. R. R. Seeber interview by L. Saphire, August 15, 1967.

21. W. W. Laurence, "Mechanical Brain Given to Science," *New York Times*, January 28, 1948, p. 25.

22.   H. H. Goldstine, *The Computer from Pascal to von Neumann* (Princeton: Princeton University Press, 1972): pp. 148-156.

23.   J. P. Eckert and J. W. Mauchly, "Automatic High-Speed Computing, A Progress Report on the EDVAC," (September 30, 1945).

24.   Nancy Stern, *From ENIAC to UNIVAC* (Bedford Mass.: Digital Press, 1981): pp. 66-182.

25.   Nancy Stern, p. 77.

26.   H. H. Goldstine, p. 196.

27.   J. P. Eckert and J. W. Mauchly, p. 48.

28.   J. von Neumann to H. P. Luhn, May 20, 1953.

29.   Nancy Stern, p. 60.

30.   J. Presper Eckert, "Thoughts on the History of Computing," *Computer* (December 1976): p. 58.

31.   J. Rajchman, "The Selective Electrostatic Storage Tube," *RCA Review* (March 1951): pp. 53-97; J. P. Eckert, Jr., "A Survey of Digital Computer Memory Systems," *Proceedings of the Institute of Radio Engineers* (October 1953): pp. 1393-1406.

32.   H. H. Goldstine, p. 312.

33.   Nancy Stern, p. 91.

34.   H. H. Goldstine, p. 317.

35.   Nancy Stern, p. 142.

36.   E. Tomash and A. A. Cohen, "The Birth of an ERA: Engineering Research Associates, Inc. 1946-1955," *Annals of the History of Computing* 1 (1979): pp. 83-97.

37.   J. W. Lacey of CDC to W. W. Jackson, May 22, 1969.

38.   S. M. Rubens interview by E. W. Pugh, May 30, 1980.

39.   Belden and Belden, pp. 218-243.

40. B. E. Phelps, "Early Electronic Computer Development at IBM," *Annals of the History of Computing* 2 (1980): pp. 253-267.

41. J. W. Birkenstock interview by E. W. Pugh, May 25, 1982.

42. C. C. Hurd, "Computer Development at IBM," International Research Conference on the History of Computing, June 10-15, 1976; C. C. Hurd interview by E. W. Pugh, September 23, 1982; *Business Machines*, November 28, 1949.

43. W. W. McDowell interview by L. Saphire, November 11, 1970.

44. J. C. McPherson to W. W. McDowell, "Retainer and License Agreement IBM and John von Neumann," August 1, 1952; J. C. McPherson to Dr. von Neumann, October 5, 1951.

45. J. C. McPherson, "IBM Engineering Program," March 28, 1950; Minutes of Engineering and Development Meeting of April 3, 1950.

46. R. L. Palmer interview by L. Saphire, July 25, 1967.

47. According to Palmer in his interview with L. Saphire on July 25, 1967, Howard T. Engstrom, cofounder of ERA, was largely responsible for pushing high-technology at the Dayton laboratory.

48. J. W. Gibson interview by E. W. Pugh, August 3, 1981.

49. B. E. Phelps interview by L. Saphire, October 12, 1967.

50. J. A. Haddad interview by C. J. Bashe, March 30, 1981.

51. R. L. Palmer, "Pluggable Support for Electron Tube and Circuit," U.S. Patent 2,637,763 (filed July 9, 1948).

52. J. C. McPherson and W. J. Eckert letter to T. J. Watson, Sr., November 12, 1946.

53. J. C. McPherson to W. W. McDowell, November 21, 1946.

54. P. E. Fox interview by L. Saphire, October 6, 1967.

55. S. W. Dunwell, "Electronic Tape Program," TR01.040.17, November 8, 1949.

56.   N. Rochester to file, "Test Assembly," August 20, 1973; W. Buchholz, "C-R Tube Storage for the Data Processing Automatic Test Assembly, Part I," December 29, 1949.

57.   N. Rochester interview by L. Saphire, October 3, 1967.

58.   J. W. Birkenstock, "Preliminary Planning for the 701," *Annals of the History of Computing* 5 (1983): pp. 112-114.

59.   J. W. Birkenstock interview by L. Saphire, November 1, 1967.

60.   H. H. Goldstine, pp. 329-330.

61.   Two other machines were announced by February 1953 with electrostatic storage tube memory and magnetic drum storage: the Ferranti machine and the TC-1 of International Telemeter Corporation. For various reasons these machines were not viewed as serious competitive threats as discussed in a memorandum from C. C. Hurd to J. W. Birkenstock et al., February 23, 1953.

Chapter 2

1.   J. C. McPherson and W. J. Eckert to Mr. Thomas J. Watson, November 12, 1946.

2.   J. C. McPherson to W. W. McDowell, "Electronic Developments," November 21, 1946.

3.   A. W. Burks, H. H. Goldstine, and J. von Neumann, "Preliminary Discussion of the Logical Design of an Electronic Computing Instrument," report to U.S. Army Ordnance Department (1946), in *Computer Structures: Readings and Examples*, by G. Bell and A. Newell (New York: McGraw-Hill 1971).

4.   P. E. Fox interview by L. Saphire, October 6, 1967.

5.   IBM did develop a magnetic drum memory for use on its highly-popular, low-cost Type 650 computer which was announced in Juy 1953.

6.   F. C. Williams and T. Kilburn, "A Storage System for Use with Binary Digital Computing Machines," *Proceedings of the Institute of Electrical Engineers*, Part III, 96 (March 1949): pp. 81-100; "The University of Manchester Computing Machine," *Proceedings of the Joint American Institute of Electrical Engineers and Institute of Radio Engineers Computer Conference*, December

10-12, 1951, pp. 57-61; J. P. Eckert, "A Survey of Digital Computer Memory Systems," *Proceedings of the Institute of Radio Engineers* 41 (October 1953): pp. 1393-1406.

7. H. H. Goldstine, *The Computer from Pascal to von Neumann* (Princeton: Princeton University Press, 1972); and private communication with J. H. Pomerene, February 1983.

8. A. L. Samuel interview by L. Saphire, December 15, 1967.

9. J. C. McPherson to J. G. Phillips, T. J. Watson, Jr., A. L. Williams, D. L. Bibby, W. L. Lewis, and W. W. McDowell, April 5, 1950; J. C. McPherson memorandum for discussion on "IBM Engineering Program," March 28, 1950; Conclusions of the Engineering and Development Meeting of April 3, 1950.

10. A. Wang and W. D. Woo, "Static Magnetic Storage and Delay Line," *Journal of Applied Physics* 21 (1950): pp. 49-54; An Wang, "Magnetic Delay-Line Storage," *Proceedings of the Institute of Radio Engineers* (April 1951): pp. 401-7; and A. Wang, "Pulse Transfer Controlling Devices," U.S. Patent 2,708,722 (filed October 21, 1949).

11. S. M. Rubens interview by E. W. Pugh, May 13, 14, 30, 1980.

12. M. K. Haynes interview by L. Saphire, September 15, 1967.

13. M. K. Haynes, "Magnetic Cores as Elements of Digital Computing Systems," Ph.D. Thesis: University of Illinois and Technical Report to the Office of Naval Research (ONR NR 048 094), August 28, 1950: pp. 24-27.

14. M. K. Haynes to A. L. Samuel, April 3, 1950.

15. R. E. Meagher interview by E. W. Pugh, January 28, 1982. The dean of the University of Illinois College of Engineering was Louis Ridenour who had previously worked on radar at the MIT Radiation Laboratory.

16. J. B. Clark to D. W. Rubridge, "Dr. Haynes' Early Experiments with Magnetic Cores," March 6, 1961.

17. R. L. Palmer, N. Rochester, and A. L. Samuel, "A Symposium on Large-Scale Digital Calculating Machinery—A Trip Report," September 29, 1949.

18. A. L. Samuel to M. K. Haynes, April 12, 1950.

19. J. H. Fraser to M. K. Haynes, May 1, 1950.

20. J. W. Forrester, "Digital Information Storage in Three Dimensions Using Magnetic Cores," *Journal of Applied Physics* 22 (1951): pp. 44-48; Project Whirlwind Report R-187, May 16, 1950.

21. R. L. Palmer interview by L. Saphire, October 10, 1967, p. 62.

22. R. G. Counihan, interview by E. W. Pugh, May 1, 1981.

23. R. G. Counihan, "Static Magnetic Volume Storage," September 9, 1951.

24. R. G. Counihan interview by E. W. Pugh, May 27, 1981, and Engineering Note Book 816, July 1951 to August 1952.

25. R. G. Counihan, M. K. Haynes, and G. E. Whitney, "Multimensional Magnetic Memory System," U.S. Patent 2,740,949 (filed August 25, 1953); M. K. Haynes, "Multidimensional Magnetic Memory Selection Systems," *Institute of Radio Engineers Transactions on Electronic Computers* 1 (December 1952): pp. 25-32.

26. E. J. Rabenda interview by L. Saphire, August 7, 1969.

27. E. J. Rabenda interview by E. W. Pugh, June 9, 1981; E. J. Rabenda and G. E. Whitney, "Intermediate Magnetic Core Storage," U.S. Patent 2,750,580 (filed January 2, 1953).

28. W. Buchholz, M. K. Haynes, and G. E. Whitney, "Magnetic Core Buffer Storage and Conversion System," U.S. Patent 2,931,014 (filed July 14, 1954).

29. E. J. Rabenda, "Response to a Request for Personal IBM History," March 1981.

30. P. W. Jackson interview by E. W. Pugh, October 7, 1981; C. J. Bashe, R. W. Murphy, and H. A. Mussell, Work Order 2-4087, 1953.

31. P. W. Jackson interview by C. J. Bashe, June 31, 1981.

32. Erich Bloch interview by E. W. Pugh, September 30, 1981, April 14, 1982.

33. M. K. Haynes interview by E. W. Pugh, April 27, 1982.

34. Erich Bloch interview by L. Saphire, October 2, 1968.

35.   M. K. Haynes to C. L. Snyder, vice president of General
       Ceramics, March 26, 1952.

36.   R. B. Arndt, interview by E. W. Pugh October 6, November 3,
       1981, recalls using 60-90 mil cores supplied to ERA by General
       Ceramics for his early experimental work. As discussed in
       Chapter 3, the first $32 \times 32 \times 17$ bit array placed on the MTC at
       MIT had 60-90 mil cores.

37.   M. K. Haynes to J. W. Birkenstock, "Early Magnetics Work at
       IBM," February 27, 1962.

38.   O. M. Scott, "IBM 774 Tape Data Selector" announcement,
       November 17, 1955; E. J. Rabenda, "Data Selector," U.S.
       Patent 3,040,300 (filed March 25, 1957).

39.   "T. J. Watson, Jr., Describes New Fellows' Achievements,"
       IBM News, June 26, 1967.

Chapter 3

1.   J. W. Forrester, "Digital Information Storage in Three
       Dimensions Using Magnetic Cores," *Journal of Applied Physics*
       22 (1951): pp. 44-48; Project Whirlwind Report R-187, May
       16, 1950.

2.   J. W. Forrester to Servomechanisms Laboratory staff members
       (M-70), "Data Storage in Three Dimensions," April 29, 1947
       (*).

3.   K. C. Redmond and T. M. Smith, *Project Whirlwind—the
       History of a Pioneer Computer* (Bedford, Mass.: Digital Press
       1980): p. 135.

4.   Redmond and Smith, pp. 33-44.

5.   Redmond and Smith, pp. 14-28.

6.   J. W. Forrester, private communication, June 13, 1983.

7.   J. W. Forrester to Engineers of Project 6345, "Conference Held
       at Naval Research Laboratories to Discuss Storage Tubes,"
       February 6, 1946(*).

8.   J. W. Forrester, Report (R-110), "Electrostatic Storage Tubes,"
       January 13, 1947(*).

9   R. F. Markel, "Gas-Discharge Gaps for Data Storage in Electronic Computers," (Master's thesis, MIT, January 16, 1948)(*).

10. Redmond and Smith, pp. 105-108.

11. Redmond and Smith, pp. 62-82.

12. Redmond and Smith, pp. 173-176.

13. Redmond and Smith, p. 183.

14. J. W. Forrester, MIT Computation Notebook, no. 47: pp. 15-27 (*).

15. W. N. Papian, Testimony before the Examiner of Interferences, March 8, 1960.

16. W. N. Papian interview by E. W. Pugh, June 18, 30, 1982.

17. W. N. Papian, Master's Thesis Proposal, (MIT, January 24, 1950)(*).

18. W. N. Papian, "Ferromagnetic Materials for Applications Requiring Rectangular Hysteresis Loops and Short Response Times," for MIT Course 6.501-2, January 1950(*).

19. W. N. Papian, Engineering Notebook, 1950: pp. 77, 84. (*)

20. Bi-Weekly Report (M-1112), Project 6345 (Whirlwind), October 13, 1950(*).

21. W. N. Papian, "Preliminary Tests on the Four-Core Magnetic Memory Array," June 18, 1951.

22. Brief for Rajchman on Final Hearing on Interference No. 88,269 on Jay W. Forrester vs. Jan A. Rajchman, September 1960.

23. Redmond and Smith, pp. 192-197. MEW is referred to as Missile Early Warning by Redmond and Smith, however, it is defined as prototype Microwave Early-Warning pulsed radar in the Servomechanisms Laboratory Summary Report 7, submitted to the Air Force Cambridge Research Laboratory (AFCRL), July 25-October 25, 1950.

24. Bi-Weekly Report (M-1357), Digital Computer Laboratory, December 21, 1951(*).

25. Bi-Weekly Report (M-1484), Digital Computer Laboratory, May 9, 1952(*).

26. Group Leaders Meeting (L-46), Digital Computer Laboratory, June 11, 1952(*).

27. J. C. McPherson to J. R. Shipman, July 17, 1952; C. P. Boberg, "Some Historical Notes" (about 1960).

28. N. P. Edwards interview by E. W. Pugh, November 2, 1981.

29. Quarterly Progress Report, Division 6, June 1, 1952 (*).

30. Digital Computer Laboratory Personnel (M-1636), September 15, 1952(*).

31   K. H. Olsen, "A Magnetic Matrix Switch and its Incorporation into a Coincident-Current Memory" (master's thesis, MIT, May 5, 1952) (*).

32. M. C. Andrews interview by E. W. Pugh, June 8, 1981.

33. Quarterly Progress Report, Division 6, Digital Computer, September 15, 1952(*).

34. Quarterly Progress Report, Division 6, Digital Computer, June 15, 1953(*).

35. Division 6 Bi-Weekly Report (M-2362), August 14, 1953(*).

36. Division 6 Bi-Weekly Report (M-2405), September 11, 1953(*).

37. J. A. Rajchman interview by E. W. Pugh, February 12, 1981.

38. J. A. Rajchman, "Computing System," U.S. Pat 2,473,444 (filed Februray 29, 1944).

39. J. A. Rajchman, "Magnetic Device," U.S. Pat 3,164,813 (filed September 30, 1950).

40. J. W. Forrester, "Multicoordinate Digital Information Storage Device," U.S. Pat 2,736,880 (filed May 11, 1951).

41. Raymond Guy to J. A. Rajchman, October 18, 1950(*).

42. W. N. Papian to Dr. Rajchman, May 14, 1951(*).

43. J. W. Forrester interview by E. W. Pugh, September 16, 1982.

44. J. A. Rajchman, "Program of Research for 1952," February 20, 1952.(*)

45. J. A. Rajchman, "A Myriabit Magnetic-Core Matrix Memory," *Proceedings of the Institute of Radio Engineers* (October 1953): pp. 1407-1421.

46. Final Hearing, Patent Interference No. 88,269, October 18, 1960, p. 12.

47. Brief for Rajchman, p. 2.

48. Brief for Rajchman, p. 27.

49. C. P. Boberg to H. T. Marcy, "Present Status of Forrester Patent No. 2,736,880," May 22, 1961. Counts 1, 2, 3, 6, 7, 8, 9, 12, 13, and 14 were awarded to Rajchman, and 4 and 5 were awarded to Forrester.

50. E. Gershuny private communication, May 13, 1982; C. McTierman to all patent managers, September 17, 1957.

51. K. J. Sixtus, "Magnetic Reversal Nuclei," *Physical Review* 48 (1935): pp. 425-430.

52. R. E. Lawhead, "Conference to Set Up General Specifications for Our Next Large Scale Calculator at IBM Watson Laboratory," June 1-2, 1948.

53. L. H. Thomas, private communication, fall 1981.

54. A. Wang interview by E. W. Pugh, May 21, 1982.

55. W. D. Gardner, "An Wang's Early Work in Core Memories," *Datamation* (March 1976).

56. F. W. Viehe, "Electronic Relay Circuit," U.S. Patent (filed May 29, 1947).

57. F. Chadurjian, private communication, May 17, 1982.

58. "Progress Report on the EDVAC (Electronic Discrete Variable Computer)," University of Pennsylvania, Moore School of Electrical Engineering, June 30, 1946, pp. 4-22, vol. II.

59. J. Presper Eckert interview by E. W. Pugh, June 9, 1981; J. A. Rajchman, "Static Magnetic Matrix Memory and Switching Circuits," *National Convention of the Institute of Radio Engineers*, March 15, 1952.

60.   R. L. Snyder interview by E. W. Pugh, May 11, 15, 1981.

61.   A 100 word by 41 bit memory of this type was developed at
       Burroughs and installed on ENIAC in mid-1953.   I. L.
       Auerbach, "A Static Magnetic Memory System for the ENIAC,"
       Proceedings of the Association for Computing Machinery, May
       2-3, 1952; *Digital Computer Newsletter* (April 1953, October
       1953).

62.   H. Billing, "On the Development of Digital Memories," in
       Digital Memory and Storage ed. Walter E. Proebster (Germany:
       Vieweg and Shon; Philidelphia: Heyden 1978).

63.   R. B. Arndt interview by E. W. Pugh, October 6, 1981.

64.   Tentative List of Invited Participants to "A Symposium on
       Magnetic Cores—Their Application, Fabrication, Testing, and
       Handling," September 10-13, 1953(*).

Chapter 4

1.   J. C. McPherson interview by E. W. Pugh, June 11, 1982.

2.   J. W. Birkenstock interview by E. W. Pugh, May 25, 1982.

3.   J. W. Forrester to Dr. A. G. Hill, "Selection of a Company to
       Work with the Lincoln Laboratory on the Transition System,"
       May 12, 1953(*).

4.   D. R. Brown, "Group Leader's Meeting, Sept. 29, 1952,"
       September 30, 1952(*).

5.   A. P. Kromer, "Engineering Relationships with IBM,"
       September 30, 1952(*).

6.   M. M. Astrahan and J. F. Jacobs, "History of the Design of the
       SAGE Computer—the AN/FSQ-7," IBM Research Report
       RJ3117, April 10, 1981.

7.   J. F. Schuehler public relations release, IBM Kingston, June
       1958.

8.   A. P. Kromer, "Summary of IBM-MIT Collaboration" (**):

       (a) December 3, 1952   (d) March 9, 1953
       (b) January 5, 1953   (e) April 3, 1953
       (c) February 3, 1953   (f) April 30, 1953

(g) June 8, 1953
(h) July 3, 1953
(i) August 26, 1953
(j) September 11, 1953
(k) October 13, 1953
(l) November 9, 1953
(m) December 7, 1953
(n) January 8, 1954

(o) February 9, 1954
(p) March 8, 1954
(q) April 8, 1954
(r) May 8, 1954
(s) June 24, 1954
(t) July 13, 1954
(u) September 9, 1954.

9.   Project High Biweekly Report, October 19-30, 1953.

10.   N. P. Edwards interview by L. Saphire, October 16, 1967.

11.   D. J. Crawford to file, "Notes Concerning the History of Core Memory," May 14, 1962.

12.   Project High Biweekly Report, March 1-12, 1954.

13.   W. M. Wittenberg interview by E. W. Pugh, May 14, 1981.

14.   N. P. Edwards interview by E. W. Pugh, June 12, 1981.

15.   J. W. Forrester to AN/FSQ-7 Engineers, "Planning, Scheduling and Administering the AN/FSQ-7 Program," July 15, 1953(**).

16.   C. W. Watt and B. B. Paine to N. H. Taylor, "Visit to IBM, Poughkeepsie, New York," December 3, 1952.

17.   Project High Biweekly Report, ending February 27, 1953. Others contributing to the solution of the vacuum tube driver problem were Haddad, Fox, and Haynes of IBM and Brown, Papian, Olsen, and Taylor of MIT.

18.   Project High Biweekly Report, March 8-20, 1953.

19.   Project High Biweekly Report, March 23-April 3, 1953.

20.   K. H. Olsen to N. H. Taylor, "A Linear Selection Magnetic Memory Using an Anti-Coincident Current Switch," May 8, 1953(**).

21.   A. P. Kromer to All Conferees, "Minutes of Joint MIT-IBM Conference Held at Hartford, Connecticut on January 20, 1953," January 26, 1953(**).

22.   A. P. Kromer and R. P. Mayer, "Project Grind Meeting of June 25, 1953 (Second Day)," June 29, 1953 (**).

23.   J. W. Forrester, Computation Notebook 47, June 1949, p. 26.

24.   J. W. Forrester, p. 26.

25.   M. K. Haynes, "Magnetic Memory System," U.S. Patent 2,881,414 (filed July 8, 1954).

26.   W. Wittenberg and J. MacDonald (H-40), "XD-1 Memory Cycle," September 11, 1953.

27.   Quarterly Progress Report, Division 6, Digital Computer, December 15, 1953, p. 61.

28.   W. M. Wittenberg private communication, June 1, 1981, September 28, 1982.

29.   A. P. Kromer to J. W. Forrester, June 9, 1953.

30.   Quarterly Progress Report, Division 6, Digital Computer, June 15, 1953(*).

31.   Biweekly Report, Division 6, July 31, 1953(*).

32.   Quarterly Progress Report, Division 6, Digital Computer, September 15, 1953(*).

33.   Quarterly Progress Report, Division 6, Digital Computer, March 15, 1954(*).

34.   Quarterly Progress Report, Division 6, Digital Computer, June 15, 1954(*).

35.   M. K. Haynes to C. L. Snyder, March 26, 1952.

36.   Quarterly Progress Report, Division 6, Digital Computer, September 15, 1952.

37.   E. Albers-Schönberg, "Square Loop Ferrite," U.S. Patent 2,981,689 (filed July 12, 1954).

38.   J. Rajchman interview by E. W. Pugh, February 12, 1981.

39.   J. W. Forrester to G. R. Solomon of IBM, May 21, 1953.

40.   J. W. Forrester to T. A. Burke, June 30, 1953(**).

41.   J. H. McCusker to D. R. Brown, "Testing Cores for WWII," March 30, 1953(**).

42.   A. P. Kromer and P. J. Gray, Biweekly Progress Report for AN/FSQ-7 (XD-1), July 24, 1953 (**).

43.   Project High Biweekly Report, September 8-18, 1953.

44.   R. R. Blessing to W. M. Wittenberg, "Test of RCA Ferrite Cores at RCA, Camden," October 27, 1953(*).

45.   Biweekly Progress Report for AN/FSQ-7 (XD-1), August 7, 1953(**).

46.   Group Leaders' Meeting, Division 6 (L-129), December 7, 1953(*).

47.   J. W. Crowe interview by E. W. Pugh, September 2, 1981. Crowe, in the electronics group, was responsible for design of the probe and John McGregor was the mey designer of the handler in Tool Engineering. Crowe later invented the cryogenic "Crowe Cell," which is mentioned in Chapter 8.

48.   Project High Biweekly Report, April 6-17, 1953.

49.   D. R. Brown to James Montgomery of IBM, September 11, 1953(*); D. R. Brown to J. W. Forrester, "Joint MIT-IBM Meeting on Memory-Core Measurement," October 13, 1953(**).

50.   Project High Biweekly Report, November 16-27, 1953.

51.   Project High Biweekly Progress Report, July 5-16, 1954.

52.   E. W. Pugh, D. L. Critchlow, R. A. Henle, and L. A. Russell, "Solid-State Memory Development in IBM," *IBM Journal of Research and Development* (September 1981): pp. 585-602.

53.   R. W. Link interview by E. W. Pugh, July 31, 1981.

54.   Group Leaders' Meeting, Division 6, October 13, 1953(*).

55.   Group Leaders' Meeting, Division 6, February 2, 1954(*).

56.   Group Leaders' Meeting, Division 6, May 10, 1954(*).

57.   Section Leaders' Meeting, Group 62, June 7, 1954(*).

58.   Quarterly Progress Report, Division 6, Digital Computer, September 15, 1954(*).

59. J. W. Forrester to J. M. Coombs and R. P. Crago, April 9, 1954; W. N. Papian and W. M. Wittenberg, "Performance Specifications for the AN/FSQ-7 Memory Element," April 9, 1954(*).

60. N. P. Edwards, W. B. Strohm, and W. M. Wittenberg interview by E. W. Pugh, June 8, 1981.

61. Central Computer, Section 4.0, Extract from Engineering Progress Report AN/FSQ-7, May 7, 1954.

62. N. P. Edwards interview by E. W. Pugh, April 23, 1982.

63. W. Wittenberg and J. MacDonald (H-40), "XD-1 Memory Cycle," September 11, 1953.(*).

64. D. C. Ross of the IBM Duplex Planning Group, (IM-97), "Memory Element for the AN/FSQ-7 Production System," July 12, 1954(**).

65. Quarterly Progress Report, Division 6, Digital Computer, December 15, 1954(*).

66. Digital Computer News Letter of Office of the Naval Research, undated.

67. R. B. Arndt, interview by E. W. Pugh, October 6, November 3, 1981.

68. D. J. Crawford to file, "Development of Ferrite Cores for Memory Purposes by IBM," May 14, 1962.

69. A. H. Eschenfelder interview by E. W. Pugh, April 5, 1982.

70. M. C. Andrews interview by E. W. Pugh, June 8, 1981.

71. Group Leaders' Meeting, Division 6, (L-87), March 16, 1953(*).

72. Group Leaders' Meeting (L-97), May 18, 1953(*).

73. J. B. Little interview by E. W. Pugh, July 31, 1981.

74. J. W. Gibson interview by E. W. Pugh, August 3, 1981.

75. J. M. Brownlow interview by E. W. Pugh, July 27, 1981. Frank Vinal was responsible for core fabrication at MIT and was the person who described the fabrication process to Brownlow and Gibson.

76.   J. W. Gibson and K. A. Lundberg, "Method of Making Ferrite Structures," U.S. Patent 2,842,500 (filed January 23, 1956).

77.   Project High Biweekly Progress Report, July 19-August 20, 1954.

78.   Group Leaders' Meeting (L-159), Division 6, July 19, 1954(*).

79.   J. W. Forrester to C. F. McElwain, April 18, 1954(*).

80.   *Poughkeepsie IBM News*, May 22, 1954.

81.   E F. Brosseau interview by E. W. Pugh, June 6, 1980, January 19, 1982.

82.   Project High Semi-monthly Report, January 16-31, 1956; *IBM Laboratory News*, Kingston, N.Y., June 12, 1974.

83.   N. P. Edwards, SAGE summary 1964; "The SAGE Computer," brochure issued by the IBM Federal Systems Division; U.S.A.F. Electronic Systems Division, news release, September 1963.

84.   IBM Advanced Systems Sales Manual, Ground Based Data Processors, October 15, 1962; *IBM Kingston News*, October 9, 1957.

85   J. W. Forrester interview by E. W. Pugh, September 16, 1982.

86.   W. N. Papian interview by E. W. Pugh, June 30, 1982.

Chapter 5

1.   W. D. Winger interview by E. W. Pugh, October 15, 1981.

2.   P. W. Jackson interview by E. W. Pugh, October 7, 1981.

3.   E. W. Bauer interview by E. W. Pugh, October 6, 1981; E. W. Bauer Engineering Notebook No. 1373, December 1953 to February 1956.

4.   K. H. Olsen to N. H. Taylor, "A Linear Selection Magnetic Memory Using an Anti-Coincident Current Switch," May 8, 1953; K. H. Olsen, "Saturable Switch," U.S. Patent 2,937,285 (filed March 31, 1953); K. H. Olsen, "A Magnetic Matrix Switch and Its Incorporation into a Coincident-Current Memory," (Master's thesis, MIT, May 1952).

5. J. A. Rajchman, "Static Magnetic Matrix Memory and Switching Circuits" presented at the National Convention of the Institute of Radio Engineers, March 15, 1952; J. A. Rajchman, "A Myriabit Magnetic-Core Matrix Memory," *Proceedings of the Institute of Radio Engineers*, October 1953, pp. 1407-1421; J. A. Rajchman U.S. Patent 2,734,187 (issued 1955).

6. E. Bloch, "Switch Core Matrix," U.S. Patent 2,947,977 (filed June 11, 1956).

7. M. K. Haynes, "Magnetic Memory System," U.S. Patent 2,881,414 (filed July 8, 1954); M. K. Haynes interview by E. W. Pugh, November 2, 1981.

8. E. W. Bauer and M. K. Haynes, "Magnetic Memory System with Disturbance Cancellation," U.S. Patent 2,889,540 (filed July 14, 1954).

9. O. M. Scott, IBM product announcements No. 4667, October 1, 1954; no. 4863, June 24, 1955; no. 4864, June 24, 1955.

10. W. N. Papian interview by E. W. Pugh, June 18-30, 1982.

11. D. J. Crawford to file, "Notes Concerning the History of Core Memory," May 14, 1962.

12. Quarterly Progress Report, Division 6, Digital Computer, June 15, 1953.

13. Quarterly Progress Report, Division 6, Digital Computer, December 15, 1953(*).

14. W. J. Canty to J. F. Jacobs, "Evidence for Increased Reliability of WWI Magnetic Core Memory over WWI Electrostatic Memory," August 11, 1954(*).

15. J. A. Little to Dr. An Wang, August 1, 1951.

16. J. J. Isole interview by E. W. Pugh, April 22, 1982. Isole was responsible for manufacturing engineering of Williams tubes at this time.

17. R. S. Partridge, "Storage Specification and Cost Sheets," April 1974.

18. P. E. Fox interview by L. Saphire, October 6, 1967; R. S. Partridge interview by E. W. Pugh, August 4, 1983. Partridge notes that the barrier-grid tube was used in the File Maintenance Machine, later called the IBM 703 and then 770

when contracted to the National Security Agency. The 770, including the memory, was so reliable that it was kept in service about seven years.

19.   M. K. Haynes interview by E. W. Pugh, November 2, 1981.

20.   T. J. Watson, Jr., to R. L. Palmer, April 22, 1954.

21.   T. J. Watson, Jr., *A Business and Its Beliefs,* (New York: McGraw-Hill, 1963).

22.   T. V. Learson, personal history sheet, about 1973.

23.   D. J. Crawford to file, "History of Core Memory Development in IBM During the Period of 1954 to 1956," May 14, 1962.

24.   D. J. Crawford interview by E. W. Pugh, July 14, 1980.

25.   P. K. Spatz interview by E. W. Pugh, October 1, 1981.

26.   The three engineers were Edward Bauer, William Lawrence, and Robert Ward.

27.   D. J. Crawford to file, "Development of Ferrite Cores for Memory Purposes by IBM," May 14, 1962.

28.   IBM Product Announcements: IBM Type 704 Electronic Data Processing Machine (letter 4571), May 7, 1954; IBM Type 701-704 EDPM-Components (letter 4666), October 1, 1954; IBM Type 705 Electronic Data Processing Machine (letter 4667), October 1, 1954.

29.   IBM Customer Engineering Manual of Instruction, 702 Core Storage, not dated.

30.   R. E. Merwin, "The IBM 705 EDPM Memory System," *Institute of Radio Engineers Transaction on Electronic Computers* (December 1956): pp. 219-223.

31.   W. W. Lawrence, "Design and Operation of a Magnetic Matrix Switch Driver for a Large Core Memory," IBM Report 004.095,586 March 15, 1955.

32.   E. C. Schuenzel, "Ferrite Cores in IBM 1951 to 1963," February 27, 1959.

33.   T. J. Watson meeting (tape recorded) with J. J. Kenny, G. I. Basile, C. C. Hurd, R. L. Palmer, F. W. Gerken, O. M. Scott, J. W. Birkenstock, W. H. Johnson, J. J. Troy, and C. J. Bashe,

August 18, 1955. As revealed in note 18 of this chapter, the storage tubes were made more relaible than Watson's statements suggested, but there is little doubt that they could never have been as reliable as ferrite cores.

34.   L. R. Johnson interview by E. W. Pugh, July 15, 1982.

35.   J. Morrissey interview by E. W. Pugh, July 22, 1982.

36.   C. C. Hurd, "Computer Development at IBM," International Research Conference on the History of Computing, June 10-15, 1976.

37.   E. Bloch interview by E. W. Pugh, September 30, 1981.

38.   J. C. Logue interview by L. Saphire, March 30, 1970.

39.   George Bruce interview by E. W. Pugh (with his Engineering Notebook No. 1034 as reference), November 10, 1982.

40.   J. E. Tilton, *International Diffusion of Technology: The Case of Semiconductors* (Washington, D.C.: Brookings Institution, 1971).

41.   D. R. Brown to J. W. Forrester, "Trip to Bell Laboratories, Whippany," October 18, 1951(**).

42.   K. H. Olsen to Memory Section, "Transistor Circuits for Driving Coincident Current Memories," January 25, 1955(**).

43.   D. J. Crawford interview by E. W. Pugh, October 2, 1981.

44.   R. S. Partridge interview by E. W. Pugh, July 22, 1981, August 4, 1983.

45.   E. Foss and R. S. Partridge, "A 32,000 Word Magnetic-Core Memory," *IBM Journal of Research and Development* (April 1957): pp. 103-109.

46.   Quarterly Progress Report, Division 6, Digital Computer, December 15, 1954(*).

47.   J. L. Mitchell and K. H. Olsen, "TX-0, A Transistor Computer with a 256×256 Memory," *Proceedings of the Eastern Joint Computer Conference* 10 (December 1956): pp. 93-101.

48.   E. W. Bauer Engineering Notebook No. 1373, December 1953 to February 1956, p. 115.

49.   H. A. DiMarco interview by E. W. Pugh, January 25, 1982.

50.   E. C. Schuenzel interview by E. W. Pugh, June 9, 1981, June 25, 1980.

51.   E. Albers-Schönberg, "Square Loop Ferrites," U.S. Patent 2,981,689 (filed July 12, 1954).

52.   E. W. Pugh to file, "History of CuMn Ferrite Core Process Development and Two Related Patents," June 11, 1982.

53.   J. M. Brownlow, "Manganese-Zinc Ferrite Cores," U.S. Patent 2,987,481 (filed October 15, 1956).

54.   J. M. Brownlow interview by E. W. Pugh, July 27, 1981.

55.   J. W. Gibson interview by E. W. Pugh, August 3, 1981.

56.   IBM-Philips agreement, internal IBM document, June 19, 1957.

57.   Agreement between IBM and Philips, May 1, 1956.

58.   A. C. A. M. Bleyenberg, A. J. DeRooy, E. C. Schuenzel, R. W. Dam, and J. W. Gibson, "Method of Manufacturing a Magnetic Core for Use as a Memory Element," U.S. Patent 3,188,290 (filed May 27, 1959).

59.   H. A. DiMarco, "Ferrite Core History," October 12, 1967.

60.   R. W. Link and D. J. Crawford interview by E. W. Pugh, January 29, 1982.

61.   H. P. Luhn, "Method for Winding and Assembling Magnetic Cores," U.S. Patent 3,134,163 (filed November 21, 1955).

62.   L. V. Auletta, H. J. Hallstead, and D. J. Sullivan, "Ferrite Core Planes and Arrays: IBM's Manufacturing Evolution," *Institute of Electrical and Electronics Engineers Transactions on Magnetics* 5 (1969): pp. 764-774.

63.   R. W. Link interview by E. W. Pugh, July 31, 1981.

64.   W. P. Shaw interview by E. W. Pugh, February 2, 1982.

65.   W. P. Shaw and R. W. Link, "Method and Apparatus for Threading Perforated Articles," U.S. Patent 2,958,126, (1960); W. P. Shaw, "Wire Inserting Machine Mechanizer Core Plane Assembly," *Automation* 5 (1958): pp. 51-54.

66.   E. W. Pugh, D. L. Critchlow, R. A. Henle¯ and L. A. Russell, "Solid-State Memory Development in IBM," *IBM Journal of Research and Development* 25 (September 1981): pp. 585-602.

67.   W. P. Shaw and R. L. Judge, "Apparatus for Winding Wire around Terminals," U.S. Patent 2,963,051 (1960).

68.   R. L. Judge interview by E. W. Pugh, January 12, 1982.

69.   W. P. Shaw, "Capstan Wire Handler," U.S. Patent 3,156,969 (filed March 13, 1961).

Chapter 6

1.   S. W. Dunwell interview by L. Saphire, March 11, 1968, pp. 83-98.

2.   S. W. Dunwell and W. Buchholz, "Objectives of the Datatron Program," October 25, 1954.

3.   C. C. Hurd to file, "High Speed Data Processing Machines," January 21, 1955.

4.   Attendees at this meeting included T. V. Learson, W. W. McDowell, J. C. McPherson, J. A. Haddad, and C. C. Hurd.

5.   B. O. Evans interview by L. M. Saphire, October 9, 1968.

6.   First Monthly Progress Report (Philco No. H-2034), "Surface-Barrier Transistors for Digital Computers, January 15-February 25, 1955 (**).

7.   L. P. Hunter interview by E. W. Pugh, December 17, 1982.

8.   H. Krömer, "Zur Theories des Diffusions-und des Drift-Transistors," Parts I, II, and III, *Arch. Elecktr. Ubertrag* 8 (1954): pp. 223-228, 363-369, and 499-504.

9.   P. K. Spatz, "The Stretch Development Program," May 1, 1959.

10.   J. C. Logue interview by L. Saphire, March 30, 1970.

11.   G. M. Amdahl interview by L. Saphire, December 14, 1967.

12.   G. M. Amdahl rejoined IBM in 1960 and played a key role in the development of IBM System/360 before he left to form the Amdahl Corporation in 1970.

13. U. S. Atomic Energy Commission Contract No. AT(29-2)-476 with International Business Machines Corporation, November 20, 1956.

14. H. A. Faw to file, "Project Stretch," February 29, 1956.

15. D. J. Crawford interview by E. W. Pugh, July 13, 1981.

16. G. Constantine interview by E. W. Pugh, July 23, 1981.

17. R. S. Partridge interview by E. W. Pugh, July 22, 1981.

18. G. Constantine and L. B. Stallard, "Matrix Switch for a Transistor Driven, High-Speed, Core Memory," Project Silo Technical Memorandum 11, January 15, 1957.

19. G. Constantine, "A Load Sharing Matrix Switch," Project Silo Technical Memorandum STM-14, August 30, 1957.

20. G. Constantine, Jr., "A Load-Sharing Matrix Switch," *IBM Journal of Research and Development* 2 (1958): pp. 204-211.

21. J. A. Rajchman, "Static Magnetic Matrix Memory and Switching Circuits," *RCA Review* 13 (June 1953): p. 183.

22. E. D. Councill interview by E. W. Pugh, July 24, 1981.

23. E. D. Councill and J. H. Widmar, "Memory Cross-Section," Series 7000 Circuit Memo 27, August 30, 1957.

24. D. J. Crawford, "Memory Array Sensing," U.S. Patent 3,142,049 (filed August 25, 1961).

25. B. N. Slade, "Device Design Considerations," in *Handbook of Semiconductor Electronics*, 2d edition, ed. L. P. Hunter, (New York: McGraw-Hill, 1962).

26. E. W. Pugh, D. L. Critchlow, R. A. Henle, and L. A. Russell, "Solid State Memory Development in IBM," *IBM Journal of Research and Development* 25 (1981): pp. 585-602.

27. R. L. Judge, "Wire Threading Method and Apparatus," U.S. Patent 3,314,131 (filed April 29, 1964).

28. J. C. Logue, private communication, July 27, 1982.

29. G. R. Monroe, private communication, July 1982.

30.   Three engineers, reporting to E. D. Councill, were responsible for assembling and debugging the three engineering models on the factory floor: Philip Lincoln, Frederick Neves, and Edward Hee.

31.   C. A. Allen, G. W. Bruce, and E. D. Councill, "A 2.18-Microsecond Megabit Core Storage Unit," *Institute of Radio Engineers Transactions on Electronic Computers* EC-10 (1961): pp. 233-237; "Three-dimensional Core-storage Memory for Computers,"*Electronics*, May 12, 1961, p. 68.

32.   R. S. Partridge, "Storage Specification and Cost Sheets," April 1974.

33.   In September 1955 E. Bloch considered the use of three-hole cores in replacement memories for the IBM 704 computer: E. Bloch to file, "Experimental Data on the Design of a Large Scale Coincidence Flux Memory," September 2, 1955.

34.   L. P. Hunter and E. W. Bauer, "High Speed Coincident-Flux Magnetic Storage Principles," *Journal of Applied Physics* 27 (1956): pp. 1257-1261; IBM Technical Report 003.111.598 (February 28, 1956).

35.   The fast switching of three-hole cores was first demonstrated in August 1955: E. W. Bauer Engineering Notebook, August 6-9, 1955.

36.   Project Silo Final Report, Contract NOBrs 63472, October 30, 1957.

37.   E. D. Councill, "A Small High-Speed Memory Model," Series 7000 Circuit Memo 13, June 25, 1957.

38.   M. A. Every interview by E. W. Pugh, July 23, 1981, and by C. J. Bashe, June 3, 1981. Moe Every joined IBM in 1952 with a bachelor's degree in power engineering; an early assignment at IBM was designing logic for E. Rabenda's Type 774 Tape Data Selector.   The otherwise calm engineer was L. A. Russell, interview by E. W. Pugh, December 14, 1981.

39.   Notes on AEC Contract No. AT(29-2)-478, date unknown.

40.   M. A. Every replaced Victor Witt who became laboratory manager in San Jose with responsibility for developing magnetic disk files.

41.   W. H. Rhodes interview by E. W. Pugh, July 25, 1980, October 15, 1981.

42.   R. M. Whalen interview by E. W. Pugh, October 16, 1981. Whalen reported to L. A. Russell, head of the Advanced Technology Group, when the two core per bit memory was developed.

43.   C. J. Quartly, "A High Speed Ferrite Storage System," *Electronic Engineering* 31 (December 1959): pp. 756-758.

44.   The first two features had been incorporated in an MIT two core per bit memory of 64 words, 19 bits each, on the TX-2 computer. It had a read time of only 0.8 microsecond. Full switching instead of partial switching was employed, resulting in a full read-write cycle of 4 microseconds for the MIT memory. See R. L. Best, "Memory Units in the Lincoln TX-2," *Proceedings of the Western Joint Computer Conference*, February 1957, pp. 160-167. Using partial switching of the cores, the Mullard engineers expected to reduce substantially the time required to write information into the memory. Partial switching of cores to improve memory speed was first proposed by researchers at MIT in February 1959, about seven months before Whalen and Crawford visited Mullard, but the MIT group had apparently not proposed a specific memory design to use partial switching. See R. E. McMahon, "Impulse Switching of Ferrite," *Digest of Technical Papers, Solid State Circuit Conference*, February, 1959, pp. 16-17.

45.   W. H. Rhodes, L. A. Russell, F. E. Sakaley, and R. M. Whalen, "A 0.7-Microsecond Ferrite Core Memory," *IBM Journal of Research and Development* 5 (1961): pp. 174-181.

46.   *New York Times*, April 27, 1960.

47.   D. R. Wright, IBM press release, April 26, 1960.

48.   T. V. Learson to T. J. Watson, "STRETCH Orders," May 18, 1961; C. G. Francis, IBM News Release "C-E-I-R Cancells Stretch Orders; will convert 7090s to 7094s," April 13, 1961. The customers were Livermore, the British Atomic Energy Commission, the Bureau of Standards (Weather Bureau), Dahlgren, C-E-I-R (two machines later cancelled in favor of IBM 7094s), and the MITRE Corporation.

49.   T. J. Watson, Jr., to T. V. Learson, April 13, 1961.

50.   W. B. McWhirter to T. J. Watson, Jr., "STRETCH Project Evaluation," June 14, 1961; F. J. Cummiskey to W. B.

McWhirter, "STRETCH Project Evaluation—Review of Reports by Dr. R. E. Meagher and C. W. Adams," June 6, 1961.

51. "The Shrinking of STRETCH," *Datamation* (June 1961): p. 17; W. B. McWhirter to T. J. Watson, Jr., "STRETCH Program," April 18, 1961.

52. J. Barton to IBM communication personnel, April 11, 1963.

53. H. Lukoff, "Were Early Giant Computers a Success?" *Datamation* (April 1969): pp. 77-82.

54. E. K. Yasaki, "Fastest in Its Time," *Datamation* (January 1982): pp. 34-47. The SOLO computer, built by Philco using its surface-barrier transistors, shipped to NSA in 1958, and debugged during the following year, may be the first large all-transistor computer built, see S. S. Snyder, *Annals of the History of Computing* 2 (January 1980): pp. 60-70.

55. "CDC 6600 in Stretch Class," *Datamation* (May 1961): p. 13.

56. S. W. Dunwell to T. J. Watson, Jr., April 8, 1964.

57. T. J. Watson, Jr., to S. W. Dunwell, April 20, 1964.

58. T. J. Watson, Jr., to A. L. Williams, February 26, 1965.

59. T. J. Watson, Jr., Annual Awards Dinner, March 15, 1966.

Chapter 7

1. B. O. Evans interview by L. M. Saphire, May 17, 1968, pp. 18-32.

2. F. A. Underwood interview by L. M. Saphire, June 12, 1968; F. A. Underwood to J. J. Ingram "Stored-Program, Variable Word-Length, Core Storage Accounting Machine Proposal," August 12, 1957.

3. IBM Pretrial Brief in USA v. IBM, US District Court, Southern District of New York, January 15, 1975, p. 337.

4. G. E. Jones, "The IBM 7070 Data Processing System" (letter 258-85), September 2, 1958.

5. Two key engineers on the 70AB project were Frederick P. Brooks and Jerry Blaauw.

6. Y. P. Dawkins, "IBM 7080 Data Processing System" (260-1), January 18, 1960.

7. J. Fairclough interview by L. M. Saphire, February 15, 1968.

8. B. O. Evans interview by L. M. Saphire, May 17, 1968, pp. 41-50.

9. T. A. Wise, "IBM's $5,000,000,000 Gamble," *Fortune* (September 1966): pp. 118-228.

10. E. Bloch, testimony in USA v. IBM, Southern District Court, New York, N.Y., October 9, 1979, p. 33.

11. E. W. Pugh, "Report of Meetings to Consider Component Needs of IBM," October 29 and November 4, 1959.

12. B. O. Evans interview by L. M. Saphire, May 17, 1968, pp. 54-57.

13. F. P. Brooks joined IBM in 1956 immediately after completing his Ph.D. dissertation under Howard Aiken at Harvard.

14. "Discussion of the SPREAD Report," *Annals of the History of Computing* 5 (1983): pp. 27-44.

15. J. W. Haanstra, B. O. Evans, et al., "Final Report of SPREAD Task Group, December 28, 1961," *Annals of the History of Computing*, 5 (1983): pp. 4-26.

16. C. J. Bashe private communication, December 10, 1981.

17. The IBM Organization Directory of 1961 notes that the Corporate Management Committee was chaired by the Chairman of the Board (T. J. Watson) and that IBM's President (A. L. Williams) served as Vice Chairman. There were six other members: the director of research (E. R. Piore), the president of IBM World Trade (A. K. Watson), the group executive who headed the divisions with primary responsibility for developing System/360 (T. V. Learson), plus two other group executives and the head of the Corporate Staff.

18. J. E. Greene interview by E. W. Pugh, January 6, 1982.

19. M. V. Wilkes and J. B. Stringer, "Microprogramming and the Design of the Control Circuits in an Electronic Digital Computer," *Proceedings of the Cambridge Pholosophical Society* 49 (1953): p. 230; M. V. Wilkes, paper presented at the

Manchester University Computer Inaugural Conference, July 16-18, 1951.

20.   S. G. Tucker, "Microprogram Control for System/360," *IBM Systems Journal* 6 (1967): pp. 222-241.

21.   G. H. Mealy, "The Functional Structure of OS/360 — Introductory Survey," *IBM Systems Journal* 5 (1966): pp. 3-11.

22.   A. Peacock interview by E. W. Pugh, September 20, 1983; A. Proudman interview by E. W. Pugh, August 16, 1983; I. Jones interview by E. W. Pugh, September 12, 1983. Peacock worked for Charles Owens and then Matthew Taub at Hursley before he became manager of the systems work. Owens and Taub contributed many early ideas on control stores, and Douglas Rae was the design engineer. Microcoding of SCAMP to make it appear as a 704 computer to the user was done by Peacock with Ivor Jones, a member of his group. S. G. Tucker, interview by E. W. Pugh, September 13-15, 1982, says the term *emulator* was proposed by Larry Moss of IBM to describe the control store, hardware, and software feature that permitted the Model 65 to perform as a 7070. The term was later applied to the control-store feature (originally called a compatibility feature) that permitted the Model 30 to perform as a 1401 and was subsequently used to describe this type of feature in any computer.

23.   I. M. Nyman and R. P. Sell, "The Honeywell 200," *Datamation* (February 1964): p. 59.

24.   M. A. McCormack, T. T. Schausman, and K. K. Womack, "1401 Compatibility Feature on the IBM System/360, Model 30" *Communications of the ACM* 8 (December 1965): pp. 773-776.

25.   J. W. Haanstra to G. F. Kennard, "1401S Versus 101 Read-Only Memory," December 27, 1963.

26.   H. F. Walsh, "SLT Processors Internal Performance Targets," January 31, 1962.

27.   R. B. Ormes, flip charts for the first SLT review, July 10, 1962.

28.   G. F. Kennard briefing for T. J. Watson, Jr., May 8, 1963.

29.   B. O. Evans to G. F. Kennard, September 23, 1963.

30.   J. A. Haddad to A. H. Eschenfelder et al., "Security," February 10, 1964.

31.   G. F. Kennard to W. C. Hume, "NPL Announcement," January 6, 1964.

32.   R. C. Warren, "IBM System/360 Product Announcement," (264-26), April 7, 1964.

33.   This was Basic Programming System (BPS) and Basic Operating System (BOS). The popular Disk Operating System (DOS) was announced later.

34.   W. J. Lynn to P. W. Knaplund, "Systems/360 Programming," September 8, 1964.

35.   B. Reisman, "Programming Report—Number 2," February 9, 1966.

36.   F. P. Brooks, *The Mythical Man-month: Essays on Software Engineering*, (Reading, Mass.: Addison-Wesley, 1975).

37.   J. W. Hinkley to P. N. Whittaker, March 12, 1956.

38.   R. S. Seymour to file, "Meeting of January 23, 1961," January 23, 1961.

39.   T. J. Watson, Jr., to J. W. Birkenstock, "Forrester Patent," May 19, 1960.

40.   W. C. Doud to A. L. Williams, October 31, 1963.

41.   J. H. Grady, Excerpts of Board of Director's Meeting of May 22, 1962; J. W. Birkenstock to D. R. McKay, July 6, 1962.

42.   J. A. Stratton, President of MIT, to J. W. Hinkley, President of Research Corporation, December 26, 1962.

43.   M. L. Wood to P. N. Whittaker, "Forrester Patent 2,736,880 issued 2/28/56, assigned to Research Corporation," October 11, 1957.

44.   P. N. Whittaker to M. L. Wood, "Forrester Patent No. 2,736,880," January 14, 1958.

45.   C. E. McTiernan, "Summary of Meeting between Representatives of IBM and Research Corp. on 11-19-59," November 24, 1959.

46.   M. L. Wood to file, " Forrester," July 20, 1959.

47.   M. L. Wood, "Summary of Forrester Calculations," August 20, 1959.

48.   G. R. Williamson to J. M. Birkenstock, "Forrester," April 20, 1960.

49.   J. W. Birkenstock to T. J. Watson, Jr., and A. L. Williams, "Forrester Patent," June 18, 1962.

50.   G. R. Williamson to file, "Meeting of Representatives of IBM and Research Corporation to Discuss the Forrester Patent on 11-30-59," December 1, 1959; G. R. Williamson to J. W. Birkenstock, "Forrester Avoidance Program," December 21, 1959.

51.   G. R. Williamson to file, "Forrester Patent," February 19, 1960.

52.   J. W. Birkenstock to T. J. Watson, Jr., "Forrester Patent," April 24, 1961.

53.   J. W. Birkenstock to A. L. Williams, "Forrester Patent License Negotiation," February 23, 1962.

54.   J. W. Birkenstock to T. J. Watson, Jr., "MIT," February 19, 1962.

55.   J. W. Hinkley to A. L. Williams, July 11, 1962; A. L. Williams to J. W. Hinkley, July 18, 1962.

56.   J. W. Hinkley to A. L. Williams, July 25, 1962; W. C. Doud to A. L. Williams, "Research Corporation Suit," August 24, 1962.

57.   M. L. Bullock to file, "MIT Visit, August 14, 1962," August 22, 1962.

58.   W. C. Doud to T. J. Watson, Jr., and A. L. Williams, "Forrester Patent, Research Corporation vs. IBM," April 5, 1963.

59.   Internal IBM memorandum, "Offer Made by Messrs. Watson and Williams on October 31, 1963 to MIT," December 24, 1963.

60.   A. L. Williams to J. W. Birkenstock et al., "Meeting Today with Doctors Killian and Floe," January 30, 1964.

61. A. L. Williams to J. R. Killian, February 26, 1964.

62. Patent license agreement between RCA and MIT, March 25, 1964.

63. A. L. Williams to J. A. Stratton, May 1, 1964.

64. "IBM's Research and Engineering Expenses for Commercial Cores and Core Memories," September, 1963.

Chapter 8

1. R. S. Partridge to E. W. Pugh, "Ferrite Core Production in IBM," May 19, 1981; R. W. Cobb, "IBM Core Usage," May 1, 1967.

2. E. C. Schuenzel to B. N. Slade, "1962 Achievement Summary," January 29, 1963.

3. R. S. Partridge, "Storage Specification and Costs," April 1974.

4. R. S. Partridge, "IBM Core Memories Shipped," 1975.

5. E. W. Pugh, "The IBM Magnetic Film Memory Development Effort," March 1981, p. 83.

6. R. E. Dehais, "A Decade of Memory 1960-1969," March 1972.

7. R. E. Elfant interview by E. W. Pugh, December 4-5, 1980. In 1967 Elfant was named the outstanding young electrical engineer in the country by the prestigeous engineering society, Eta Kappa Nu; but in 1963 he was just an inexperienced young engineer, buffeted by the pressures of a newly structured, rapidly growing organization in which rapid progress was expected.

8. E. W. Pugh, pp. 153-165.

9. J. W. Crowe interview by E. W. Pugh, September 15, 1982; D. A. Buck, "The Cryotron—A Superconductive Computer Component," *Proceedings of the Institute of Radio Engineers* 44 (1956): p. 482; J. W. Crowe, "Trapped-flux Superconducting Memory," *IBM Journal of Research and Development* 1 (1957): pp. 295-303; J. W. Crowe, "Superconductive Devices," U.S. Patent 3,271,585 (filed August 27, 1957).

10. E. W. Pugh, pp. 55-71.

11.   E. W. Pugh, pp. 95-118.

12.   J. C. Sagnis, Jr., P. E. Stuckert, and R. L. Ward, "The Chain
       Magnetic Memory Element," *IBM Journal of Research and
       Development* 9 (1965): pp: 412-417.

13.   G. S. Burgess, "Read-only Memory Systems," IBM TR 12-036,
       April 16, 1962.

14.   D. M. Taub and B. W. Kingston, "The Design of Transformer
       (Diamond Ring) Read-only Stores," *IBM Journal of Research
       and Development* (September 1964): p. 443.

15.   W. A. Warwick to N. A. Killgren (UK Pat. Dept.) "Proposed
       Transformer Read Only Memory," April 12, 1962.

16.   J. E. Greene cable to J. W. Fairclough, October 17, 1963,
       Engineering Justification for Use of CCROM in the 101,
       November 26, 1963.

17.   P. A. Lord interview by E. W. Pugh, September 16, 1982.
       Lord worked with Haskell before being transferred to Hursley to
       continue work on CCROS. He alerted the Endicott group to
       the problems in Hursley, causing them to initiate a product
       development effort in Endicott under Carl D. Southard.

18.   J. W. Haskell, "Design of a Printed Card Capacitor Read-only
       Store," *IBM Journal of Research and Development* 10 (March
       1966): p. 142.

19.   J. Fairclough, to D. E. Slattery, "Use of CCROM in the 101
       System," December 6, 1963.

20.   C. J. Bashe to H. T. Marcy, "Possibility of Using CCROM
       Instead of TROM in NPL Systems," December 9, 1963; F. M.
       Trapnell to H. T. Marcy, "CCROM for 101," December 2,
       1963.

21.   D. B. Havens to Frizzell and H. T. Marcy, October 6, 1964;
       TROS Product Highlight Report, September 1964.

22.   E. Brosseau interview by E. W. Pugh, January 19, 1982.

23.   J. E. Greene interview by E. W. Pugh, January 6, 1982.

24.   Stuart G. Tucker served briefly as the first manager of the
       Model 65 (then called the 400) computer project before being
       replaced by a sequence of managers ending with J. L. Brown.
       In January 1963 F. P. Brooks agreed to use conventional

controls on the 400 machine as recommended by Tucker in September 1962. Late in 1963 Brown took over the project and made the shift to control store. He also asked Tucker to work on the conversion problem; see note 22 of Chapter 7. S. G. Tucker interview by E. W. Pugh, September 13, 1982; S.G. Tucker to R. P. Case, "ROM and the 400," September 5, 1962; F. P. Brooks to S. G. Tucker, January 8, 1963.

25.   F. Neves interview by E. W. Pugh, December 21, 1981. The two engineers who agreed to fund work on BCROS for the Model 50 were Peter Fagg, engineering manager for System/360 processors, and John Hipp, engineering manager for the Model 50. Bruce Felton is the second-level manager who took over management of the BCROS effort in Kingston.

26.   A. Proudman interview by E. W. Pugh, August 5, 1983.

27.   S. A. Abbas et al., "A Balanced Capacitor Read-only Storage," *IBM Journal of Research and Development* 12 (1968): pp. 307-317.

28.   R. C. Warren, "IBM System/360 Product Announcement," (264-26), April 7, 1964.

29.   J. R. Opel, "IBM System/360, Models 65 and 75 Product Announcement (265-40)," April 22, 1965.

30.   R. S. Partridge interview by E. W. Pugh, December 19, 1981.

31.   R. J. Flaherty et al., "MECCA, A Preliminary Report," December 15, 1961.

32.   R. J. Flaherty interview by E.W. Pugh, January 4, 1982.

33.   R. J. Flaherty, H. J. Halstead, R. J. Judge, C. J. Schug, R. L. Vaudreuil, and J. W. Wyckoff, "Core Matrix Winding Pattern," U.S. Patent 3,381,282 (filed April 6, 1964).

34.   R. L. Judge, "Wire Threading Method and Apparatus," U.S. Patent 3,314,131 (filed April 29, 1964).

35.   R. L. Judge interview by E. W. Pugh, January 12, 1982.

36.   R. D. Peterson interview by E. W. Pugh, January 14, 1982. Thomas S. Cooper was the manager of the Endicott memory group that developed the Model 30 memories using Mecca technology.

37.   Pretrial Brief for Defendant IBM in U.S.A. v. IBM, U.S. District Court, Southern District of N.Y., January 15, 1975. The IBM Product Announcement of April 1964 said shipments would begin in the third quarter of 1965. The Models 30 and 40 were shipped in the second (earlier) quarter and the Model 50 was shipped in the predicted third quarter.

38.   E. R. Hee interview by E. W. Pugh, January 15, 1982.

39.   E. D. Councill interview by E. W. Pugh, December 17, 1981.

40.   A. H. Eschenfelder (using diary) interview by E. W. Pugh, April 12, 1982. Erich Bloch headed SLT and memory development in the fall of 1963, reporting to Eschenfelder; and Robert E. Markel was appointed manager of SLT, reporting to Erich Bloch.

41.   L. A. Russell interview by E. W. Pugh, December 14, 1981.

42.   E. C. Schuenzel, "Summary of 1963 Achievements," January 30, 1964, and "1964 Achievement Summary," January 18, 1965.

43.   L. P. Schab interview by E. W. Pugh, January 18, 1982.

44.   *IBM News* (November 1967); L. P. Schab, "Press History," October 9, 1967.

45.   L. Novakowski interview by E. W. Pugh, January 22, 1982.

46.   E. W. Pugh, D. L. Critchlow, R. A. Henle, and L. A. Russell, "Solid State Memory Development in IBM," *IBM Journal of Research and Development* 25 (1981): pp. 585-602.

47.   Gene O. Baker, Robert H. Cadwallader, and Charles P. Marinelli, "Handling and Testing Miniature Magnetic Elements," U.S. Patent 3,539,004 (filed June 17, 1968).

48.   E. W. Pugh, "Memory Use on System/360," presented to A. K. Watson on October 15, 1965.

Chapter 9

1.   T. A. Wise, "IBM's $5,000,000,000 Gamble," *Fortune* (September 1966): pp. 118.

2.   E. K. Friedli interview by E. W. Pugh, April 23, 1982.

3. E. C. Schuenzel, "1964 Achievement Summary MR, Mask and Memory Products," January 18, 1965.

4. R. W. Cobb, "IBM Core Usage," May 6, 1964, May 1, 1967.

5. A. H. Eschenfelder interview by E. W. Pugh (dates and facts from diary), April 5, 1982.

6. W. Newman interview by E. W. Pugh, April 29, 1982.

7. J. T. Ahlin to C. E. Branscomb et al., "System/360 Orders," May 7, 1964.

8. I have personal knowledge of these vendor programs.

9. J. Haanstra, "Monolithics and IBM," September, 1964.

10. *IBM News* (September 1965).

11. E. W. Pugh, "The IBM Magnetic Film Memory Development Effort," March 1981, p. 190.

12. E. W. Pugh, D. L. Critchlow, R. A. Henle, and L. A. Russell, "Solid State Memory Development in IBM," *IBM Journal of Research and Development* 25 (1981): pp. 585-602

13. J. W. Gibson interview by E. W. Pugh, April 7, 1982.

14. E. Bloch interview by E. W. Pugh, April 14, 1982.

15 M. A. Every interview by E. W. Pugh, April 23, 1982.

16. N. P. Edwards interview by E. W. Pugh, April 23, 1982.

17. J. W. Birkenstock interview by E. W. Pugh, May 25, 1982.

18. M. K. Haynes interview by E. W. Pugh, April 27, 1982.

19. T. J. Watson, Jr., *A Business and Its Beliefs* (New York: McGraw-Hill, 1963).

20. H. A. DiMarco interview by E. W. Pugh, January 25, 1982.

21. F. Neves interview by E. W. Pugh, December 21, 1981.

22. T. J. Watson, Jr., interview by J. B. Rochester, *Computerworld* (June 13, 1983): pp. 10-17.

23. L. P. Schab interview by E. W. Pugh, January 18, 1982.

24.   J. W. Forrester interview by E. W. Pugh, September 16, 1982.

25.   H. A. Simon, *Models of Man* (New York: John Wiley, 1957); J. G. March and H. A. Simon, *Organizations* (New York: John Wiley, 1958).

26.   G. Schussel, "IBM vs. RemRand," *Datamation* (May 1965): pp. 54-57, (June 1965): pp. 58-66.

27.   G. F. Perry to E. W. Pugh, April 29, 1982.

28.   M. K. Haynes interview by L. Saphire, September 15, 1967.

Chronology

1911	The Computing-Tabulating-Recording (CTR) Company is established.
1914	Thomas J. Watson, Sr., is hired as president of CTR.
1924	CTR name is changed to International Business Machines (IBM).
1942	IBM Plant in Poughkeepsie, New York, is built for munitions production.
8/44	Dedication of the IBM Automatic Sequence Controlled Calculator (ASCC), also known as the Harvard Mark I.
8/44	John von Neumann begins collaboration with John William Mauchly and John Presper Eckert at the Moore School.
3/45	Wallace J. Eckert is hired as director of IBM's first Department of Pure Science.
8/45	World War II formally ends as Japan accepts terms of surrender.
8/45	Robert R. Seeber joins IBM and becomes the chief architect for the IBM Selective Sequence Electronic Calculator (SSEC).
9/45	"A Progress Report on the EDVAC" is submitted by Eckert and Mauchly as a classified government document, three months after von Neumann's "First Draft of a Report on the EDVAC" was distributed by Herman Goldstine.
1/46	Engineering Research Associates (ERA) is founded.
1/46	T. J. Watson, Sr., authorizes construction of the IBM SSEC.
1/46	Jay W. Forrester proposes use of a digital computer instead of analog techniques for the Aircraft Stability and Control Analyzer (ASCA) project at MIT. The approach is based on P. O. Crawford's thesis published in 1942.

2/46   The Electronic Numerical Integrator and Computer (ENIAC) is dedicated at the Moore School.

2/46   Ralph L. Palmer establishes an electronics laboratory in Poughkeepsie after returning to Endicott from the navy in late 1945.

6/46   Eckert and Mauchly found the Electronic Control Company, which later became the Eckert-Mauchly Computer Company.

1/47   James W. Birkenstock is appointed manager of the IBM Future Demands Department.

4/47   Jay W. Forrester proposes a three-dimensional storage array using gas glow discharge tubes.

12/47   The transistor is invented by J. Bardeen and W. H. Brattain at the Bell Telephone Labortories.

1/48   T. J. Watson, Sr., dedicates the IBM SSEC, which has since been characterized both as a "kludge" and as the world's first operational stored-program computer.

7/48   The IBM Type 604 Electronic Calculating Punch is announced, with over 1400 electronic vacuum tubes and 50 decimal digits of storage.

9/49   An Wang describes a shift register using magnetic toroids of Deltamax.

6/49   Jay W. Forrester begins documentation in his notebook of a three-dimensional memory using toroids made of square-loop characteristic magnetic materials such as Deltamax.

1/50   William N. Papian writes a thesis proposal for work on magnetic devices needed for Forrester's proposed three-dimensional memory array.

2/50   The Eckert-Mauchly Computer Company (EMCC) is purchased by Remington Rand.

3/50   J. W. Forrester is advised that his digital computer project will receive Air Force funding for the newly proposed air defense system, later known as SAGE.

4/50   M. K. Haynes describes his proposal for a magnetic core memory while interviewing for a job at IBM.

4/50	W. N. Papian reports "first real gleam of possible future success" in his work on magnetic core memories.
6/50	Wallace W. McDowell replaces John C. McPherson as IBM director of engineering.
8/50	M. K. Haynes's thesis is submitted with the first written description of his coincident-current magnetic core memory proposal.
9/50	Programs are run successfully on the IBM stored-program Test Assembly in Poughkeepsie.
9/50	Jan Rajchman of RCA files a patent application for a "Magnetic Device," which is a coincident-current magnetic memory.
10/50	Preliminary operation of $2 \times 2 \times 1$ array of Deltamax cores is reported by W. N. Papian at MIT.
10/50	M. K. Haynes joins IBM to work on magnetic core logic and memory devices.
10/50	J. W. Forrester initiates ferrite material development work at MIT based on square-loop magnetic ferrite materials reported by Albers-Schönberg in 1949.
12/50	The Atlas I stored-program computer is delivered to the government by ERA. It contained 2700 vacuum tubes, 2385 crystal diodes, and a magnetic drum main memory. Commercial computers based on this machine were named the ERA 1101.
1/51	A 250 word Williams tube memory is successfully tested on the IBM Test Assembly in Poughkeepsie.
2/51	Haynes learns of Forrester's proposal for a coincident-current 3D memory using magnetic cores.
3/51	Whirlwind achieves 90 percent useful operation using electrostatic storage-tube memories.
3/51	The first Universal Automatic Computer (UNIVAC) is accepted by the U.S. Census Bureau. It contained a mercury delay-line memory.
5/51	J. W. Forrester files for a patent on his magnetic core memory. A patent interference results with Rajchman's application of September 30, 1950.

6/51   M. V. Wilkes of the University of Cambridge, England, proposes the use of control stores for microprogramming computers.

9/51   Richard G. Counihan completes his analysis of various magnetic core memory organizations, two months after joining Haynes's group.

12/51   Successful operation of a 16×16 array of metallic cores is reported by W. N. Papian at MIT.

1/52   John von Neumann is hired as an IBM consultant, a position he retained until February 3, 1955.

1/52   Erich Bloch joins IBM.

1/52   A 2×2×2 ferrite core memory built in Haynes's group at IBM operates in the XY selection, 3D mode.

1/52   Thomas J. Watson, Jr., is appointed president of IBM.

4/52   Edward J. Rabenda and Gordon E. Whitney of IBM build a 960 bit ferrite core buffer memory and test it on a Type 407 accounting machine.

5/52   A 4×4×4 ferrite core memory operates at IBM in what Haynes describes as a five-dimensional (5D) selection mode.

5/52   Successful operation of a 16×16 array of ferrite cores is reported by Papian at MIT.

6/52   John von Neumann's Institute for Advanced Study (IAS) computer is publicly announced.

6/52   N. H. Taylor of MIT discusses manufacturing problems of the proposed air defense system with J. C. McPherson of IBM.

7/52   MIT representatives tour IBM laboratories and plant in search of a contractor to build the proposed air defense system.

9/52   M. C. Andrews and A. H. Eschenfelder initiate ferrite core fabrication at IBM.

10/52   IBM is notified that it has been selected to work with MIT on the proposed air defense systems, later called Project SAGE.

11/52   A ferrite core buffer is proposed by W. D. Winger and P. W. Jackson for the IBM 702.

12/52	Nathen P. Edwards joins Project High and is given responsibility for memory systems.

1952   Engineering Research Associates (ERA) is purchased by Remington Rand.

1/53   First shipment of an IBM 701 computer to an external customer. Williams tubes are used for its main memory.

1/53   First Project Grind meeting is held in Hartford, Connecticut.

2/53   The ERA 1103 is announced with electrostatic storage tube memory.

2/53   Erich Bloch successfully demonstrates a product prototype memory on the IBM Tape Processing Machine. The memory has an 80×12 array of 60 mil inside diameter, 90 mil outside diameter (60-90 mil) ferrite cores made by General Ceramics using dies ordered by Haynes in March 1952.

3/53   A decision is made to use Williams tube memories on the IBM 702 computer, about this time.

4/53   The IBM 701 is formally dedicated. Ultimately nineteen were built.

5/53   K. H. Olsen of MIT suggests that a memory array wiring scheme, similar to that proposed by M. K. Haynes of IBM, is superior to the one proposed by J. W. Forrester.

5/53   The world's first ferrite core main memory operates on the MIT Memory Test Computer (MTC). It has a $32 \times 32 \times 17$ array of 60-90 mil cores made by General Ceramics using dies first ordered by Haynes of IBM.

6/53   J. W. Gibson joines IBM. His first assignment is to establish a ferrite core production pilot line.

8/53   The first experimental 64×64 bit ferrite core plane is assembled at MIT for project SAGE.

8/53   The first bank of $32 \times 32 \times 17$ bit ferrite core memory is removed from the MTC and placed in Whirlwind I.

9/53   David R. Brown reports successful use of an IBM automatic core handler with MIT automatic core-selection electronics.

10/53   J. Rajchman reports on his 100×100 bit ferrite core memory array using 34-54 mil ferrite cores made at RCA.

11/53   Project High staffing reaches 300.

11/53   IBM has three semiautomatic testers, each producing an average of 1000 good cores per two-shift day.

11/53   Erich Bloch is assigned to build a ferrite core buffer memory for use with IBM 702 magnetic tape units.

12/53   Error-free operation of thirty-seven days is reported for MIT's 32×32×17 bit memory on the MTC.

2/54   The first 64×64×17 bit ferrite core array is operational in the MTC at MIT.

4/54   T. Vincent Learson is appointed director of Electronic Data Processing for IBM.

4/54   Design specifications for the XD-1 SAGE prototype memories are approved by J. W. Forrester.

4/54   T. J. Watson, Jr., urges greater use of ferrite core memories on the IBM 702.

5/54   The IBM 704 is announced as a replacement for the 701. Like the 701 it is announced with electrostatic memories. Before shipment the electrostatic memories were replaced by ferrite cores.

6/54   David J. Crawford transfers from Project High to head the development of ferrite core memories for commercial machines.

7/54   486,000 good ferrite cores are available, and sixty planes of 4096 cores each have been wired at IBM for the SAGE memories.

7/54   Peter K. Spatz urges W. W. McDowell and T. V. Learson to use ferrite core main memories on commercial machines.

8/54   P. K. Spatz is assigned to put ferrite core memories on the IBM 704 computer.

9/54   J. W. Gibson's ferrite core pilot line at IBM produces cores of exceptional quality.

9/54   Richard E. Merwin is assigned to put ferrite core memories on the IBM 705 computer.

10/54   Ferrite core memories for the IBM 704 and 701 computers
          are announced.

10/54   A ferrite core manufacturing facility is established in the
          IBM plant in Poughkeepsie.

11/54   International Telemeter installs a 4096 word ferrite core
          memory on the Rand Corporation's Johnniac computer,
          and ERA ships a 32×32×36 bit memory on its 1103
          computer to the National Security Agency.

1/55   The XD-1 SAGE prototype computer with two 64×64×36
          bit arrays is shipped by IBM to Lincoln Laboratory.

2/55   The first IBM 702 computer is accepted by a customer.
          Ultimately fourteen are built. These systems employ the
          ferrite core buffer memories, with 2D selection, based on
          E. Bloch's product design and the pioneering work of
          M. K. Haynes, E. J. Rabenda, and G. E. Whitney.

4/55   IBM proposes a ten megapulse instead of a two megapulse
          machine for the Livermore Automatic Research Computer
          (LARC) and looses the contract to Remington Rand.

6/55   The IBM 776 tape buffer, with a 40×20×7 bit array of
          ferrite cores, is shipped to Commonwealth Edison.

7/55   IBM starts a development effort to find a ferrite core
          composition not covered by the General Ceramics patent.

7/55   Erich Bloch develops plan for a megabit ferrite core
          memory, later called the Type 738.

7/55   A brainstorming session defines ferrite core memory
          approaches developed for Stretch.

12/55   The first IBM 704 computer is shipped to IBM
          headquarters.

1956   Cryogenic logic and memory and flat magnetic film
          memory efforts are started in the IBM Kingston Military
          Products Division as part of an effort to provide new
          technologies for an improved SAGE.

1/56   The first IBM 702, 704, and 705 computers, with ferrite
          core memories, are shipped to customers.

1/56   IBM signs a contract with the National Security Agency
          (NSA) for a memory technology development effort,
          called Project Silo.

3/56   Negotiations on the Forrester patent begin between IBM and MIT's patent assignee, Research Corporation.

5/56   IBM obtains the right to use the CuMn ferrite core material developed by Philips.

6/56   Thomas J. Watson, Sr., dies of a heart attack.

9/56   E. R. Piore is hired as director of research for IBM.

9/56   Patent interference is declared between the Forrester and Rajchman patent applications.

10/56   A 60 percent yield on CuMn ferrite cores is achieved by the IBM manufacturing group.

11/56   The core threading machine is first used in production at IBM about this time. It reduces XY core threading time from twenty-five hours to twelve minutes.

11/56   IBM signs a contract with the Atomic Energy Commission for delivery of the Stretch computer.

1/57   Ferrite core development and product engineering activities are transferred to the IBM Poughkeepsie plant.

1/57   Gregory Constantine documents his first version of a load-sharing matrix switch, which facilitates the use of transistor drive of ferrite core arrays.

4/57   IBM signs the final agreement with General Ceramics on the purchase of MgMn ferrite cores. It specifies 49.5 million cores at an average price of 3.4 cents each.

4/57   The first Type 738 memory with 1 million bits and transistor sense amplifiers is shipped on the IBM 704.

5/57   IBM agrees to buy 90 million CuMn ferrite cores from Ferroxcube (a Philips subsidiary) at an average price of 1.5 cents each.

7/57   IBM negotiates a patent cross-license agreement with RCA, which covers computer-related technologies including magnetic core memories.

11/57   The decision is made not to use magnetic core logic in any part of Stretch.

12/57   The first IBM 608 calculator is shipped with a small ferrite core memory having all semiconductor support circuits. The 608 is the first commercial electronic calculator produced with all solid-state circuitry and memory.

7/58   The first production SAGE system is declared operational at
            McGuire Air Force Base.

7/58   IBM contracts to supply transistorized 709s, later called
            7090s, for the Ballistic Missile Early Warning System
            (BMEWS) by the end of 1959.

6/59   Divisionalization of IBM divides the Data Processing
            Group into three divisions: the Data Systems Division, the
            General Products Division, and the Data Products
            Division.

7/59   The Atomic Energy Commission (AEC) agrees to
            eliminate the requirement for a 0.5 microsecond memory
            on Stretch.

9/59   D. J. Crawford and R. M. Whalen observe a two core per
            bit memory prototype at Mullard.

11/59   Research Corporation offers to license IBM under
            Forrester's patent at two cents per core. IBM rejects price
            as too high.

12/59   The first IBM 7090 with a Type 7302 memory is shipped
            to Sylvania for the BMEWS program.

12/59   M. A. Every is appointed manager of Nonmechanical
            Memory (later called Solid-State Memory) Development
            for the IBM Data Systems Division.

5/60   Two cores per bit replaces three-hole cores for the 0.5
            microsecond memory committed to the NSA Harvest
            computer.

10/60   The U.S. Patent Office Board of Interferences awards ten
            of the broadest claims of the Forrester patent to Rajchman
            of RCA.

12/60   Two memories using two cores per bit are completed and
            attached to Harvest.

1/61   M. A. Every is given responsibility for solid-state memory
            development in the Data Processing Group.

4/61   T. J. Watson, Jr., requests frequent reports on the Stretch
            problem.

4/61   Erich Bloch's Advanced Technology Study Committee
            recommends IBM use Solid Logic Technology (SLT) in
            future computers.

5/61	William Norris, president of the Control Data Corporation (CDC), makes an off-the-record remark that announces the CDC 6600 computer.
5/61	The Data Systems Division 8000 series project in Poughkeepsie is terminated, a decision that helped trigger a series of events leading to the IBM System/360.
6/61	Price reduction on Stretch is announced by T. J. Watson, Jr., to compensate for lower than anticipated performance. Stephen W. Dunwell is removed as manager of Stretch.
6/61	Rotary presses with sixteen stations are introduced into manufacturing for making 19-30 mil cores.
8/61	The IBM Components Division is established with John W. Gibson, manager.
10/61	Sperry Rand announces the UNIVAC 1107 for delivery in April 1962 with a small, high-speed magnetic-film buffer memory.
11/61	The Mecca task force is initiated by M. A. Every; Robert J. Flaherty is the task force leader.
12/61	The SPREAD task force report is completed after three months of meetings chaired by John W. Haanstra and co-chaired by Bob O. Evans. The New Product Line (NPL), later called the IBM System/360, is proposed.
1/62	The Harvest computer is shipped to NSA.
5/62	IBM's Corporate Management Committee formally approves the NPL (System/360) proposal.
6/62	MIT makes a patent settlement offer to IBM, which IBM rejects as too high and Research Corporation rejects as too low.
9/62	A development effort on flat magnetic film memories is started jointly in the IBM Components and Data Systems Divisions.
9/62	F. Neves initiates the Balanced Capacitor Read-Only Store (BCROS) project for the Model 50 computer of System/360.
12/62	Robert F. Elfant initiates the Flute memory project in IBM Research.
12/62	MIT terminates its contract with Research Corporation because of differences over patent negotiations with IBM.

4/63	The first BCROS bench model is successfully tested with a 0.3 microsecond cycle.
5/63	M. A. Every takes over direct leadership of the flat magnetic-film memory project and transfers the troubled cryogenic memory development effort to the Components Division.
9/63	F. Neves agrees to design an improved BCROS (C-13) for the Model 60 and 62 processors, an approximate date.
11/63	E. Bloch replaces M. A. Every as manager of Solid-State Memory Development, A. H. Eschenfelder replaces J. W. Gibson as manager of the Components Division, and J. W. Gibson is promoted to a group executive.
11/63	Honeywell announces its H-200 computer with Liberator software designed to translate IBM 1401 programs into H-200 machine language.
12/63	The Hursley Laboratory is asked to develop CCROS in addition to TROS for the IBM System/360.
1/64	The decision is made to use 13-21 mil cores in the M-4 memory instead of the larger 19-32 mil cores.
2/64	IBM and MIT reach a patent license agreement, by which IBM pays $13 million to MIT.
4/64	The IBM System/360 is announced. Within the next four weeks, orders are received for more than one thousand computers plus peripheral equipment.
6/64	The improved BCROS (C-13) enters product test.
8/64	The first M-4 memory achieves a read-write cycle of 0.75 microsecond.
9/64	John W. Haanstra issues his report, "Monolithics and IBM," which urges rapid development and use of semiconductor technology with ten to one hundred circuits per chip versus less than one circuit per chip then being produced for the IBM System/360.
9/64	The minimum memory size required to use the operating system OS/360 is increased from 16K to 32K bytes.
9/64	The IBM Hursley Laboratory stops its effort on CCROS and concentrates on its own TROS technology. Endicott reinitiates its own CCROS development project.

12/64   Rotary presses with thirty-two double stations are
             introduced in manufacturing. They produce 30-50 mil
             cores at a rate of forty-two cores per second.

1/65   IBM development activities are reorganized, combining
             three divisions into one, to permit focus on advanced
             technologies, especially monolithic semiconductors.

4/65   IBM System/360 Models 60, 62, and 70 are withdrawn
             and replaced by Models 65 and 75 which use the new 0.75
             microsecond cycle main memory.

4/65   The first IBM System/360 Model 40 is shipped.

6/65   The first IBM System/360 Model 30 is shipped.

8/65   The first IBM System/360 Model 50 is shipped.

11/65   The first IBM System/360 Model 65 is shipped.

1/66   The first IBM System/360 Model 75 is shipped.

10/66   Rotary presses with thirty-two double stations are used in
             IBM to produce 13-21 mil cores at a rate of 102 cores per
             second.

1/68   The primary development program on ferrite core
             memories is terminated in IBM so resources can be
             focused on monolithic semiconductor memories.

1968   Ferrite core testers used in IBM manufacturing achieve a
             rate of 180 cores per second.

1970   The manufacturing cost of tested cores made by IBM is
             0.03 cents each, one thousand times less than the price
             charged by General Ceramics in 1953.

6/71   IBM introduces the world's first commercial computer with
             an all-semiconductor main memory, the IBM System/370
             Model 145.

1979   IBM begins shipping its 4331 computer with main memory
             composed of silicon chips about 6 mm on a side and
             containing 65,536 bits each, the largest number of bits per
             chip achieved to that time.

Index